TELOS

NUMBER 148   FALL 2009

POLITICAL THEOLOGIES

FROM SCANDINAVIA

PHILOSOPHY AND SOCIETY

NOTES AND COMMENTARY

REVIEWS

Introduction

When asked whether the U.S. government considers Mahmoud Ahmadinejad to be the "legitimate president" of Iran, White House spokesman Robert Gibbs responded laconically that "he's the elected leader," according to an AP report of August 4. The phrasing—and the omission of any reference to the brutal suppression of Iranian protests—offers an insight into key political orientations of the current regime. What counts is the outcome, not the process; what matters are the ends, not the means; and what is of greatest importance is the state and its apparatus, not society and its complexities. No doubt, the Obama administration's caution on this matter reflects its effort to emphasize diplomacy, as the opportunity for states to talk with states, and to back off from the democratization agenda of its predecessor. The way it has taken sides in Iran is, at least, consistent with its values. Diplomatic negotiations take place over the heads or behind the backs of society, which is why state departments and foreign ministries frequently find themselves at odds with the values of the polities they purport to represent.

This priority of state-to-state relations internationally corresponds domestically to the priority of the state over society. None of the expansion of policing powers of the previous era has been significantly retracted, while the management of the economy proceeds at a brisk pace, with the prospect of a biopolitical administration increasingly likely. Current events are breathing new life into Critical Theory's nightmare of a "totally administered society." Anxiety about the growth of the managerial state defined classical Critical Theory, and this was frequently enough one of the key issues that separated it from the orthodox left. For *Telos*, the political developments of the last third of the twentieth century seemed to indicate various rollbacks in the state apparatus and the potential emancipation of society. Has that historical episode come to an end?

The current discussion of political theology has erupted out of the renewed attention to Carl Schmitt, which *Telos* pioneered. Schmitt's theorem that modern political categories derive from the secularization of theology provides powerful insights, but, as with all academic discussions, this one too is susceptible to a flattening out into an anemic history of ideas. The constellation of articles in this issue should contribute to a recovery of the radical insight: politics not merely as the concepts that inhabit the desiccated carcass of secularized theology, but theology as the marker of the inescapable limitation on politics and state power. The theological turn can be as consistent with Foucault's exhortation to defend society against the state as it is with Adorno's insistence on considering all things from the standpoint of redemption. Yet those positions belong to an era of theory and society increasingly distant. What we need now is a political theology of the new bureaucratic regime. This issue is a first step.

The issue opens with Bassam Tibi bridging the decades between his encounters with his teacher Max Horkheimer in the days of the student movement and his own evaluation of contemporary Islamism. A self-described liberal Muslim, Tibi denounces Islamism as a new totalitarianism. This is however not an attack on Islam as religion but on its deformation into a politics of oppression. Islamism is to Islam as ideology is to ideas: a form of betrayal. Yet for Tibi, an even more urgent concern than Islamism is its leftist defenders in the West. Here, too, Tibi sees betrayal, the jettisoning of the ideals, which he suggests a left tradition ought to honor. It is precisely at this point however where further discussion could begin. In the current fascination of parts of the left with jihad, what can one make of the willingness of progressives to deep-freeze their long-held beliefs—in civil rights, in gender equality, in free speech, and so forth—in order to enter alliances with reactionary Islamists due to their veneer of anti-imperialism? Is this a tactical blunder (reminiscent of parts of the Iranian left and its misplaced enthusiasm for Khomeinism in 1979)? Or is there not a repressive streak within the left with a much longer genealogy, stretching back at least to 1793? That is where a discussion of terror ought to begin.

James V. Schall provides a systematic foundation to the possibility of political theology through a reflection on the relationship between reason and revelation. Both forms of knowledge can concern themselves with the "best city," the possibility of political excellence. But the revelational tradition surpasses the law, even if it tries to guide it. Politics remains incomplete, and necessarily so; the aspiration for a total politics, a full management of human affairs, runs counter to human limitations. Hence the importance of his conclusion with Aristotle's warning: "For it would be absurd for someone to think that political science or intelligence is the most excellent science, when the best thing in the universe is not a human being…"

Arthur Versluis undertakes an inquiry into the intellectual lineage of Schmitt's account of modernity. Rather than placing him primarily in relation to early modern political theory (Hobbes), Versluis traces discussions back to late antiquity and conflicts between an orthodoxy emerging around the Church and the mystical radicalism of Gnostic heresies. For Versluis, secular modernity results from an institutionalist emphasis on historicity over transcendence. The consistent marginalization of gnosis eliminates transcendence and "one is left only with a historical horizon," which becomes the space in which the total state operates. "Totalitarianism results from pursuing a distant mirage of enforced historical utopia, the pursuit of which left behind the bodies of many 'heretical' victims or scapegoats." Islamism, despite its opportunistic appeals to religion, fits into this model of a secularizing modernity because it has little to do with transcendence—consider its distance from Sufism—and everything to do with an immanentist "paradise on earth"—as lugubrious as that so-called paradise turns out to be. Against this enforced management of life, Versluis appeals to mystical and anarchic (i.e., anti-statist) traditions, as far apart as Böhme and Péguy.

Telos has a long history of transmitting international intellectual opinion, so following the explicit discussions of political theology, a set of essays presents critical voices from contemporary Scandinavia. The Scandinavian social model has of course long been the paradigm of the administered society, the most fully developed welfare states, in part due to unique circumstances of demography and culture, but in part as well because social-democratic advocates regularly invoke it as the template to emulate elsewhere. Some of the emergent tensions in contemporary Northern Europe—and therefore in the paradigm of the welfare state—are reflected in these essays. Frederik Stjernfelt's argument that secularism is not a fundamentalism responds to the rise of culturalist or multiculturalist agenda that have called for limitations on free speech: in Denmark this issue came to a head around the cartoon controversy, but it is indicative of a wider anthropological turn in culture that erodes the ability and will to make distinctions, even between democratic and totalitarian politics. For Stjernfelt, this represents "a major political step backward, which threatens to erode 250 years of enlightenment and to open the door to never-ending religious wars," a critique compatible with Tibi's attack on the western apologists for Islamism.

The paradox however is the alliance between statist expansionism and multicultural fragmentation. Kasper Støvring explores the transitions in cultural agenda in Denmark, from the (social) democratic radicalism aligned with modernism through the contradictions of elitist modernization to the more recent turn to a national conservatism. Støvring places this transformation in a European context and explicates it with references to Roger Scruton's positive evaluation of national community. Because of an implicit populism, it stands closer to elements of popular culture than did the radical advocacy for modernism, with its frequent avant-garde and therefore elitist profile. Klaus Solberg Søilen moves the discussion to Sweden and to social policy. He traces the ideological origins of the Scandinavian welfare state, its ultimately depoliticizing impact, and its capacity to provide bountifully for the "new class." The Scandinavian model is less about radical redistribution than about the preservation of the status of a bureaucratic managerial class: "the welfare state today is less about solidarity than it is about self-interest," or in other words, an organized *status quo* with a high degree of inefficiency. For the new class, it serves as "a modern version of Robin Hood. Unlike in Sherwood Forest, however, most of the funds today go to the middle class, not to the poor."

A final trio of articles presents some contemporary treatments of philosophy and society. Rossen I. Roussev traces the decline of philosophical and more broadly humanistic education in colleges and universities and mounts a robust and appropriately philosophical defense of the need for a program to rectify this cultural impoverishment. He invokes Derrida's insistence on a "right to philosophy" and the importance of educational reform. Matthew Rampley provides a comprehensive discussion of art and society in the work of Niklas Luhmann, with striking contrasts to the accounts associated with Bourdieu and Foucault. Rampley also shows how Luhmann's emphasis on micro-social events rather than on larger frameworks can shed light on specific problems, such as the particular evanescence of contemporary art. Peter Gratton provides a comprehensive profile of Derrida's thought with regard to the internal tensions within democracy, the implications of sovereignty, and the possibility of a "non-sovereign freedom." That however can only imply a politics that escapes the constraints of a totalizing state.

Gábor T. Rittersporn provides an elaborate discussion of David Ost's *The Defeat of Solidarity*. At stake are the vicissitudes of post-Communism in Poland and the fraught relationship between liberal intellectuals and social movements. Even more, however, this discussion concerns the status of liberalism in general and its limits, especially in the face of the social devastation left by Communism. Gerhard Richter follows with a critical reply to Ulrich Plass's review of recent Adorno scholarship in *Telos* 146. Three book reviews conclude the issue. Mark Wegierski presents Paul Gottfried's anatomy of the conservative movement. Shafiq Shamel discusses Bassam Tibi (whose article opens this issue) and his strident critique of jihadism. Finally, Matthew Congdon explores Derrida's essay on the blind hubris of anthropocentrism. The humanism that denies its limits is akin to the limitless state.

Russell A. Berman

The Political Legacy of Max Horkheimer and Islamist Totalitarianism

Bassam Tibi

Some theorists on the left believe that "Islamism is a creative space for political articulations of protest against present inequalities" and that "Islamism is not a religious discourse, but a political one. It is a debate about modernity."[1] Other left apologists for Islamism treat it solely as a contestation of capitalist globalization and therefore attribute a progressive character to it.[2] To do so, however, they have to remain blithely oblivious to the fact that a religious fundamentalism,[3] and not a progressive movement, is at work. Scholars of the left like Susan Buck-Morss could not be more wrong when they invoke Critical Theory to endorse Islamism. As a liberal Muslim and a former student of Max Horkheimer, I adamantly reject such views. On the contrary, in the tradition of the Frankfurt School, I view Islamism as the new totalitarianism and follow Horkheimer's view that it is obligatory to resist totalitarian ideologies, regardless of their origin and shape. Yet the contemporary left is no longer loyal to this tradition

1. Susan Buck-Morss, "Critical Theory and Islamism," ch. 2 of *Thinking Past Terror: Islamism and Critical Theory on the Left* (London: Verso, 2003), pp. 41–56; here, pp. 52, 43.

2. Frank Lechner and John Boli, the editors of *The Globalization Reader* (Oxford: Blackwell, 2008), chose two opposing views on Islam and Islamism, one of which is mine. My interpretation of Islamism (political Islam) as a variety of religious fundamentalism appears on pp. 358–63. There, I look at religion in terms of a politicized politics that "religionizes" conflict. This view runs counter to Buck-Morss, who in *Thinking Past Terror* claims that "Islamism is not a religious discourse" (p. 43) and that "Islamist politics increasingly transcends theological splits" (p. 53). Such statements are not only utterly wrong, but they are deeply uninformed.

3. See Bassam Tibi, *The Challenge of Fundamentalism: Political Islam and the New World Disorder*, updated ed. (Berkeley: Univ. of California Press, 2002).

of Western humanism.[4] What has happened to the left? Why is it rushing into the welcoming arms of Islamism? And why does it display such an untroubled affinity for Islamist antisemitism?[5]

The love affair of the contemporary left with Islamism derives from the earlier new left romanticism about the "third world."[6] The real postcolonial developments dealt a severe blow to the illusion that a universal liberation would emerge from "third-worldism." Yet neither the postwar developments in Vietnam nor dictatorships in Africa (e.g., Idi Amin and Robert Mugabe) nor even the Pol Pot regime ever induced the left to reconsider its exotic fascination with non-European revolutions. Instead, the Islamic Revolution in Iran was celebrated, and the left consistently overlooked its totalitarian character (even when it persecuted Iranian leftists). Critical Theory can help cut through this obfuscation. Horkheimer was my academic teacher, and I am also a Muslim living in Europe. Today, the credibility of the left is at peril, and it is urgent to protect Critical Theory from being distorted into a defense of Islamist totalitarianism, misogyny, and antisemitism.

Horkheimer, the Left, and the "Third World"

At the height of the Vietnam War and the protests against it, we students of the Frankfurt School were organized in the Sozialistischer Deutscher Studentenbund (SDS), which represented the new—or critical—left. Some of us went to Horkheimer, our highly revered teacher, to ask him to endorse our pro-Vietcong and anti-U.S. declaration. He politely turned us down, and in turn, we were impolitely outraged. But he explained his refusal:

4. "The Grammar of European Humanism" is the theme of a special issue of the Dutch journal *Nexus* 50 (2008). The issue was presented at an international congress on humanism that took place in Amsterdam in June 2008. In my conference presentation, based on my contribution to the issue, "The Grammar of Islamic Humanism" (pp. 592–616), I argued that an Islamic version of humanism existed in medieval Islamic rationalism, and that it could serve today as a cultural bridge that offered an alternative to the polarizing impact of Islamism.

5. On Islamist antisemitism, see Matthias Küntzel, *Jihad and Jew-Hatred: Islamism, Nazism and the Roots of 9/11*, trans. Colin Meade (New York: Telos Press Publishing, 2007), and Bassam Tibi, "Public Policy and the Combination of Anti-Americanism and Antisemitism in Contemporary Islamist Ideology," *The Current* (Cornell University) 12, no. 1 (2008): 123–46.

6. On the cultural roots of third-worldism see Peter Worsley, *The Third World*, 2nd ed. (Chicago: Univ. of Chicago Press, 1970).

while he too opposed the war, he neither admired the Vietcong nor did he share our anti-Americanism. He documented his reservations with press reports of Vietcong torture, and he argued more broadly against the third-worldist mind-set. There was no ambiguity in Horkheimer's dismissal of our third-worldist romanticism, which he regarded as a recycling of the fantasy of the "noble savage." He did not hesitate to speak of "the free world," although he made it clear that this notion should not be equated simplistically with capitalism. He was dismayed about the way that the left dismissed Western humanism altogether, in order to pursue its anti-capitalist agenda: to oppose Western capitalism, the left felt that it had to reject the Western tradition and its ideals.

To make matters worse for us, Horkheimer attended that year's American Independence Day celebrations, while we were in the streets furiously shouting anti-American slogans. Now, four decades later, it is clear to me that I—though a non-European—was participating in an old tradition of European anti-Americanism, culturally alien to me. I had internalized the "noble savage" mythology. As a person from the "third world," I actually felt flattered, during those years of ugly racism, to be upgraded via that romanticism from a lowly Arab into a "theorist of the third world," publishing articles in the Marxist Berlin-based journal *Das Argument* and even joining its board. Now, however, as a Muslim who fled from "Oriental despotism," i.e., the authoritarianism of Middle Eastern dictators, I defend an alternative reading of Horkheimer's legacy in the light of the spread of Islamism. I am profoundly concerned about the apologetic misrepresentation of Islamism by the left, which treats this totalitarianism as if it were a liberation movement. Horkheimer teaches us otherwise. For while he could certainly be critical of the West by holding it up to its own ideals—its *Begriff*—he consistently opposed the anti-Western ideology that intertwined anti-Americanism and antisemitism:

> America, regardless of its motives, saved Europe from complete enslavement. The response today from everywhere, not only in Germany, has been a widespread profound hostility toward America. There has been a great deal of puzzling over the origin of this. Resentment, envy, but also the errors made by the American government and its citizens: all play a role. It is especially startling to notice that everywhere where one finds anti-Americanism, antisemitism flourishes. The general malaise caused by cultural decline seeks a scapegoat, and for the aforementioned

reasons, it finds the Americans, and, in America itself, once again the Jews who supposedly rule America.[7]

Today this anti-Americanism is shared by strange bedfellows: right-wing Islamists—in the tradition of Sayyid Qutb—and parts of the European (and American) left, paradoxically prepared to jettison all progressive ideals in order to forge an alliance with Islamist reactionaries. Of course, Horkheimer understood the catastrophes that had had their origins in the West, especially in Europe: the Crusades, colonialism, two world wars, genocidal Hitlerism, and, last but not least, Communist Stalinism. Yet in 1968, Horkheimer was prepared to designate the West as an "island of freedom surrounded by an ocean of violent regimes,"[8] and to add to this favorable judgment his view that it is an obligation on those who subscribe to Critical Theory to defend the West against its totalitarian enemies.

In 2008, forty years after my education in Frankfurt in 1968, I joined the Center for Advanced Holocaust Studies in Washington, DC, to study the Islamization of European antisemitism. In the course of my research, I was shocked to see how Islamists embrace *The Protocols of the Elders of Zion* and give them an Islamist cast. Islamists view liberation as an uprising against the "Jewish conspiracy."[9] They denounce the Enlightenment as a "Jewish idea."[10] They believe that U.S. policies are steered by "world Jewry," thereby merging antisemitism and anti-Americanism, in the spirit of Sayyid Qutb.[11] Of course, Horkheimer did not witness Islamism, but his legacy informs the fight against the new totalitarianism of political Islam. Islamism is certainly modern—as Buck-Morss insists—but she fails to inquire into the specific nature of its modernity. Islamism is favorable only

7. This statement by Max Horkheimer is included in *Horkheimers Gesammelte Schriften*, and it is quoted here in the excellent translation by Andrei Markovits, *Uncouth Nation: Why Europe Dislikes America* (Princeton, NJ: Princeton UP, 2007), p. 199.

8. Max Horkheimer, *Kritische Theorie*, 2 vols. (Frankfurt am Main: S. Fischer, 1968), 1:xiii.

9. Anwar al-Jundi, *Ahdaf al-Taghrib* [*The Targets of Westernization*] (Cairo: al-Azhar, 1987).

10. For an influential example for this mind-set, see the work of the Islamist Anwar al-Jundi. In his view, "Enlightenment is a Jewish Idea," and his books call for a purification of Islam from the "Jewish virus." See for example his *al-Mu'asara fi itar al-Asalah* [*Modernity in the Framework of Authenticity*] (Cairo: Dar al-Sahwa, 1987), for instance pp. 79 and 83.

11. See S. A. al-Khalidi, *America min al-dakhil bi minzar Sayyid Qutb* [*America from Inside Viewed Through the Lenses of S. Qutb*] (al-Mansura [Egypt]: Dar al-wafa', 1987).

to the instruments, but not to the values, of modernity: it is a version of "reactionary modernism" [12] and has nothing to do with "the philosophical discourse of modernity."

Islamism is the most recent and also the most powerful variety of a third-worldist ideology, expressing a new totalitarianism. It is not about liberation. For early Islamists, the primary concern was a remaking of the world in the pursuit of establishing a religious order: *hakimiyyat Allah* or "Allah's rule." The goal was based on an invented *sharia* elevated to a political state law.[13] It is an ideology, represented by a movement based on transnational religion, which is poised to establish a political rule. It is a transnational movement organized along the lines of a religious ideology. It enjoys global networks and acts across borders. In Islamism, politics and religion are completely intermingled. This takes place in the pursuit of remaking the world, a world-conquering totalitarianism with religious rhetoric. This Islamism not only thrives the world of Islam but also takes pains to hijack the Islamic diaspora in Europe, where Islamists have been successful in establishing their power through all kinds of networks, while they are abusing the freedom that civil society guarantees.[14]

In the past, liberal and left-wing humanists who dared to criticize Soviet Communist practices that violated human rights had to run the risk of being accused of "anti-Communism." The left engages in a similar terminological policing today in order to censor any free and critical discussion, for instance, about Islamism and its violations of individual human rights. When even Muslim reformers criticize the excesses of Islamism, they face accusations of "Islamophobia." The ideological mechanisms in the use of anti-Communism and Islamophobia are nearly identical. By indulging in this self-repression, the left undermines whatever claims it may still have

12. On this kind of instrumental modernity, see Roger Griffin, *Modernism and Fascism* (London: Palgrave, 2007), and Jeffrey Herf, *Reactionary Modernism: Technology, Culture and Politics in Weimar and the Third Reich* (New York: Cambridge UP, 1984). This instrumental modernity rejects the values of cultural modernity outlined by Jürgen Habermas in *The Philosophical Discourse of Modernity: Twelve Lectures*, trans. Frederick Lawrence (Cambridge, MA: MIT Press, 1987).

13. See Bassam Tibi, "The Return of the Sacred to Politics: The Case of Shari'atization of Politics in Islamic Civilization," *Theoria* 55 (2008): 91–119.

14. See Lorenzo Vidino, *Al Qaeda in Europe: The New Battleground of International Jihad* (Amherst, NY: Prometheus, 2006), and Bassam Tibi, *Political Islam, World Politics and Europe: Democratic Peace vs. Global Jihad* (New York: Routledge, 2008), chs. 5 and 6.

to progressivism and the Enlightenment tradition. I write this as a Muslim scholar committed to enlightenment in Islam and to intercultural bridging between civilizations, but also to enlightening the left about its own shortcomings in a radically changed world in which politicized religion has come to represent a counter-enlightenment. Islamism is the foremost case in point. Supporting it, the left betrays itself and the related ideals. The left needs to understand that Islamism is nothing but a variety of the global phenomenon of religious fundamentalism.[15]

To be sure, Islamism does have a social dimension, and this is what creates its appeal for both the left in the West and disaffected Muslims. As Buck-Morss rightly argues, Islamism is a "protest against present inequalities." Yet this contestation is articulated through a religionized politics with reactionary contents. Political Islam essentializes the binary division of humanity into "Muslims" and "unbelievers." The traditional Islamic worldview determines the ideology of these religious fundamentalists, albeit in a new configuration, joining modernizing politics with inherited faith. Any explanation of Islamism that focuses solely on the non-religious social agenda—which is how its left apologists misrepresent it—is absolutely wrong. The Islamist articulation of social discontent in religious terms is much more than a cover for a social concern because it also includes an irreducible meaning: the religious doctrine of jihad and the concept of *sharia* were reinvented in the course of the return of the sacred in a political garb. The traditional Islamic worldview is thereby recast and modernized:[16] Islamism is not Islam in general, but it is certainly based on a view of Islamic faith and on an eccentric, radicalizing interpretation of it.

No doubt, Islamist movements are movements of contestation and protest, but it is perilous to ignore the goals of this protest. There is a de-secularization as well as a de-Westernization of society within the

---

15. See Tibi, *The Challenge of Fundamentalism*. To be sure, Islamism, as a political Islam, is a variety of the global phenomenon of religious fundamentalism. See the five-volume series *The Fundamentalism Project*, ed. Martin E. Marty and R. Scott Appleby (Chicago: Univ. of Chicago Press, 1991–95). On "Remaking of the World," see vol. 3, *Fundamentalisms and the State: Remaking Polities, Economies, and Militance* (Chicago: Univ. of Chicago Press, 1993), pts. 1 and 3. In vol. 2, *Fundamentalisms and Society* (Chicago: Univ. of Chicago Press, 1993), see Bassam Tibi, "The Worldview of Sunni-Arab Fundamentalists," pp. 73–102.

16. On the Islamic worldview, see Bassam Tibi, *Islam between Culture and Politics*, ch. 2 (New York: Palgrave Macmillan, 2005), pp. 53–68.

framework of a new "Revolt Against the West," understood as a purification.[17] Totalitarian Islamism intends to carry out a cultural purge directed
against all Western values and—as the Islamist Anwar al-Jundi states
clearly enough for even Buck-Morss to understand—against the Jews who
"stand behind them." The Jewish philosopher Horkheimer taught us to
defend humanistic values, and I follow him as a Muslim. Islamism does
not only contest Western political hegemony but also the cultural idea
of the West itself and the core of humanism. Unlike decolonization, the
new revolt relates the rejection of Western dominance to the dismissal of
all cultural patterns associated with Europe at the core of the West. The
suggestion that cultural modernity and European humanism ought not be
reduced to European political hegemony is discarded by Islamists as a
"Jewish idea."[18]

   To date, the highest authority in Islamist thought is Sayyid Qutb. His
book *Milestones* (*Ma'alim al-tariq*) provides directions that are understood
to be valid not only for all Muslims but for all of humanity. He pursues the
establishment of *hakimiyyat Allah*, with *dar al-Islam* (again: this is neither
the caliphate nor "Islamic democracy") as the first stage of a global jihad,
practiced in its new meaning as a comprehensive Islamic world revolution.[19] This right-wing revolutionary ideology provides the grounds for an
Islamist internationalism. As Qutb asserts, it is an "obligation" (*farida*) to
pursue jihad as a world revolution of Islam. In contrast, Horkheimer asserts
that it is obligatory for the supporter of Critical Theory to defend the West
against any totalitarianism. In that sense, the left has two options today:
to learn from Horkheimer or to submit to Qutb! The cultural modernity

17. Bassam Tibi, "Secularization and De-Secularization in Islam," *Religion-Staat-
Gesellschaft* 1, no. 1 (2000): 95–117. See also Hedley Bull, "Revolt against the West,"
in Hedley Bull and Adam Watson, eds., *The Expansion of International Society* (Oxford:
Clarendon Press, 1984), pp. 217–28, which continues to provide guidance for understanding this revolt. See also the chapters in Bassam Tibi, *Islam's Predicament with Modernity*
(New York: Routledge, 2009), on the Islamist drive against secularization (ch. 6) and pluralism (ch. 7), legitimated as "authenticity" (ch. 8), understood as an act of purification.

18. See al-Jundi, cited above, who follows a drive toward de-Westernization advo-
cated by Sayyid Qutb, the mastermind of Islamism. See Sayyid Qutb, *Ma'alim fi al-Tariq*
[*Milestones*], "legal ed." (Cairo: Dar al-Shuruq, 1989), pp. 5–10 and 201–2. On the place of
Qutb, see Roxanne Euben, *Enemy in the Mirror: Islamic Fundamentalism and the Limits of
Modern Rationalism* (Princeton, NJ: Princeton UP, 1999), pp. 54–55.

19. See Sayyid Qutb, *al-Salam al-Alami wa al-Islam* [*World Peace and Islam*] (Cairo:
Dar al-Shuruq, 1992), pp. 171–73, on jihad as world revolution. See also Qutb, *Ma'alim
fi al-Tariq*.

praised by Horkheimer is among the targets of Islamism, so how could anyone defend Islamism in the name of Critical Theory?

It is sad to see that some American supporters of Critical Theory who fail to understand the nature of Islamism end up using leftist arguments to support a religious fundamentalism. The Islamist politicization of religion, as a type of fundamentalism, discards the tradition of cultural modernity to which Critical Theory subscribes. True, Islamic fundamentalists are a minority within Islam. However, it is not only a vocal but also a very powerful minority, one that is empowered by global networks. It is the best organized opposition throughout the Islamic countries and, as already noted, in the Western diaspora as well.

To be sure, the conflict is not between Islam and the West. In contrast to Huntington, I argue that there is a better Islam that derives from the rationalist medieval philosophers Avicenna and Averroës. The Marxist-Jewish philosopher Ernst Bloch, who knew Islam well, defended Avicenna and the Aristotelian left [20] against the orthodoxy of Islamic Salafism. These Muslim rationalists defined both Islamic and Hellenized medieval culture, which unfortunately did not endure as a lasting tradition. It is worth being revived [21] as the alternative to a fundamentalism that pursues a return of the sacred into politics. At present, as in the past, civil Islam and its humanism could promote democracy and human rights and turn into a civilizational bridge. This tradition exists today in Indonesia. [22] The revival of the Islamic rationalism of Averroës and Avicenna could incorporate Muslim cultures into a universal humanity along pluralist lines. If, however, fundamentalism were to prevail, the current crisis will not end soon. Political Islam legitimates its resort to violence by reference to an "Islam under siege," [23]

20. See Ernst Bloch, *Avicenna und die Aristotelische Linke* (Frankfurt am Main: Suhrkamp, 1963). On Islamic rationalism, see Herbert A. Davidson, *Alfarabi, Avicenna and Averroes on Intellect: Their Cosmologies, Theories of the Active Intellect, and Theories Of Human Intellect* (New York: Oxford UP, 1992). See also Bassam Tibi, *Der wahre Imam: Der Islam vom Mohammed bis zur Gegenwart* (Munich: Piper, 1996), pt. 3, and Franz Rosenthal, *The Classical Heritage in Islam* (New York: Routledge, 1994).

21. Mohammed Abed al-Jabri, the Moroccan Muslim philosopher of a true Islamic modernity, argues that Muslims are at a crossroads: for a better future, they need to revive the heritage of Ibn Rushd (also known as Averroës). See al-Jabri, *Arab-Islamic Philosophy: A Contemporary Critique* (Austin, TX: CMES, 1999), pp. 124–29.

22. Robert Hefner, *Civil Islam: Muslims and Democratization in Indonesia* (Princeton, NJ: Princeton UP, 2000).

23. Graham Fuller, *A Sense of Siege: The Geopolitics of Islam and the West* (Boulder, CO: Westview Press, 1995), and Tibi, *Political Islam, World Politics and Europe*.

encircled by "Jews and crusaders." Neither the left nor any other group should tolerate this caricature of Islam, which crudely and propagandistically equates it with Islamism. Islam is not Islamism.[24] Moreover, the left has no valid reason to support such a movement, which is based on a totalitarian ideology, defined by religion and imbued with reactionary ideology. It explicitly defames the West as a marketplace "for Jews and crusaders." No self-respecting left should be defending reactionary Islamism, unless of course the left itself has abandoned all of the progressive values once central to the Critical Theory of Max Horkheimer. A question to the apologists: which side are you on? Are you on the side of an open society, or the side of its totalitarian antisemitic enemies?

---

24. Bassam Tibi, *Islam and Islamism* (New Haven, CT: Yale UP, forthcoming).

Revelation and Political Philosophy: On Locating the Best City

James V. Schall, S.J.

For it would be absurd for someone to think that political science or intelligence is the most excellent science, when the best thing in the universe is not a human being...

Aristotle, *Ethics*, 1141a20–22

The word "revealed" refers not only to the future—as though the Word began to reveal the Father only when he was born of Mary—it refers equally to all time. From the beginning the Son is present to creatures, reveals the Father to all, to those the Father chooses when the Father chooses, and as the Father chooses. So, there is in all and through all one God the Father, one Word and Son, and one Spirit, and one salvation for all who believe in him.

Saint Irenaeus, *Against Heresies*, book 4

After they have been carried along to the Acherusian lake, they cry out and shout, some for those they have killed, others for those they have maltreated, and calling them they then say to them and beg them to allow them to step out into the lake and to receive them. If they persuade them, they do step out and their punishment comes to an end; if they do not, they are taken back into Tartarus and from there into the rivers, and this does not stop until they have persuaded those they have wronged, for this is the punishment which the judges imposed on them.

Plato, *Phaedo*, 114a–b

I.

Philosophy is the quest for knowledge of the whole by a being who is himself a whole but not the whole. The quest is given with our very being. It makes us be what we are, both acting and thinking beings. It explains

16

the constant dynamism that charges through our being whether we like it or not. Further, it incites us to know what we are in order that we might choose to be what we are. We are the only beings in the universe that cannot be what we are without our own decision actually to be what we are. Not even the gods can change this status, nor do they wish to. The gods want us to be what we are. The question is whether we want this "whatness" also, or do we wish to be ourselves gods?

The gods are not philosophers, as they already know the whole. We love wisdom; they are wisdom. Philosophy begins with not knowing, the *tabula rasa*. Philosophy is a human enterprise, the activity of leisure, the contemplative life. Philosophy is the articulation in conversation of what we know about *what is*. The truth of what we know is measured by the intelligibility within *what is*. The truth is, as Plato observes, to say of *what is* that it is, and of what is not, that it is not. *Veritas est adaequatio mentis et rei.* Truth only "exists" when something is actively being affirmed as true by a being with the power of intellect.

Philosophy wants to know how and why things are, rather than are not; why they are this and not that. Our mind is defined by Aristotle as the faculty that is *capax omnium*, the power by which we are all things not ourselves while still being ourselves. We are not deprived of *all that is* by being, within the whole, a particular *that which is*.

"Know thyself," the great Delphic admonition that sent Socrates forth on his lifetime mission, his quest, includes first knowing what is not "thyself." This self-knowing results when Socrates ventures forth in the streets of Athens to find out who was wise since he knew he was not. Thus, I am not the first object of my intellect. I know myself indirectly through first knowing what is not myself. The world, what is not myself, gives me myself, both in being and in knowledge. Ultimately we are "gifts" even to ourselves.

In following Socrates, the philosopher does not know, or claim to know, what he does not really know. He knows that he does not know; he knows that he knows little or nothing. But, if he could, he does want to "know" what he does not know. He knows that he does not know all there is to know about anything that he does know. In this sense, he does not know. He is not a skeptic. That is to say, the philosopher's ignorance of *what is* becomes itself an incentive to pursue the light, wherever it can be found. No one is immune to the charm of things. They are designed, by their very being, to unsettle us. And they do unsettle us if we really look at them, especially, as Plato said in the *Symposium*, if they are beautiful things. *Omne ens est pulchrum.* When they have unsettled us enough, we wonder why such things exist in the first place.

Philosophy's own incompletion in its own order is not a form of despair. It knows that it possesses a partial light. What we do not know by our own powers of knowing does not necessarily mean that what is unknown, as such, is unknowable. It just means that we do not yet know it, that our intellects are not the highest of the intellectual powers that be.

Philosophy itself falls within the mystery of the whole that is the intelligible light. We are the weakest of the intellectual beings. But we do know and know that we know. We shine by our own light, by our own *intellectus agens*, as Aristotle told us. We really are beings who know. We are rational animals in all that we do and do not do, even in our sins and errors. No one can do something wrong without doing something right. But this "right," as Aristotle says in the seventh book of the *Ethics*, is itself out of order, and chosen to be so.

II.

Revelation presents before our minds, whether we "believe" it or not, what has been given by God and what is subsequently handed down to us. Atheists can understand basically what it is said to maintain. We do not need to be believers to know what believers hold. Revelation is not itself philosophy. Philosophy cannot be what it is, philosophy, if it cannot reach its own limits with its own powers. Revelation wants philosophy to be what it is, that is, philosophy. Revelation is only safe if philosophy is philosophy, though not all "philosophies" are based on *what is*.

Revelation contains its own articulated corpus of what it presents as true. Theology (*theo-logos*) is this articulation. Revelation can be articulated for it contains *logos*. What is revealed, on examination, is strangely open to reason, itself something that provokes our reason. We are unsettled by our not knowing even when we realize that we will die not knowing all there is to know.

Reason can recognize what is reasonable even when its source is not finite reason. The principle of contradiction always holds, even for revelation. This is why an intelligible connection can exist between philosophy and theology without denying the validity of either. Revelation, among other things, addresses itself to reason, active reason. Reason is open to what is reason as such.

We are beings who can choose either to know or not to know the truth of things. We can reject *what is* when *what is* itself is addressed to reason. The philosophy that results from this rejection becomes a description of the world minus its inner intelligibility to which the mind is by its nature open. This is the immediate source of all ideology. Such philosophy becomes an account of a reality that exists only in mind, with no basis in *what is*.

Reason can only know that something is addressed to it if it is itself actively philosophizing, if it is pursuing the truth in its own order, if it has reached the "limits" of its own order. While revelation's content is accepted by faith, it is articulated through reason, a reason that is open to *logos*, to *what is*. Reason, as a given power in our being, does not know only itself. It cannot even know itself unless it knows that what is not itself stands before it, stands in front of its finite existence in a body. Only the divine reason knows all things in knowing itself. Human reason, in its very self-reflection on itself, knows that by its proper activity what is not itself becomes itself, without changing what it knows. What is not ourselves can be given to us because we are particular, individual beings endowed with reason.

Augustine says, in the nineteenth book of the *City of God*, that there is "no other reason for a man to philosophize except in order that he might be happy." We are not made for ourselves alone even when we are indeed made for ourselves. Man is by nature a political animal. He seeks to live in the polity, the best polity. Does this mean, then, that revelation, to address him in his nature, is about the "perfect city"? In some sense it does. What are actual cities? What kind of happiness, if any, can we expect in them? What does it mean that most people, most of the time, do not live in perfect cities? Do only those in perfect cities live human lives? Are perfect cities the only cities "by nature," as Plato seemed to indicate?

Aristotle, that clear-minded man, in the last book of the *Ethics*, said that there are two kinds of happiness, one political, one contemplative. The political exists both for itself and as preparation for the contemplative. The city is not safe unless there are within it those who devote themselves to contemplation, as Aquinas says. Why is this so? Does someone in actual cities, for the human good itself, need to know that this actual city is not the best city? "Do not listen to those who tell us that, being mortal, to look only on mortal things and, being human, to look on human things." It was not a believer who said these things, but Aristotle, the philosopher.

Thus, being human we should look at things beyond the human and being mortal, immortal things. How remarkable that we read in this same Aristotle, "If the gods give any gift at all to human beings, it is reasonable for them to give happiness also; indeed, it is reasonable to give happiness more than any other human good, in so far as it is the best of human goods" (1099b12–14). Notice that Aristotle himself said that it was "reasonable" to do this.

At the end of this extraordinary passage, Aristotle adds: "However, this question is more suitable for a different inquiry." What would the "different inquiry" be, we wonder, that would be able properly to locate the "happiness" that Aristotle, the philosopher, intimated? If it is a "gift" of the gods, is it also directed to the philosopher as philosopher seeking to know *what is*? Can anything other than happiness itself give happiness?

Plato, in the end, did not think that the best city existed among actual men who did live in cities. It existed rather in speech, in mind, in argument. The purpose of liberal education was to know this location, which is what book seven of the *Republic* was about. But it did exist there, in speech, he thought. In the *Republic*, again and again the location of this city, whether it actually exists, comes up.

The *Laws* of Plato wish to retain philosophy in a city less than the best, the second best, in the sort of cities that actually exist, in cities that kill their philosophers. The very life of Socrates hinted that the philosopher could exist, for a time at least, as a private citizen, in a democracy, because people with disordered souls, souls free to do whatever they want, the Greek definition of democracy, could not tell the difference between the philosopher and the fool.

But the myths of Plato about what happens to immortal souls that have lived disordered lives in any existing city, those myths in the *Phaedo*, the *Statesman*, and the *Republic*, tell us that none are exempt from judgment, no matter what sort of city he lives in. The city in speech still rules all actual cities, even the worst. The great theme of the Platonic myths of the end times joins Aristotle's wonderment about the inquiry that locates our real and ultimate happiness in the realm of gift. The real question of the relation of philosophy and revelation, then, has to do with whether gifts can be also intelligible. If what is presented to us as a gift is also intelligible to reason, what does this signify about the whole that is the object of the philosophical quest?

III.

Aristotle said that political things are not the highest things as such because man is not the highest being in the universe. Political things are the highest things of the practical order, not the theoretical order. This is why there is a natural law that indicates to politics what it is. "Man does not make man to be man," Aristotle said, "but, taking him from nature to be already man, makes him to be a good man." Aquinas said that the natural law is the eternal law as it exists among creatures. It is the "normalcy of their functioning," as Maritain put it. If man were the highest being, as happens in those philosophies that deny transcendence, politics does become the highest science. Positive law is then the highest law. Science becomes subject to politics.

The political animal deals with man as finite, as the mortal. Aristotle wondered in the *Politics*: What is the best or most reasonable or most feasible regime for this people at this time with these virtues and vices? Politics also knows about vices; and, as Aristotle said in the second book of the *Politics*, it is aware of and must account for human "wickedness." Most people, most of the time, in most regimes would live and die amidst imperfections and disorders in their own polities, in their own souls. If there were a "best regime," it would not be in this world.

Augustine read Plato correctly. He did not give up the search for the best city. Plato was right; there was such a search. Augustine did not reject it because it was a gift. Indeed, this is precisely what he thought it must be if it were to exist. But he did not locate it in this world. Thus he wrote the *City of God*, not the *Republic*, which had already been written. Augustine knew that the pagan philosophers knew what the virtues were. Their real frustration concerned why it was that men did not practice them. This is why he is the doctor of grace and not simply a Platonic philosopher, though he is that too.

The most important book written in political philosophy in recent years is called, ironically, the *Law of God*. It deals with the Jews, the Muslims, and the Christians, with their wars and their hopes. It deals precisely with the difference in theologies and their effect in the world. Rémi Brague, its author, writes: "Our societies, with their agenda of a law with no divine component, are in fact made possible, in their final analysis, by the Christian experience of a divine without the law. Even atheism as 'unbelief' presupposes the primacy of faith in the definition of the religious."[1] A "law with no divine component" is what we call modernity.

What Brague says here is in the direct line with what Benedict XVI writes in the last half of *Deus Caritas Est*. What human beings need in all polities at all times is beyond what the state can provide even for its own good. Political philosophy is not to be rejected, but it is not a complete understanding of the actual men who are likewise political animals by nature. Each political man has a contemplative life, that is, an end that is beyond politics. But it is a real end; it is what charges his being.

We have often read: "He who loves God has no law." The politics of modernity is an effort to achieve the kingdom of God in this world without divine revelation or even without knowing about it. They have retained the elevated end, eternal life, without the revelational means to attain it, as I believe Strauss intimates in his book on Machiavelli. This, too, is what Voegelin writes in *Politics, Science, and Gnosticism*.[2] The men who lose supernatural faith turn to this-worldly utopianism. That is, they turn to the creation of the best regime on earth. Brague's point is subtle. When he says that the modern desire of a polity for a law "with no divine component"—the positive law state—he implies the secularization of grace. What is needed is within our human powers.

What was it Strauss said? "[Modern political philosophy] is the highest form of the mating of courage and moderation. In spite of its highness or nobility, it could appear as Sisyphean or ugly, when one contrasts its achievement with its goal. Yet it is necessarily accompanied, sustained and elevated by *eros*. It is graced by nature's grace."[3] *Eros* is itself always a grace. Nature's grace is itself graced. It is not its own cause. It lies open to further grace in the line of why man exists in the first place. This is what the Prologue of John is about.

The intention of God in creation in the first place was to associate each man and all men with His own inner life. Nature's grace as such is not sufficient for this, and Aristotle suspected it wasn't. The "unbelief" of modern atheism unknowingly accepts this original purpose of creation.

1. Rémi Brague, *The Law of God: The Philosophical History of an Idea*, trans. Lydia G. Cochrane (Chicago: Univ. of Chicago Press, 2007), p. 263.

2. Eric Voegelin, *Science, Politics, and Gnosticism: Two Essays* (Chicago: Regnery, 1964).

3. Leo Strauss, *What Is Political Philosophy?* (Glencoe, IL: The Free Press, 1958), p. 40.

This is why, in Brague's sense, its divine is without law. This is why modern political philosophy is busy recreating man in his own image. It does not know that natural law is the reflection of the eternal law. The "law of God" is *Logos*. This *Logos* has dwelt among us. The purpose of the creation is being carried out.

IV.

Irenaeus, the great second-century theologian, said that the word "reveal" referred not only to the future but to all time. There is one Word, one God, one Spirit, one salvation. Plato, too, is concerned with salvation, the perplexity of what happens to the wicked. He tells us that those who murder and commit great crimes must first be forgiven by those against whom they commit them. The unpunished crimes of the universe, the great enigmas that pierce the Platonic corpus, are not redeemed in this world, in politics.

In *Spe Salvi*, Benedict cites Adorno as saying that the only way justice can be restored once we die in our crimes is through the resurrection of the body (§42). This position on personal resurrection Adorno himself rejects as true, even when he sees its necessity or logic. Aristotle implies much the same thing when he says that ultimately we do not wish our friends to be anything other than themselves, neither gods nor kings. *Eros* in friendship penetrates to the being of the other as other. That is to say, we hope our sins can be forgiven so that we can be. It is no accident that the Gospel of Mark begins with the notion of "repent." We hope we can be what we are, even if we are not perfect.

Political philosophy, as Strauss says, is not primarily the philosophical discussion of political things, but rather the political discussion of philosophical things. That is to say, what is the place, if any, of philosophy within the city? Some "philosophies" can and do destroy cities. A polity cannot be indifferent to the dangers of philosophy to its order. But disordered regimes need a true philosophy, even if it is only in speech.

The reconciliation of philosophy to the city would require, on the one hand, granting that our mortal lives are by right four score and ten. The scientific project cannot replace our natural being. A "city" may be "immortal" in the sense that it outlasts the lives of the mortals within it. But few cities do last very long in fact. Political philosophy, on the other hand, must be open to those forces in being that would help it overcome its own difficulties with the achievement of the very virtue it can know by reason, with what assists it to have a reasonably good city, even if its impetus is beyond politics.

Most of all, political philosophy would have to acknowledge, without denying its own competence, that the highest things are not political. Indeed, the political things, the decent regime, exist to enable the highest things, including grace and *eros*, to be present in the city. The common good, the object of the polity to achieve, allows what is more than itself to appear and flourish. The highest things are not political. The politician is always a servant.

The Word, the *Logos*, is present to creatures and reveals *what it is* to them. The relation of political philosophy to *Logos* is nothing less than the recognition that *Logos*, too, belongs within the city, not directly to correct the city, but to save its citizens as persons with transcendent destinies to which they are called by their very creation. The effect of revelation on the city is real but indirect. Its exclusion from the city is not neutral to the city. The "liturgy" of the city was always a search for the proper form of the worship of God who is not the city. This proper rite or liturgy, as it turned out, was not something man could give himself. This is the real meaning of Catherine Pickstock's *After Writing* and Josef Ratzinger's *The Spirit of the Liturgy*.[4]

Plato says, in the myth at the end of the *Republic*, that there are politicians who do not choose well even when they live under good constitutions because they do not philosophize except by habit. What does this not to philosophize well mean? Aristotle was content to separate politics and metaphysics as separate disciplines for purposes of understanding the whole. The rulers of the city did not have time or occasion or even interest to be philosophers. This is why they needed music and poetry. This is why, in the *Republic*, Plato understood why he had to "out-charm" even Homer.

The most dangerous man was the politician with a disordered soul who also claimed to be a philosopher. Surely this was the significance of Alcibiades, the young friend of Socrates. This phenomenon of the philosopher who wants to impose his theories is more a modern than an ancient problem, though its roots are classic. The reason for this danger was that such a politician did not really know *what is*. The right order of things,

---

4. Catherine Pickstock, *After Writing: On the Liturgical Consummation of Philosophy* (London: Blackwell, 1998); Joseph Cardinal Ratzinger, *The Spirit of the Liturgy*, trans. John Saward (San Francisco: Ignatius Press, 2000).

ultimate things, must thus be known and kept for the good of the city and its politicians. Augustine, the author of the *City of God*, was thus not wrong to be so concerned with pride, the placing of the cause of all things, including political and transcendent things, in oneself. Voegelin rightly called this "ideology."

"According to the modern project, philosophy or science was no longer to be understood as essentially contemplative and proud but as active and charitable," Strauss wrote in *The City and Man*. "It was to be in the service of the relief of man's estate; it was to be cultivated for the sake of human power; it was to enable man to become the master and owner of nature through the intellectual conquering of nature."[5] Here the "contemplative" is contrasted to the "active," the "proud" to the "charitable." The "modern project" is when charity itself, the gracious alleviation of all wrongs, becomes political, not something from transcendence. It is not just that man becomes the "owner" of all human things. He also becomes owner of all "superhuman" things.

When the word "charity" appears in the famous passage above, it was not necessarily in contrast to the word "proud," but rather joined with it. Indeed, its inclusion is the height of pride; it is Brague's atheist society with a "law with no divine component." The "estate"—a word from Bacon—of man that we are seeking is now not under the *City of God*. It is autonomous, but somehow recognizes that a transcendent end once defined the proper limits of the city. With the transcendent end gone and now replaced within the world, the supernatural means to this end remained. It was necessary to recognize that man could not achieve his end simply by his own powers. Nietzsche's superman has theological origins. Charity reappears but secularized and located within the polity, with no divine or civil law other than itself.

We can ask, with Heidegger, "What Is Philosophy?" Dietrich von Hildebrand asked the same question. Leo Strauss asked, "What Is Political Philosophy?" What has concerned me is "What Is Roman Catholic Political Philosophy?"[6] This last question is only meaningful within the line of a philosophy open to *Logos* both in reason and revelation. There is, in other

---

5. Leo Strauss, *The City and Man* (Chicago: Univ. of Chicago Press, 1964), p. 3.

6. Martin Heidegger, *What Is Philosophy?* trans. William Kluback and Jean T. Wilde (New Haven, CT: College and University Press, 1956); Dietrich von Hildebrand, *What Is Philosophy?* (Milwaukee, WI: Bruce, 1960); James V. Schall, *Roman Catholic Political Philosophy* (Lanham, MD: Lexington Books, 2004).

words, a "whole." Philosophy begins with *what is*. Political philosophy begins with man who is already man, what he is, from nature.

"Roman Catholic political philosophy"—is it a contradiction in terms? I intend it certainly as a paradox and a provocation. We have, all of us, lived so long without taking together, in one intellectual whole, the rather uncanny body of knowledge that constitutes both political philosophy and Roman Catholic thought about *what is*. Aquinas does not ask first "Quid sit Deus?" but rather "An sit Deus?" He begins from *what* is.

What political philosophy is, finally, is not merely the question of the philosopher and his art in the city, in a place where he will not be killed for pursuing the truth. It includes its own awareness of its own questions as political philosophy. It is aware of its own inability to answer its own highest questions. But, and this is significant, it can recognize an answer when it hears one. We are "hearers" of the Word we do not ourselves make.

Its next step, as philosophy, is to ask whether any of its unanswered questions have answers proposed that are both intelligible and answers to its own questions as posed. If this relationship is noticed, a place can be found for revelation within the city. It is the Christian view, moreover, that when this question was in fact posed within the greatest cities of the ancient world, in Athens, Rome, and Jerusalem, the *Logos* was crucified with the cooperation of philosophers, priests, and politicians.

It is this same *Logos*, to return to the final myth in the *Phaedo*, that forgave us our sins. We could not simply forgive each other, though we are to do that too. The fact that rewards and punishments could not be finally meted out in existing cities was what led Plato to pose the immortality of the soul in the first place. Plato was "half" right, for the soul, as Aristotle would say, is the form of the body.

What is presented to our reason, following Adorno, is whether the resurrection of the body is not a more reasonable solution to the same question of rewards and punishments. Ultimately, we want our friends to remain what they are, that is, human, even in eternal life. This seems to be, to recall Brague's title, "the Law of God." It is likewise the rule of reason. The briefest and most succinct statement of this was formulated under a Roman Emperor in a Near Eastern city called Nice, located in what is today a Muslim state, Turkey.

Reason and revelation both concern themselves with the location of the best city. Political philosophy exists to find a place for both within the city on terms proper to both. Those terms must allow for a place wherein reason and revelation can recognize that they are in the same world. We are concerned with the salvation of individual souls in even the worst regime and virtue even in the best. Philosophy, political philosophy, and theology are all "architectonic" sciences. The order of one to the other is not necessarily antagonistic.

Today, political philosophy, at its best, is the discipline strategically located to reflect on how God, cosmos, man, and polity belong together. Philosophical *eros* is indeed what most drives us on. But we are aware from the revelational tradition that both charity, the friendship with God, and grace that guides law to its particular and highest end unaccountably exist among us. They, too, guide us to be what we are intended to be and remain, that is, rational beings with a transcendent end. We pass through our cities and sometimes kill the philosophers. Our politicians sometimes want to be like gods; we want them to remain but men with solid reasons to do so.

Sophocles said that man learned by suffering. The Crucifixion tells us that God teaches by suffering. As it says in the last book of *The Chronicles of Narnia*, "It's all in Plato."[7] It was Plato who worried about the location of the best city. We will not easily find its final location, I suspect, until we again ask his questions and wonder why it is not enough that we forgive one another, as the myth in the *Phaedo* intimated that it was.

Let me cite again one final time what Aristotle has said in the beginning: "For it would be absurd for someone to think that political science or intelligence is the most excellent science, when the best thing in the universe is not a human being..." Sometimes I think it's all in Aristotle too. We just need a few answers to questions he posed to us as we dwell in cities that kill philosophers and do not wonder what it is that consummates their philosophy and restores their politics.

7. C. S. Lewis, *The Last Battle* (New York: Collier, 1956), p. 170.

Carl Schmitt, Modernity, and the Secret Roads Inward

Arthur Versluis

Understanding intellectual lineages is vital if we are to understand our own era more clearly and deeply. It is not enough to investigate this or that figure in isolation. An author who is worth reading embodies many forebears, so by recognizing them, one comes to understand not only the work of a given individual but also much larger currents that have shaped and that continue to shape the often hidden intellectual architecture of our time. Carl Schmitt is particularly instructive in this regard, because he drew upon—indeed, foregrounded—political and religious figures with much in common. At the same time, what he rejected is also extremely revealing. In what follows, we will disentangle and tease out from the skein two primary hidden lines shaping the substructure or intellectual infrastructure not just of Schmitt but also more broadly of "secular modernity."

In order to understand the intellectual substructure that we see in Schmitt's work, we must recognize that informing and shaping it is a struggle that took place at the origin of Christianity. This struggle emerged from the rejection of mysticism as represented in those works that today are often categorized as "Gnostic," and from the concurrent insistence on the primacy of Christ's historicity. It eventuated in the rejection of those deemed "heretical," who asserted the paramount importance of direct inner spiritual experience, and in the creation of an imperial Christianity seated in the very center of the Roman Empire, which itself had formerly persecuted Christians.

One can understand why comparatively little attention has been given to such themes in contemporary scholarship. The opprobrium heaped upon "Gnosticism," "gnosis," and related subjects by the ante-Nicene Church

Fathers, such as Irenaeus, Tertullian, and Epiphanius, was quite successful in keeping those topics outside the realm of acceptable discourse through the medieval period and right into modernity itself. Indeed, even today, one finds the largest conference of medievalist scholarship in the world has in its program virtually nothing on the theme of mysticism. The fulminations of heresiophobes in late antiquity were remarkably successful in rendering gnosis and mysticism mostly *outré* right up into our own time.

This struggle of the self-styled "orthodox" against the "heretics" manifests itself in Schmitt's prose. It is not accidental that in *Political Theology II*, Schmitt specifically identifies one of the most anti-heresiological and polemical of the Church Fathers as the prototype of theologically informed juridical thinking.[1] In fact, Heinrich Meier remarks that "Tertullian's guiding principle *We are obliged to something not because it is good but because God commands it* accompanies Schmitt through all the turns and vicissitudes of his long life."[2] Tertullian bitterly attacked what he perceived as "heresy," and especially those termed "Gnostics," who insisted on mystical or gnostic experience over historicism, that is, over faith in a historical Christ as sufficient for salvation.

Schmitt's friend/foe distinction reflects the orthodox/heretic dynamic built into early Christianity by Tertullian and other definitive figures of late antiquity. For Tertullian, as for Schmitt, historicity has absolute precedence over the docetic view that Christ did not come in the flesh but belongs to another world. Tertullian bitterly attacks those he deems heretics, venomously likening them to scorpions. Echoing this, in an aside in "The Visibility of the Church," Schmitt remarks "every religious sect which has transposed the concept of the Church from the visible community of believing Christians into a *corpus mere mysticum* basically has doubts about the humanity of the Son of God. It has falsified the historical reality of the incarnation of Christ into a mystical and imaginary process."[3] For Schmitt, too, mysticism is congruent with docetism; it is "imaginary." Mysticism is false because, he imagines, it has "falsified" history.

1. See Carl Schmitt, *Political Theology II: The Myth of the Closure of any Political Theology*, trans. Michael Hoelzl and Graham Ward (Cambridge: Polity Press, 2008), p. 111, to wit: "Tertullian is the prototype of a reflection on the theological possibilities of specific legal thinking."

2. Heinrich Meier, *The Lesson of Carl Schmitt* (Chicago: Univ. of Chicago Press, 1998), p. 92.

3. See Carl Schmitt, "The Visibility of the Church," in *Roman Catholicism and Political Form*, trans. G. L. Ulmen (Westport, CT: Greenwood, 1996), p. 52.

It becomes clearer, then, why Schmitt endorsed Tertullian as the prototypical political theologian. Both Tertullian and Schmitt insist on the primacy of the historical. In *The* Nomos *of the Earth*, Schmitt proposes the *historical* importance within Christianity of the concept of the *katechon*, or "restrainer," that creates the possibility of Christian empire, brought about by "the historical power to *restrain* the appearance of the Antichrist and the end of the present eon."[4] The notion of a *katechon* is taken from an obscure Pauline verse, 2 Thessalonians 2:6–7: "And you know what is restraining him now so that he may be revealed in his time. For the mystery of lawlessness is already at work; only he who now restrains it will do so until he is out of the way." The *katechon* represents, for Schmitt, a "historical concept" of "potent historical power" that preserves the "tremendous historical monolith" of a Christian empire, and it does so by opposing the perceived activity of Satan in others.[5] One can hardly avoid the paramount importance of historicity here.

Schmitt is a political and geopolitical theorist whose political theology represents an insistence upon antagonism and combat as the foundation of politics, reflecting Tertullian's emphasis on antagonism toward heretics as the foundation of theology. A confirmed dualist, Tertullian even wanted to continue his orthodox/heretic (friend/enemy) dynamic into the afterlife, asserting that "There will need to be carried on in heaven persecution [of Christians] even, which is the occasion of confession or denial."[6] Likewise, Schmitt writes, in *The Concept of the Political*, that "a theologian ceases to be a theologian when he . . . no longer distinguishes between the chosen and the nonchosen."[7] When he writes "the high points of politics are simultaneously the moments in which the enemy is, in concrete clarity, recognized as the enemy," the theological antecedent of this statement is that, from Tertullian's perspective, the high point of theology is the recognition of "heretics" or of "heresy."[8] Schmitt insists on "the fundamental theological dogma of the evilness of the world and man" and rejects those who deny original sin, i.e., "numerous sects, heretics, romantics, and anarchists."[9]

4. See Carl Schmitt, *The* Nomos *of the Earth in the International Law of the* Jus Publicum Europaeum, trans. G. L. Ulmen (New York: Telos Press, 2003), pp. 59–60.

5. Carl Schmitt, *The Concept of the Political*, trans. George Schwab (New Brunswick, NJ: Rutgers UP, 1976), p. 60.

6. Alexander Roberts and James Donaldson, eds., *Ante-Nicene Fathers*, vol. 3 (Edinburgh: T&T Clark, 1989), p. 643. See Tertullian's treatise "Scorpiace" in ibid., 3:633–48.

7. Schmitt, *The Concept of the Political*, p. 64.

8. Ibid., p. 67.

9. Ibid., p. 65.

It is interesting, then, that Schmitt lays considerable emphasis on the political philosophy of Thomas Hobbes, whose somewhat pessimistic views emerged in part as a response to the chaos of the English Civil War, but also in the historical context of what can only be termed a remarkable efflorescence of esotericism not seen since late antiquity. Hobbes's *Leviathan* arguably signals an intellectual point of origin for the modern secular state, and it is little surprise that Schmitt devoted considerable space to Hobbes in his 1938 *The Leviathan in the State Theory of Thomas Hobbes*. Schmitt accepted the Hobbesian emphasis on the authority of the sovereign, and the Hobbesian belief in original sin was congenial too. But Schmitt also recognized the larger esoteric context in which Hobbes emerged—that is, he understood that the early modern period represented what can best be described as an esoteric renaissance.[10]

In his discussion of Hobbes, Schmitt revealingly cites the influential French esoteric author René Guénon's *La crise du monde moderne* (1927), and specifically Guénon's observation that the collapse of medieval civilization into early modernity by the seventeenth century came about because of secret forces operating in the background.[11] Guénon saw the early modern period as inaugurating the progressive decline that modernity represents for him, which would conclude in the appearance of the Antichrist and the end of the world. For Guénon, as for Schmitt, individualistic Protestantism entailed a deterioration from prior medieval unity, and accordingly in *Leviathan*, Schmitt is especially critical of "secret societies and secret orders, Rosicrucians, freemasons, illuminates, mystics and pietists, all kinds of sectarians, the many 'silent ones in the land,' and above all, the restless spirit of the Jew who knew how to exploit the situation best until the relation of public and private, deportment and disposition was turned upside down."[12]

At this point, we can see Schmitt's perspective is implicitly critical of the subjectification and inward or contemplative turn characteristic of those who travel "the 'secret road' that leads inward." Romantics, mystics, Jews, Schmitt holds, "as differently constituted as were the Masonic

10. For an extensive historical survey, see Arthur Versluis, *Magic and Mysticism: An Introduction to Western Esotericism*, (Lanham: Rowman & Littlefield, 2007). Some scholars of esotericism, notably Antoine Faivre, have argued in effect that esotericism begins in the early modern period, around 1600. See Antoine Faivre, *Access to Western Esotericism*, (Albany: SUNY, 1993).

11. Carl Schmitt, *The Leviathan in the State Theory of Thomas Hobbes*, trans. George Schwab (Westport, CT: Greenwood, 1996), p. 29.

12. Ibid., p. 60.

lodges, conventicles, synagogues, and literary circles, as far as their political attitudes were concerned, they all displayed by the eighteenth century their enmity toward the leviathan elevated to a symbol of state."[13] Esoteric groups and individual figures, like Romantic poets, represented an inward turn that was also skeptical and perhaps even hostile to centralized state power.

Like Hobbes, Schmitt is pessimistic about the human condition. The leviathan symbolizes the awful but, in his view, necessary power of the centralized state, necessary because it can restrain or postpone the larger decline that modernity represents. Man is inclined toward evil by nature and must be controlled by an outside force (the centralized state). In *Leviathan*, Schmitt deplores the split between inner and outer life represented by esoteric groups and individuals, and by the subjectification represented by Romanticism during the early modern period. Those who represent the "inward turn" are viewed as that which the *katechon* restrains; they represent fragmentation and decline. To restrain such fragmentation was the task enjoined by Juan Donoso Cortés in his defense of the Inquisition, and by Dostoyevsky's Grand Inquisitor in *The Brothers Karamazov*.[14]

It is interesting to consider Schmitt's later (1949) linking of Hobbesian statist philosophy with none other than "the domestication of Christ undertaken by Dostoyevsky's Grand Inquisitor." For, Schmitt continues, "Hobbes gave voice to and provided a scientific reason for what the Grand Inquisitor is—to make Christ's impact harmless in the social and political spheres, to dispel the anarchistic nature of Christianity while leaving it a certain legitimating effect, if only in the background."[15] Of course, it is a charmingly perverse interpretation of Dostoevsky's great character, the Grand Inquisitor, to assert that his purpose was to "make Christ's impact harmless in the social and political spheres." Dostoevsky's novel reveals something rather different about the Grand Inquisitor, and "harmless" doesn't quite describe it.

What conclusions and inferences might we draw from this adversarial, prosecutorial lineage within Christianity that clearly helped shape Schmitt's

13. Ibid., p. 62.

14. These are themes and figures discussed at length in Arthur Versluis, *The New Inquisitions: Heretic-hunting and the Intellectual Origins of Modern Totalitarianism*, (New York: Oxford UP, 2006).

15. See G. L. Ulmen, "Introduction," in Schmitt, *Roman Catholicism and Political Form*, p. xv, citing Schmitt, *Glossarium: Aufzeichnungen der Jahre 1947–1951*, ed. Eberhard Freiherr von Medem (Berlin: Duncker & Humblot, 1991), p. 243 (May 23, 1949).

work? Without doubt, this intellectual lineage has larger implications, perhaps even implications for the origins of "modernity." As we will see, I am not the first to observe the connections between the emergence of "secular modernity" and the struggles that gave birth to historicist Christianity in late antiquity. But my interpretation is rather different from its antecedents. At this point, therefore, we must move from these themes within the work of Schmitt to some of their implications.

Far from belonging only to a mostly forgotten and distant era of late antiquity, questions concerning "heresy" and "orthodoxy," "gnosis" and "anti-gnosis," are of great importance if we are to more clearly understand what we may call the intellectual substructure of our own time. Here I am not referring only to what we may call the "secularization hypothesis," meaning the view that modernity emerged from the secularization of Christian theology and culture. Such a perspective is certainly visible in the work of Max Weber on Protestantism and capitalism, as also in Schmitt's work on what he termed "political theology," which is more allied to Roman Catholicism. There is much to be said for the "secularization hypothesis" as a way of interpreting why and how secular modernity came into existence.

Understanding the origins of secular modernity, and in particular understanding the emergence of secular modernity's most concentrated form—totalitarianism—requires understanding the history of Christianity, going all the way back to late antiquity and the formation of Christian "orthodoxy." Such connections have been recognized before: one thinks here of the work of Eric Voegelin or Hans Blumenberg, for instance, who posited modernity as a renewed battle of the "orthodox" against the dreaded "Gnostics."[16] Voegelin and Blumenberg were entirely misguided in their emphases, but they did recognize that there is a profound connection between modernity and the struggle in late antiquity between the "orthodox" and the "Gnostics." Where they went wrong was to uncritically accept the anti-gnostic rhetoric of late antiquity—thus, effectively, they recapitulated the heresiophobic dynamics of early "orthodox" Christianity. What they claimed was "legitimate" in modernity, or what "legitimated" modernity, was what Blumenberg termed the "second overcoming of Gnosticism."[17]

16. See Arthur Versluis, "Voegelin's Anti-gnosticism and the Origins of Totalitarianism," *Telos* 124 (Summer 2002): 173–82.

17. See Hans Blumenberg, *The Legitimacy of the Modern Age*, trans. Robert Wallace (Cambridge, MA: MIT Press, 1983), pp. 125ff.

Hence we are not surprised to find that Blumenberg began his *The Legitimacy of the Modern Age* by directly alluding to Voegelin's claim "the modern age 'would be better entitled the Gnostic age.'" He adds that "the old enemy who did not come from without but was ensconced at Christianity's very roots, the enemy whose dangerousness resided in the evidence that it had on its side a more consistent systematization of the biblical premises."[18] We also should not be surprised at the language here, at terms like "the old enemy," as though the "Gnostic" were synonymous with the devil himself, for this is precisely the transposed and unexamined language of heresiophobia carried over from antiquity. What is to be feared? Most of all, an "escape into transcendence."[19] Modernity is "legitimated" by an emphasis on this-worldliness, on historicity, which is also to say, on eschatology transposed into the teleology of technical/historical progress.

But when we reverse this thesis, we gain some interesting results. What if secular modernity is the logical result of the prevailing tendency in "orthodox" Western Christianity to emphasize historicity over transcendence, indeed, to anathematize as "heretical" those who insisted on transcendence of subject and object dualism? This would make secular modernity, especially in its worst, totalitarian forms, the triumph of heresiophobia. Once transcendence or gnosis is driven to the margins and excluded, then one is left only with a historical horizon. If gnosis is demonized, then there remains only the flat plain of historicity, at the far end of which hovers the specter of millennium or apocalypse. It is not far, then, once one is out on this plain, to the strictly secular millennialism of modernity as reflected in various forms of twentieth-century totalitarianism. Totalitarianism results from pursuing a distant mirage of enforced historical utopia, the pursuit of which has left behind the bodies of many "heretical" victims or scapegoats.

What I am suggesting here is that "secular modernity" owes much, perhaps even almost everything, to a much earlier battle that was mostly, but never completely won in late antiquity. This is the battle against gnosis that was fought by Tertullian, Irenaeus, Epiphanius, and some others among the Ante-Nicene Fathers, but a battle in which even some of their own number, notably Clement of Alexandria, took the other side and defended the value of an orthodox gnosis. A certain ambivalence remained

18. Ibid., p. 126.
19. Ibid., p. 137.

in Western Christianity, emblematized in the works of such figures as Dionysius the Areopagite, under whose auspices there remained at least some room for mysticism within the tradition. It was only in the emergence of "secular modernity" that the battle against gnosis was won again, a bit more thoroughly this time.

It is true that on the cusp of modernity, Protestantism gave birth to its greatest mystic, the inexhaustible Jacob Böhme, who died in 1624. But Böhmean theosophy, which sought to restore to Christianity its metaphysical mooring, did not establish dominance or even much of a foothold or influence in the universities or in any established churches. Indeed, Böhmean theosophy is strikingly anti-sectarian.[20] By the nineteenth century, "secular modernity" had taken hold thoroughly enough that we can hardly think of a single great mystic during the nineteenth and twentieth centuries. I discuss this problem in my historical survey *Magic and Mysticism*, and note a few major exceptions, among them Franklin Merrell-Wolff in the mid-twentieth century, who was inspired by Vedanta, and Bernadette Roberts, a Roman Catholic gnostic of the late twentieth century. But the exceptions prove the rule: who has heard of them? Even specialists in the recent history of religion overlook them.

My point here is this: "secular modernity" in the West emerged out of an even more complete banishing of gnosis than that which took place in late antiquity. What we term "secular modernity"—with all its technological prowess, its extraordinary capacity to mobilize people and machinery into a greater mechanism that can lay flat the entire earth (*mobilmachung*), to exploit and dominate other people and nature without qualms—derives from a fundamental schism within us, a profound dualism so deeply a part of society that we hardly even recognize that it is there. This division is between subject and object, a dualism upon which the exploitation of the world entirely depends.

To use the terms of Charles Péguy, when *mystique* is banished, that is the triumph of *politique*. *Politique* is the political philosophy of combat and calculation that remains completely engrossed in the historical and that rejects out of hand those who are drawn to the secret roads inward. *Politique* has religious antecedents, no doubt. But it is not and cannot be religious except in the sense of affirming and defending a religion devoid

---

20. See on this point Arthur Versluis, *Wisdom's Children: A Christian Esoteric Tradition* (Albany: SUNY Press, 1999).

of mysticism, that is, devoid of inwardness and transposed into a language of empire that unfolds in history.

And there is an interesting parallel here with the emergence of Islamic fundamentalism, especially of the al-Qaeda species, because here, too, one finds the assertion of an imperial and historicist religion whose millennialism is transposed into the historical notion of a grand caliphate, sometimes mingled with the notion of a coming Mahdi. For the Islamic fundamentalist, too, the world is a field of combat: an historical plain on whose distant horizon hovers the hazy mirage of an imagined utopia, if only one could impose by force one's vision on others, kill those whom one imagines to be the minions of Satan, and so forth. For the Islamic fundamentalist of this variety, Sufism, the mysticism of Islam, is to be rejected precisely because it turns one's attention inward, away from the projected enemy, away from the dualistic world of combat.

I mention this because the various fundamentalisms, in particular those of Islam, belong to so-called secular modernity too. They belong as much as "secular modernity," and perhaps even more, to the realm of *politique*. At least "secular modernity" has a libertarian ethos built into it, the concepts of civil liberties, of individual freedom. But the bastard children of "secular modernity," the various fundamentalisms, they are not so welcoming of those who disagree with them, nor of the rights of others. In truth this is because they have turned, even more than have "secular moderns," against the very notion of gnosis, that is, of inwardness. For them, what matters above all is indeed exactly what Schmitt recognized, the need for the "enemy," for the projected "other" who is hardened into a mere target, who is to be annihilated. Reacting against the alienation endemic to "secular modernity," they choose as a remedy an even more intense and total alienation. They are the avenging shade of "secular modernity" itself.

What then has *mystique* to offer us? Of what value are these "secret roads" inward? (I write "roads" because, given the numerous forms of esotericism, there is not only one road inward.) Let us look back at the early modern period that Guénon and Schmitt rightly recognized as pivotal. There was at that time, in the seventeenth and eighteenth centuries, an efflorescence of esoteric movements, notably alchemy, but also astrology, Christian theosophy, and various other movements like Rosicrucianism. What did these movements have in common? They sought bridges between self and other, between us and nature and spirit; to them belonged the desire for union or reunion with the Divine as it appears in us and in nature. Little wonder that they were rejected—they had to be rejected, if the subject-object division was accepted to the extent necessary to make possible the technical apparatus of industrial modernity. But they offered then, and still offer now, alternatives to the subject-object dualism that underlies, and makes possible, the condition of "secular modernity."

Indeed, one can go further. It may well be that "secular modernity" taken as a whole, recognizing both its positive and negative dimensions, nonetheless derives from and exemplifies a fundamental alienation of self and other. It is possible that the one thing needful, the rejected keystone, cannot be found in any external, technical solution, nor does it belong to the endless concatenation of dualistic combat, but rather belongs to consciousness, more specifically to the turn inward toward what Böhme called the *mysterium*. Such a turn does not belong either to a political Right or to a political Left; it belongs, rather, to a re-orientation of a being toward realizing that which is beyond being.

As Böhme recognized, we live in a dualistic world, one in which love and wrath, friendship and hostility alternate with one another. But he also suggested, just when "modernity" was emerging, that another way of being is also possible. Such a way of being has its origin not in dualism but in a non-dualism that derives from gnosis, or direct insight into what he termed the *Ungrund*, or divine "not-ground." The word *Ungrund* is itself a refusal of objectification: it embodies *via negativa* mysticism that goes back to Meister Eckhart, to Dionysius the Areopagite, and before him, to Basilides. Does such insight—attested to in Christianity, from late antiquity onward—have political implications? Undoubtedly it does. But the rejection of mysticism built into Christianity from early on, and if anything, intensified in modernity, created an environment highly unconducive to exploring such implications.

And so here we are. The modern period has given birth to a vast array of possibilities, which is also to say, choices. It has created a space in which, for the first time in millennia, it is possible to explore openly and thoughtfully what before could not be investigated—the excluded, the suppressed, the "heretical" and esoteric currents of the past and present. Now, like in the Russian Silver Age (as John Milbank attests with his work on Sophianic Christianity), it is possible to look into the implications not just of this or that imposed political regime, but into the intellectual architecture that informs what and how we see, but that we rarely recognize or acknowledge.

The temptation is always there to recoil against the array of choices, of possibilities, to turn back toward the fixed, the comfortable, the literal, the twin familiar realms of faith and reason, even if they too often give birth to monsters. Fundamentalism is such a recoil: it is a recourse to an extreme form of dualism, seductively comforting because it provides the familiar rhetoric of believers and unbelievers, the chosen and the obdurate heretics. It is indeed the twin of technological-industrial rationalism, as evidenced by the technological sophistication of the jihadists with their digital video webcasts of murderous attacks, mirroring the cameras embedded in the noses of American missiles. Dualism is the foundation of modernity, as Schmitt testifies. Is it not possible, now, to begin exploring gnosis, that hidden third pillar of the West, there from antiquity and still unspoken? Or are we rather on the brink, as the Russian Silver Age was, of descent into yet another bout of totalitarian brutalism?

Secularism is a Fundamentalism! The Background to a Problematic Claim

Frederik Stjernfelt

The claim in the title of this article is now heard more and more frequently. It often comes from religious people who have themselves been targets of attack for fundamentalism, and they feel compelled to pay back this criticism in the same currency. Secularists, too, they claim, hold fast to a point of view, and this tenacity of belief is in itself deemed a fundamentalism, the religious person argues. The character of the point of view in question is of no importance; the very fact that it is held is sufficient to denounce it as fundamentalism. This is a smart strategy, for if it is fundamentalism merely to have a point of view, then a pleasant darkness descends in which "all cows become grey"—i.e., in which all points of view become equally legitimate. "Fundamentalism" ceases to mean anything precise, and thus the criticism of certain radically religious points of view becomes diluted. From this perspective, we are all fundamentalists to the extent that we seriously mean anything at all.[1]

1. This rhetorical trick corresponds to the argument that science is but another form of belief: the concept of science is thereby diluted, and sooner or later any claim can pass for being equally scientific. The leading Danish daily *Politiken*—a former bastion of Enlightenment thinking—has also introduced this argument. It was presented by the former rationalist Peter Wivel in a so-called "Politiken comment," under the title "Science Rests on Belief" (Peter Wivel, "Videnskab hviler på tro," *Politiken*, January 3, 2007). Here, theory, hypothesis, and faith are made into one and the same thing—all, of course, under the headline of "faith." In this way, all differences between literal belief in revelations and holy books, on the one hand, and critical construction and investigation of hypotheses and theories, on the other hand, are obliterated. Similarly, the differences between the corresponding institutions, churches and universities, are also swept away.

Yet it is only possible to claim that secularism is a fundamentalism by closing your eyes to some basic differences. Fundamentalism refers to a specific type of religious practice that accords to special holy writings a non-negotiable status wherein the text must be read and followed in practice in a literal way. Views of this kind are well known from Christianity and Islam. They often appear in more recent currents within these old religions, currents that see their own religious tradition as desolate and devoid of spirit. For that reason, tradition needs to be revived by means of a return to its sources and a new, more literal, and more faithful belief in the religion's holy writings. In Islam, for example, we know of Wahhabism and Salafism, neither of which dates back more than a couple of centuries (the Muslim Brotherhood, e.g., dates from 1928). In Christianity, many of the American fundamentalist sects are not much older than a century ("Dispensationalism," for instance, dates from the late nineteenth century). Thus, it is a normal part of large, text-based religions that they now and then give rise to reformist fundamentalist currents that insist on a firm and faithful re-reading of the holy texts.[2] These holy writings are most often strongly heterogeneous texts, comprising claims about the existence of sacred beings, narratives about the origin and ontological status of world and mankind, as well as directives for human life of very differing degrees of generality, ranging from general demands for faith and prayer to very specific juridical and moral instructions that govern types of food, dress, impermissible actions, inheritance laws, punishments, treatment of non-believers, and so on. If you claim that all of these different aspects of your holy text must be understood and obeyed literally, then you are a fundamentalist.

It follows from this that secularism cannot possibly be a fundamentalism. Secularism does not point to any body of sacred writings, it does not refer to revealed knowledge, and it makes no claim about the existence or non-existence of gods, demons, or other suprasensible beings. It makes no ontological assertions about the deepest fundament of the world. It does not provide detailed behavioral codices for any congregation. Secularism, in general, has no congregation. Secularism is merely a social and political

---

2. This is also why fundamentalists may portray themselves as adherents of the "reform" of religion—yet without this indicating any movement toward democracy and secularism. A prominent example on this strategy is the "reformist" "Euro-Islamist" Tariq Ramadan. See Caroline Fourest, *Frère Tariq: Discours, stratégie et méthode de Tariq Ramadan* (Paris: Grasset, 2004).

doctrine that makes certain claims about how society can be formed so that different believers and non-believers may live together. It claims that this is optimally possible if the political system is not, in itself, religiously motivated and is not constructed according to the directives of any of the competing deities. Secularism therefore only demands a very small, but a nevertheless decisive, contribution from citizens living within a secular society: namely, that they tolerate the coexistence of widely different forms of belief and non-belief.[3] Secularism may even be said to be supported by a certain amount of empirical evidence. Religious tensions in the democratic societies that have experimented with secularism in recent centuries have lessened considerably when compared to those same societies in earlier times. Secularism is thus a political principle whose practical effects are supported by objective observation.[4]

It is very important to understand that secularism does not support any doctrine about the existence or non-existence of gods or related beings. It can not make any claims about such matters; it only addresses the political structuring of modern societies. It has no idea about whether the world is created or not, whether revealed or sacred texts exist, or which values individuals should choose in order to orient their lives. In a certain sense, secularism is a meta-value or a meta-principle that deals with the regulation of the interaction between different values. It does not demand any specific type of behavior but instead provides a framework for the encounter between different values and behaviors.

3. Thus, secularism is closely connected to the Enlightenment tradition for tolerance as well as to democracy and human rights (especially freedom of belief and freedom of speech). The very notion of "secularism" is due to the Englishman G. J. Holyoake, who uses it for the first time in the 1840s and subsequently develops the concept in *The Principles of Secularism* (London, 1860) and *The Origin and Nature of Secularism* (London, 1896). Holyoake supposed "the practical sufficiency of natural morality apart from Atheism, Theism or the Bible" (Holyoake, *Principles of Secularism*, p. 17).

4. Just as secularism is not atheist—it has no stance on that issue—it does not in any way preclude public religious manifestations. In the current anti-secular crusade, it is often claimed that secularism demands the withdrawal of religion from the public sphere. This is not correct. In a secular state, religions may, just like any other social group, organize demonstrations, make publicity, publish books, magazines, and newspapers, participate in public discussions, and so forth. They may even form parties (like the European Christian Democrat Parties) whose candidates run for democratic elections. In a Danish context, theologians have often played very central roles in public debate. Secularism has nothing to say against this. It simply claims that religious arguments have no privileged role at all and that public space, and the norms for behavior in that space, can not be regulated by any religion.

This is why it is inherently mistaken to put secularism and funda-mentalism on equal footing. Even if you strongly support secularism, you do not become a fundamentalist by virtue of that support. But how have things developed such that classical Enlightenment commentators—like those of the Danish daily *Politiken*—suddenly find themselves called upon to claim that secularism and religion are identical?

My hypothesis is that it has its roots in the spreading of a specific notion of *culture* in public debate. Recall the political Left and its many analyses of societies, ideologies, and politics from twenty or thirty years ago. At that time, the talk was about economics, ideology, politics, social structures, history, geography, resources, and much more—but only rarely about "culture." In the present, the conversation has changed completely. Now the talk focuses almost exclusively on different groups, countries, or even civilizations in terms of their "culture," and where other aspects are involved, "culture" is typically given explanatory priority. The concept of "culture" is considered the deepest level of analysis when the thoughts, ideas, motives, habits, and acts of people are described.

How in the world has this happened? Nowhere on the political Left, during the past thirty years, has there been a significant debate between proponents for "society" and "culture," respectively, where the latter have ended up victorious. Yet the concept of culture has ever so slowly sneaked into the discussion and body-snatched large parts of the once so-critical Left. Now, "culture" is probably one of the most ambiguous words in the English language, and it is well known that it may mean just about anything, from yeast production and agriculture to habits, the arts, and personal refinement. But the use of the word that has distorted the debate is a specific one. Here, culture refers to a group of human beings that shares a set of values that determines their access to the world. The grammatical form "a culture" is characteristic of this use of the word and is used as if it were simply a given that such groups exist and are easily distinguished from one another. Culture, in this sense of the word, is sup-posed to form homogeneous bubbles, where the individuals trapped in one bubble all share the same fundamental values and worldviews. In this understanding of culture, you can only understand and access the world and society when you shape them through the optics of your own culture. Thus, culture is more basic than the individual, and in relation to other cultures, it forms similarly closed bubbles, homogeneous on the inside and heterogeneous on the outside. There is no place outside of culture

SECULARISM IS A FUNDAMENTALISM! 43

from which the different cultures may be compared or judged, and for this reason their "sets of values" are incommensurable and equally valid. The celebration of human sacrifice, war, stoning, and the cutting off of hands is one set of values, while the striving for art, science, and democracy is another, and it is impossible to claim that one is superior to the other. Moreover, this concept of culture asserts the unchangeable character of culture, both as a fact and as a norm. It dramatically exaggerates the external differences between cultures, and it diminishes the internal differences within a culture. Cultural change is consequently seen as degeneration, and it is presumed that cultures exert mechanisms that prevent individuals from changing their culture, mixing their culture with others, or jumping to a different culture entirely. This concept of culture is consistent with the most conservative forces in a given culture, i.e., those forces that claim the right to call individuals to order who belong to the group but who do practice the culture correctly or to a sufficient degree.[5]

It is an important task for the history of ideas to trace the development of this concept of culture. It has an obvious root in Herder and his idea of the nation as an organic being and a fundamental destiny, and the romantic nationalisms of the nineteenth century constitute a strong variant of this notion of culture. The political history of nationalism is well charted.[6] However, the concept also has a left-wing sense, which is more recent and less well known, but which is informed by, among other influences, a certain variant of the anthropological concept of culture. Anthropology and ethnology had to turn away from the tendency of the discipline to evolutionism and from the claim that the white man was the end of evolution while all other societies correlatively were seen as more or less primitive earlier stages. In that tendency, the concepts of "race" and "culture" were used interchangeably. Instead, a more sober methodology was assumed, where the field worker was expected to bracket his or her own prejudices and neutrally chart and analyze the findings. In the study of different societies, this method naturally appeared to reflect great progress. In certain parts of anthropology, however, this methodology was

5. Thus, it is a conception of "cultures" that systematically overlooks how societies and groups of human beings are constantly in a some degree of evolution, internal disagreement, exchange, and hybridization. The inherent conservatism in this notion of culture has, strangely, not led the political Left to find it unpalatable.

6. Cf. Ernest Gellner, *Nations and Nationalism*, 2nd ed. (Malden, MA: Blackwell, 2006).

given an ontological interpretation: cultures are necessarily fundamentally autonomous, unique, and incommensurable. From Radcliffe-Brown and structure-functionalism, a tradition for radical holism has been thriving in parts of anthropology, claiming that cultures are organism-like, self-organizing structures, which are closed around themselves. In certain periods, other cultures might even play the role of utopian ideals, serving as a basis for the criticism of one own's culture—a famous example of which is Margaret Mead's use of Oceania for attacking Western sexual mores in *Coming of Age in Samoa*. Mead's friend Ruth Benedict framed the anthropological concept of culture in her highly influential *Patterns of Culture* (1934), which has since been reprinted numerous times and now enjoys the status of a classic text.[7] The book had the noble aim of arguing against contemporary racism, but like many others Benedict ended up arguing against the idea of the roots of culture in racial biology, absolutizing the differences on the cultural level instead. Cultures were "cultural patterns," and each culture had its own distinct "personality," which could only be understood on its own terms. The absolute differences between races, as claimed by racism, were replaced with equally absolute differences between cultures. Zygmunt Bauman has fruitfully pointed to the similarities between racism and this new doctrine on the absolute cultural difference between people. The latter may appropriately be called "culturalism."

On the Western Left, there have always been a number of different ideas about the basis of critique. One was grounded in Marxism, in its communist and social democratic variants, and viewed the economic issue of distribution as the decisive consideration. However, a constant undercurrent of culturalist and vitalist alternatives tended to see economics as less important and chose to focus instead upon cultural aspects of life forms. The vitalist critique of bourgeois society did not attack the basic economic and political structures, as did Marxism; instead, it attacked the bourgeois lifestyle, the bourgeois "culture." In doing so, it was closely aligned with conservative criticism that also attacked bourgeois values: both assumed that the decisive issue was not to see the bourgeoisie as the

---

7. See, for instance, Alan Barnard's judgment regarding the history of anthropology: "While Tylor's definition [of culture] has remained at the heart of considerations of culture in the abstract, the perspective which emerged as most crucial to its position as the quintessential anthropological concept was that of Ruth Benedict. The key text is her *Patterns of Culture...*" Alan Barnard, *History and Theory in Anthropology* (Cambridge: Cambridge UP, 2000), p. 102.

class responsible for capitalism as an economic system, but rather to attack the bourgeois culture and to replace it with another. Bourgeois life was supposed to be shallow, superficial, one-dimensional, inauthentic—and a more authentic life, rather than the mere redistribution of wealth, should be the basis of critique. On the Left, this idea came to the fore in the years around 1968, when the Western working classes enjoyed the benefits of an unprecedented economic boom and economic issues seemed less relevant. It is well known how Marxism subsequently withered away as an intellectual framework, both in its university variants in the West and as "realized socialism" in other countries around the globe. And what was left for the Left other than the concept of "culture"? The baby boomers had experimented with a "counterculture," whose primary aim was not a political or economic struggle but rather a vitalist struggle in terms of dress codes, dietary habits, consumption, lifestyle, travels, music, metaphysics—exactly those "sets of values" described by anthropologists.[8] The counterculture of the baby boomers had disappointingly little real political impact but rather provided a new set of Bourdieuian "distinctions" for an emergent academic elite, by means of which it became possible to distinguish oneself from ordinary, inauthentic people. Meanwhile, capitalism developed further without any hindrance.[9] This implies, however, that when Marxism, along with a whole body of sophisticated theory, withered away, only this vulgar version of the anthropological concept of "culture" remained on the Left—without any similarly refined body of theory, it must be added. During the 1980s and 1990s, this concept of culture slowly assumed the place previously occupied by Marxism, a transformation that was neither explicitly discussed nor noticed to any large degree.

This is how the Left gradually became "multicultural,"[10] which led it to embrace a long series of anti-Enlightenment ideas that previously it had fiercely attacked. But it is a decisive peculiarity, without which

8. The 1968 icon Herbert Marcuse incarnates this turn. As a figure influenced by both Heidegger and the Frankfurt School, he left Marxism behind to the benefit of a criticism of "one-dimensionality" in the culture of Western societies.

9. As described by Joseph Heath and Andrew Potter in *Nation of Rebels: Why Counterculture became Consumer Culture* (New York: HarperBusiness, 2005).

10. This unfortunate concept is almost as imprecise as the notion of culture. Does it mean that different cultures may coexist if they assume the rule of law, democracy, and secularism as a common frame? If so, then it is a completely different from the claim that cultures may coexist unmodified and without such a framework. The latter is the idea of "strong" multiculturalism, and it is that version which is discussed here.

the actual political tensions may not be understood, that this concept of (multi-)culturalism has exactly the same structure as that of the resurgent right-wing nationalism and its ideas of national culture. Both celebrate the idea of culture as a homogenous set of values that precedes the individual and which has the right to govern and punish the individual if it does not conform. The right-wing version of this concept of culture is a revival of nineteenth-century nationalism and conceives of the bubble of culture as something characteristic of a group of people who inhabit a territory—typically a nation-state. The left-wing version celebrates the very same homogenous cultural bubbles but claims that they may be smaller and can and must thrive in parallel on the same territory—without proposing any way of accommodating the presence of other such bubbles, i.e., without any secularism that would provide a framework for their coexistence. On the contrary, this version of (multi-)culturalism celebrates the pluralization of the law, such that a single group must have the opportunity to introduce its own laws and courts, which have jurisdiction over the group's members only.[11] In this version, the principles of enlightenment and human rights are not universal but must be shaped to fit culturalist demands. These rights pertain to individuals, but in culturalism, the rights of cultures are seen as more basic than individual rights, which must consequently yield in cases of clashes between the two. In Denmark, we heard such demands in the debate around the Danish caricatures of Muhammad, where it was claimed that the constitutional freedom of speech (paragraph 77 in the Danish constitution, which corresponds to the First Amendment of the U.S. Constitution) must be restricted because

---

11. It requires a considerable amount of political naïveté not to see the dangers in a juridical pluralism of this sort. Obviously, it will lead to different rights for different individuals in the same society (cf. the Islamic ideas of half-inheritance for women only, prohibition of interests, the husband's legal right to marital violence, and the prohibition and punishment of apostasy). Even more problematic, any legal system with courts presupposes the existence of a police force to ensure the decisions of the courts are carried out. A pluralization of law necessarily implies the pluralization of the police force and consequently the partitioning of the state's "monopoly of violence" (Weber) and its sovereignty over its territory. Islamist groups have realized this and have begun to argue for, and in some cases to create, a religious police charged with enforcing the observation of Islamic norms in certain immigrant neighborhoods in Western Europe. In situations of tension, it is hardly a good thing that different groups of citizens will thus have access to their own standing armies or militias. The implications of such policies in peacetime can be seen in Malaysia, with a segregation that borders on apartheid. Bosnia serves as an example of these policies during wartime.

of Islamist demands.[12] In such cases, it is not the Enlightenment and secularist principle of toleration that is maintained. Here, the party expected to tolerate other parties is the one that might otherwise be shocked by the strange customs of other parties. Instead, a principle of "respect" is invoked, according to which other people and cultures may be forced to respect central rules and ideas in a single culture—such as the Islamic prohibition against pictures of the prophet. The party expected to show "respect" is not the party that may otherwise be shocked but rather the party that other parties might see as shocking. The tolerant party must restrain its own tendency to be shocked; the respectful party must yield to the demands of other easy-to-shock parties. This is why toleration and respect are not the same thing, even if they are often identified with each other when people try to find an easy solution to religious and cultural tensions. Toleration is a demand made on the party that might otherwise be shocked; respect is a demand made on the party that might otherwise cause other parties to be shocked. This is why the demand for toleration is intimately connected to freedom of religion and the freedom of speech, while the demand for respect, by contrast, is connected to the demand for limits on freedom of speech and religion. For the time being, radical versions of Islam are very aggressive regarding this "respect," as evident in the Salman Rushdie case, the Theo van Gogh case in Holland, the Mohammed crisis in Denmark, and the case of the Pope in Germany and Italy. Yet Christian fundamentalism in the United States, with its demand for the teaching of "creation science" in biology classes, has the same character.[13]

12. Even though such claims from Islamic countries were numerous throughout the crisis, and even though the twelve illustrators were forced to go into hiding to protect themselves against death threats, most of the Danish Left, including the traditionally Enlightenment daily *Politiken*, claimed that the case was not at all about freedom of speech. Instead, the case was seen as a purely Danish issue, and the main point was Prime Minister Fogh's tackling of the case and the arguments for or against him—as if it were not rather unimportant on a larger scale who is prime minister in a country half the size of London. This should be mentioned here, because it shows how a culturalist focus on Denmark only makes the international, cosmopolitan aspects of the case vanish. Like the extreme Danish Right, which is obsessed with Denmark exclusively, the Danish Left saw the case in a purely Danish perspective and thus missed the principal, international aspect of the case: the question of freedom of speech. The American media, however, is not free of blame. Its timid refusal to reprint the caricatures is a shameful case of not living up to the central ideals of Western democracy.

13. "Respect" is also an example of polysemy. "Respect" may mean the recognition of a person or a group that has achieved something praiseworthy, and it may mean a fear that you feel toward a person or group that has the ability to hurt you. The kind of "respect"

It is very important to emphasize that the concepts of culture maintained by the nationalist Right[14] and by the multiculturalist Left are very closely related. In both cases, culture is seen as preceding the individual, as something essentially static, as something venerable that should be protected, and as an entity that in itself should form the basis for the allocation of political rights and privileges on the group level. The difference between the two cases pertains merely to the distribution of cultures within the territory. In both cases, the basic counterargument is that one group's privileges are another group's repression. The tension between the two types of culturalism—national culturalism and multiculturalism—is a war between brothers and does not constitute a basic opposition in actual politics. That opposition, instead, is to be found between the culturalism of these two parties (mono- or multi-), on the one hand, and political liberalism and its emphasis on the individual and democratic institutions, on the other hand. Both of these culturalist currents are, in a deep sense of the word, conservative and aimed against individual human rights. Neither of them are concerned with the decisive issue of apostasy—which in even relatively mild versions of Islam is prohibited and results in severe punishment, ranging from a loss of rights to imprisonment to, in extreme cases, even death.

The human rights principle of freedom of religion is thus silently reinterpreted so as to cover the right of groups—"cultures"—to cultivate their religion (including forcing individuals into submission), rather than being concerned with the right of individuals to choose, change, or even abandon religion. In this widespread Newspeak reinterpretation, freedom of religion now means exactly the opposite: the freedom of religious authorities to repress individuals.

In both left-wing and right-wing versions of culturalism, human rights and democracy are not seen as universal and "thin" structures that only furnish a framework for the lives and choices of individuals. Quite to the contrary, they are seen as a deplorable ersatz religion that sanctifies human beings instead of God. Such a doctrine may be found in very different religious groups, from right-wing Christian groups to al-Qaeda. The left-wing

---

that is called for in connection to the different Islamist threats has the latter character, of course, and thus it has nothing to do with real recognition. It is more closely related to the mafia idea of "respect," which arises from offers you can not refuse.

14. In Denmark, e.g., by the so-called "Danish People's Party," which forms part of the parliamentary basis of the actual government and appeals to 10 to 15 percent of the electorate.

version of the attack on human rights is that human rights and democracy are merely "Western values," which the imperialist West attempts to force onto other cultures—thus making universalism and totalitarianism one and the same thing. The connection to the anthropological concept of culture can be observed in the fact that, in 1947, none other than the American Anthropological Association protested against the preparation of the 1948 United Nations Human Rights Charter with culturalist arguments.[15] The protest was aimed at the UN Human Rights Commission and claimed that "It must also take into full account the individual as a member of the social group of which he is a part, whose sanctioned modes of life shape his behavior, and with whose fate his own is thus inextricably bound."[16] As is evident by the word "inextricably," this claim rejects the possibility that the individual might leave or change his culture. Today, a similar campaign is being waged to change the UN Human Rights Charter through the addition of a paragraph that criminalizes the critique of religions. The Organization of the Islamic Conference (OIC) has over many years repeatedly proposed the inclusion of such a paragraph. The instrumentalization of the Danish caricature crisis by the Arab world must be seen in this context: that crisis was utilized by the campaign to advance such a prohibition. Related demands are now seen in the cross-religious "high-level" Alliance of Civilizations initiative assembled by former UN general secretary Kofi Annan, which includes Christians, Muslims, and Jews, and is led by former Iranian president Mohammad Khatami (who, as president, supported the death penalty for homosexuality). The group presented a much-discussed report on November 13, 2006, which claimed that the actual tensions between Islamic and western countries are purely political and have nothing to do with religion.[17]

15. Lawrence Harrison, *The Central Liberal Truth: How Politics Can Change a Culture and Save It from Itself* (Oxford: Oxford UP, 2006), p. 8.

16. American Anthropological Association, "Statement on Human Rights. Submitted to the Commission on Human Rights, United Nations, by the Executive Board, American Anthropological Association," *American Anthropologist* 49, no. 4 (1947).

17. It is too rarely emphasized that the pressure on Denmark and the burning of Danish embassies in Islamic countries around February 1, 2006, coincided with a fateful vote in the British House of Commons. On January 31, the Blair government was on the brink of confirming a radical prohibition against many kinds of religious criticism, the so-called "Racial and Religious Hatred Bill," effectively delimiting freedom of speech in a very radical manner. The bill was supported by radical British Islamists. The House of Lords had changed the bill to avoid free-speech implications, but the majority in the House of Commons seemed to agree in voting against these changes. Blair went home early, convinced the

The vulgar version of the anthropological concept of culture is dangerous because it tends to depoliticize issues that are essentially political. Political ideologies are necessarily partial—liberalism, conservatism, social liberalism, social democracy, socialism, etc., are posed against each other—even if they (as a rule) stand together on a more basic level, where they oppose fascism, communism, Islamism, and other totalitarianisms. But if a political current is categorized as "culture," it is immediately preserved and protected against criticism. It is no longer seen as one partial and debatable point of view among others, because according to culturalism, cultures are organic, irreducible entities worthy of protection. Thus, cultures have a right to exist, they must be respected, they can claim privileges, and they have the right to unchanged survival. This is, in fact, the tourist's descending gaze on the natives, which must be there to supply an experience of "difference," "authenticity," and "otherness"—the tourist busily forgetting them when the postcard has been mailed and he is safely back home. If, for instance, a political current like Islamism (whose different reformist, revolutionary, and terrorist variants all share the belief that society should be constructed on Islamic political principles) is categorized as "culture," then it becomes immediately exempted from critique.[18] Hence, political criticism of Islamism may be discarded as "Islamophobia"

vote was safe. He and his party's "whip" had not, however, counted on a group of Labour back-benchers who decided to vote against the law, which fell with just one vote. Had that bill been passed in England—the country of origin for free speech—the implications might have been disastrous in the EU, if not worldwide. The caricature crisis must be seen is this wider context: a decade-long controversy over free speech between Islamists, on the one side, and democratic principles, on the other, and including such controversies as the Salman Rushdie case, the Theo van Gogh murder, the Muslim campaign against the Pope, and, of course, the OIC pressure to truncate the UN Human Rights Charter.

18. It is a widespread defense among non-terrorist Islamists to point to the many different versions of Islamism, which have different strategies for the Islamization of society and also differing ideas about which domains of society should be subjected to *sharia* law. The overall goal of Islamists maintains the same principal character, however: to make (Islamic) religion the basis for society instead of democracy. In the same way, there were also many different political strategies in Nazism. Hitler's (winning) strategy, as is well known, was the mildest, reformist strategy, which refrained from revolution or terror but sought Nazification through democratic elections. This does not, of course, make Nazism as such a democratic movement. The very existence of different strategies, including strategies that utilize democracy, does not prove that Islamism can be democratic. The decisive issue is not whether you will make use of democracy to achieve your goal, but whether you will dismantle democracy or preserve it when you achieve power.

or "racism" because it does not "respect" a "culture." Nazism attempted something similar when it claimed to continue an age-old Germanic culture, but left-wing critics at that time were better equipped to see through the nonsense. Now, extreme Islamist movements like wahhabism, salafism, and the Muslim Brotherhood (which was directly influenced by European fascism) may be preserved with the "culture" argument: these movements are not political programs but rather "cultures" that must not be attacked. But as soon as "culture" enters the field of politics, it becomes exactly as debatable and open to criticism as any other organization, grouping, party, or movement that makes political demands. And priests, clerks, and imams of all sorts are not entitled to a single grain more of respect than any other person just because they use divine curses in their political discourse.

Religiously motivated policies may use this escape to avoid criticism because the vulgar anthropological concept of culture has a certain affinity to religion. In many of the societies studied by classic anthropology, the different distinctions, institutions, and modularizations in later high cultures were unknown—such as the distinctions between religion, politics, science, arts, etc. In these societies, a single worldview generally prevailed, where religious ideas occupied the central position (even if the tendency of anthropology to homogenize intracultural differences probably was not always without effect). This gave rise to the idea that religion constitutes the basis for the culture of a given society, and that other cultural levels only mirror that religious foundation—a mirror reflection, so to speak, of the vulgar Marxist belief in the economic basis of society. If you buy the vulgar anthropological concept of culture, religious ideas have a privileged status and are particularly apt to be preserved as "culture," no matter which horrible ideas, demands, and consequences are implied by them. A sober understanding of societies would instead stop searching for one basic level that everything else reflects, and face the much more complicated issue of trying to grasp the interplay between sociology, politics, religion, culture, economics, science, language, history, biogeography, etc.—which may vary considerably from one society to another.

The sneaking religiousification of political discourse by means of the vulgar anthropological concept of culture may be observed quite directly in some cases. Very often, the argument is made that the problem of the West is that we are unable to meet "the Other" or even "the radically Other." Now I have never encountered the "radically Other," and I seriously doubt it exists anywhere in the universe. All known cultures are created by human beings, who possess a large biological uniformity, even if an impressive cultural variation has indeed developed. You can easily encounter something "other"—other ways of eating, governing, exchanging, and dressing—but never anything "radically Other." The awe-inspiring capital "O" is telling: the very concept of the "radically Other" is important from science of religion and from theology. The concept originates in the writings of the German Rudolf Otto in the 1910s, in his interpretation of religion as such as built on the encounter with "das ganz Andere," the "radically Other"—the sacred, the divine, the holy.[19] This "radically Other" is an example of modern syncretism between religions (it holds for all religions, in Otto's doctrine) and shows how religious the thoughtless idea of "respect" for "other cultures" is—in contradistinction to the Enlightenment idea of toleration.[20]

The new emphasis on religion and culture in the explanation of the behavior of human groups also constitutes a decisive step backward in terms of science. By the phrase "set of values" it is often presupposed that no matter which combination of value ideas some group might decide to fancy, it would give rise to a viable culture. It is as if politics did not possess its own structures and constraints, not reducible to "culture"; it is as if economic relations and laws did not play a central role in the understanding of a society and its possibilities. The proponents for the hard concept of culture thus presuppose that politics, economy, sociology,

19. The revival of the concept in the identity politics of the 1990s seems to be due to an argument by Jacques Derrida: the sacred, pertaining to "the wholly other [le tout autre]," is generalized to refer to everywhere that "the wholly other" appears, including the encounter with other cultures. Jacques Derrida, The Gift of Death, trans. David Wills (Chicago: Univ. of Chicago Press, 1995).

20. A good example of how this meta-religious syncretism thrives within the science of religion appears in Mensching's history of the science of religion (Gustav Mensching, Geschichte der Religionswissenschaft [Bonn: Universitätsverlag Bonn, 1948]). He sees the whole of the development of the science of religion as one great struggle to overcome its origins in Enlightenment and its criticism of religion. The one scholar who after all succeeds in fighting Enlightenment is Rudolf Otto, who decisively pushes through irrationalism in the science of religion (ibid., p. 87) by focusing on the very object of religion: the sacred (mysterium tremendum et fascinosum). The religious scientist must, in this account, be a believer himself, otherwise he has no access to this object of religions. But at the same time, his faith must aim at the sacred as such—beyond the different religious orthodoxies. Both rationalism and the orthodoxies of the single religions are, according to Mensching, opponents of the religious scientist. This religious tendency within the science of religion is, of course, highly problematic and may, with its antimodernity, approach fascism (as in the case of Mircea Eliade).

and so on are nothing but a freely variable surface to the basic choice of religious "values" in a society—a strongly idealist hypothesis, in fact. For that reason, the hard concept of culture tends to occult completely the fact that different "cultures" may be compared according to criteria such as whether their economy, politics, bureaucracy, or production of knowledge functions—criteria that are not themselves "cultural." Maybe certain cultural patterns contribute to preventing individual societies from becoming democratic, wealthy, and enlightened—a Weberian thought that is currently being investigated by the "Culture Matters" project in the United States. Here, culture in the anthropological use of the word *does* mean a lot for a society, but without the vulgarizations of culturalism and its ideals of the closedness and relativism of cultures. On the contrary, one may research which aspects of culture support economical and political development and which do not.

The critical political issue in this context is, of course, the growing fundamentalism within many different religious groups and the threat that it poses to democratic and enlightened principles. But an acute higher-level problem among intellectuals of the West is that culturalism in politics, both in its right-wing and left-wing variants, accepts fundamentalisms on the basis of the vulgar anthropological concept of culture. Culturalism completely lacks the intellectual tools necessary to distinguish fundamentalism and secularism. It can not distinguish faith and knowledge, religion and science. It can not distinguish democratic and totalitarian politics. All in all, it constitutes a major political step backward, which threatens to erode 250 years of enlightenment and to open the door to never-ending religious wars.

As to this particular concept of culture, the conclusion must be: Down with Culture!

The Turn from Cultural Radicalism to National Conservatism: Cultural Policy in Denmark

Kasper Støvring

Cultural policy in Denmark has undergone a change in recent years. A liberal cultural policy has dominated throughout the entire postwar period, under the influence of the movement called "cultural radicalism." In this article I will try to explain the main characteristics of this movement in Danish postwar history, and I will argue that the consensus concerning cultural policy has more recently been challenged. This has been possible because of certain flaws in the ideology of cultural radicalism. The liberal, culturally radical attitude toward cultural policy has traditionally had the purpose of emancipating citizens and subsequently educating them to become rational, independent individuals who are able to take part in the democratic process.

The current Danish right-wing government, which was elected in 2001, has instead promoted a national conservative cultural policy as an alternative to cultural radicalism. At the conclusion of this article I will explain how this has been done. I will argue that according to national conservatives, the state cannot be neutral precisely because it must actively give support to the national culture by means of a cultural policy. The purpose of conservative cultural policy is, in fact, to preserve the unity of the nation.

The Ideology of Cultural Radicalism

The arguments in favor of cultural policy that have been put forward by the cultural radical movement are bound to a certain point in time and to a certain understanding of art and culture. Therefore, these arguments may seem rather obsolete today. This has first and foremost to do with the

54

fact that cultural radicalism works with certain edifying categories when it comes to understanding the nature and social function of art.

Cultural radicalism started out during the interwar period as a reformist movement. It conceived of itself as a movement that advanced an enlightenment project. By means of rationalism, the movement sought to promote the emancipation of the individual. Cultural radicalism argued for a pacifistic and open-minded view of life in a cultural struggle against what was perceived as aggressive militarism, reactionary nationalism, clerical Christianity, and a narrow-minded Victorian sexual morality. All of this was regarded by cultural radicals as chains of the past that tied the individual to a form of mental slavery.

One of the chief figures of the cultural radical movement was the energetic and optimistic intellectual Poul Henningsen (1894–1967). The key issues in Henningsen's cultural emancipation project were jazz in the field of arts, a new minimalist building style in the field of architecture, and a reformist theory of education in the field of educational policy. Henningsen's views can be summed up in the following proposal: Leave the old lifestyles behind and embrace functionalism, modern teaching, and modern art instead.

Henningsen argued in favor of his project in several articles and books. Especially noteworthy is the pamphlet entitled *What about the Culture?* (*Hvad med kulturen?*) from 1933.[1] In this pamphlet, Henningsen criticizes conservative cultural policy and conservative art as being the art

that does not provoke controversy, the art that tells people what they want to have confirmed, such as class romanticism as it is cultivated on grounds of thick dumbing-down speculation in Danish movies. Here, the *large* population is dulled, not by means of conscious conservative propaganda; no, it is much worse. *The capitalistic society is naturally conservative.* If we let free enterprise prevail, all mediocre spiritual life will find its natural center of gravity in the conservation of the present state of affairs. Everyone who writes, paints, and makes movies for the sake of success or money will automatically create conservative art. Everyone who only wants to entertain creates conservative propaganda. Everyone who lacks talent, but who still produces art, supports conservatism. Ninety-nine percent of all art is a pure and dismal imprint of our time without any glimpse of hope for a better future.[2]

1. Poul Henningsen, *Hvad med kulturen?* (Skovlunde: Thaning og Appel, 1969).
2. Ibid., p. 29.

Hence it follows that valuable art is necessarily radical art, and that radical art serves progress, which is characterized as "personal liberty, liberal mindedness, tolerance, sense of justice, egalitarianism, honest sexual morality, internationalism, atheism—in short, the total bright summer program of democracy."[3]

Henningsen was primarily engaged in cultural radicalism during the interwar period, but cultural radicalism continued as a cultural policy project in the postwar period. A central element in this cultural policy and theory of art is a certain version of Freudian psychoanalysis. It teaches that the human being can become emancipated from his or her repressions through a confrontation with irrational feelings: anxiety, neurosis, etc.—all the mental diseases and fixations. Art serves precisely this emancipating purpose, and therefore art has a therapeutic use for the individual as well as for the democratic system because democracy needs emancipated citizens in order to function smoothly.

Legitimating Modernism

The project of cultural radicalism could therefore prove useful in articulating a cultural policy that aims at legitimating a new modernistic art in a political framework defined by the rise of the welfare state. This new modernistic art was in fact identified with the radical modernism that originated in Denmark during the 1950s and 1960s. It was represented by such writers and intellectuals as Klaus Rifbjerg and Villy Sørensen, among several others.[4]

According to Torben Brostrøm, one of the most prominent literary educators of modernism in Denmark, postwar cultural and artistic radicalism is defined by a break with the previous art and culture theory promoted by the so called "Heretica" movement.[5] The "Heretica" movement was quite influential in the years immediately following the Second World War. The new cultural radicals rather unfairly regarded this cultural movement as a kind of inbreeding representative of an outdated rural idyll. And by doing so, Brostrøm and other cultural radicals introduced new standards in

3. Ibid., p. 45.
4. Cf. Villy Sørensen, *Hverken-eller: Kritiske betragtninger* (Copenhagen: Gyldendal, 1961).
5. Cf. Torben Brostrøm, "Det umådelige mådehold," in Anne Borup, Morten Lassen, and Jon Helt Haarder, eds., *Modernismen til debat* (Odense: Syddansk Universitetsforlag, 2005), pp. 254–64; and Ole Wivel, ed., *Heretica: en antologi* (Copenhagen: Gyldendal, 1962).

cultural radical aesthetics. These standards primarily included the norma-tive idea that the break with tradition is a crucial criterion of valuable art. This new—and valuable—art was thus labeled "modernism of confronta-tion" by Rifbjerg.

Now, this new dogma of radical transgression is theoretically joined together with the Freudian idea of psychoanalytic therapy, and the whole concept fits adequately with the Social Democratic welfare policy. This policy prescribes the transformation of the individual's traumatic emo-tional life through the acquisition of "unpleasant" modernistic art. By being confronted with traumas, the individual is cured from mental illness (and in this political agenda, to be reactionary, intolerant, and myopic is, in a sense, to be mentally ill). Only then can the individual be mature enough to take part in the democratic political process.

This shows that the project of cultural radicalism is, in overall terms, concerned about the question of how the state is able to educate the reaction-ary and narrow-minded human being to become a good democratic citizen. This was the guiding purpose of the cultural policy of cultural radicalism, which necessarily included support for modernistic art. For, according to the influential liberal educator Hal Koch, democracy is not only a form of governance but a certain lifestyle, a project of emancipation.[6]

The idea that Social Democratic cultural policy was an integral part of welfare policy was articulated in a report from 1953, entitled "Focus on the Individual Citizen: Contribution to an Active Cultural Policy" (*Men-nesket I centrum: Bidrag til en aktiv kulturpolitik*), which was edited by Julius Bomholt, who was later to become Minister of Cultural Affairs. In this report, Hans Hedtoft, the Social Democratic prime minister at that time, stated that

> any democratic cultural policy must consistently aim to break down all barriers that prevent the self-improvement of the people. A true democracy cannot continue indefinitely, if its foundation is not based on educated, responsible, and independently minded citizens... and general education has to be based on guaranteed freedom of thought, speech, and criticism. Each and every citizen must not just be trained to cope with practical aspects of life. They must also have the opportunity to satisfy the love of beauty, artistic desires, the need for all that lies beyond the boundaries of time and space. A real democratic cultural policy must protect all this in order to guarantee humanity, tolerance, and farsightedness in our modern

6. Hal Koch, *Hvad er demokrati?* (Copenhagen: Gyldendal, 1991).

society, which otherwise threatens to leave us isolated, specialized, one-sided—intellectually and spiritually myopic.[7]

So, cultural radicalism canonizes a certain view of art, and this canonization has been very resistant. It has therefore settled numerous unquestioned issues: that valuable art is modernistic, useful, and edifying while at the same time difficult, critical, and anti-authoritarian. Yet paradoxically it is also supported by the state.

This unity of modernism and cultural radicalism places art in a politically progressive service in which it consequently is bound together with the construction of the Social Democratic welfare state. It was simply the official art theory of the welfare state that Brostrøm and other new cultural radicals articulated in the early 1960s. Hence the ground was paved for a cultural hegemony in Denmark. Hegemony in this sense has to do with the circumstance that a certain intellectual constellation has obtained a dominant position that has entailed a marginalization of diverging movements. And what has been marginalized in Denmark in the postwar period is precisely national conservatism.

This is due to the fact that cultural radicalism in the postwar period is no longer a movement in opposition to the ruling power. On the contrary, it gained power by becoming institutionalized, and this is especially so in the educational and cultural system and in the media. So cultural radicalism is no longer a movement with certain representative figures; the ideology of cultural radicalism is, on the contrary, omnipresent in the institutions of the state and society. And, as I have mentioned, it has also dominated Danish cultural policy—until recently, at least.

The Flaws of Cultural Radicalism

In an anthology from 2001 entitled *The Challenge of Cultural Radicalism* (*Den kulturradikale udfordring*), several Danish intellectuals attempt to revitalize the cultural radical movement. Among the contributors is Klaus Rifbjerg, whose article pays tribute to Poul Henningsen.[8] As the tribute demonstrates, Rifbjerg inherits the emancipation project of cultural radicalism, but along with several other contributors, he also inherits the flaws of cultural radical ideology.

7. Quoted in Peter Duelund, ed., *The Nordic Cultural Model* (Copenhagen: Nordic Cultural Institute, 2003), pp. 37f.

8. Klaus Rifbjerg, "Med højt humør og løftet hale," in Klaus Rifbjerg et al., eds., *Den kulturradikale udfordring* (Copenhagen: Tiderne Skifter, 2001), pp. 9–25.

Rifbjerg accepts Henningsen's statement that "if you want democracy, then you also need democratic art." But cultural radicalism thereby makes itself blind to the fact that great works of art do not necessarily express democratic ideals in an edifying manner. Conservative poets, such as T. S. Eliot, and politically suspicious poets, such as the fascist poet Ezra Pound, have created great works of art. Art does not always serve democratic purposes, and readers of modernism do not necessarily become better citizens by consuming art.

Henningsen's statement reveals the idealism that underlies the emancipation project of cultural radicalism. This idealism is based on an element of mental "sanitation," as the Danish art critic Poul Vad vividly expressed it in an article in the Danish journal *KRITIK*.[9] The phrase "sanitation" refers to the belief that the correct use of therapy and education will unproblematically clean up the messy elements of irrationalism that suppress the individual. When these irrational elements have been washed away, the truly good and harmonious individual will come through, emancipated from the chains of tradition and religion and liberated from the suppression of nationalism and sexual morals. The individual is simply to be emancipated "to an existence in harmonious balance between sense and intellect and of course liberated from all the metaphysical nonsense," according to Vad, summing up the project of cultural radicalism.

But time has long ago revealed the flaws of this cultural optimism. All of these edifying concepts presuppose in fact that the human individual is good by nature, so to speak. This is clearly a simplistic understanding of human nature, something that most individuals—and, by the way, most artists and critics, too—have recognized, at least secretly. (It has not been considered politically correct to express it openly.)

The Critique of "Democratism"

Yet this skeptical attitude has not gained ground in cultural radicalism. Still, cultural radicalism has enjoyed enormous public attention and power. This is due to the fact that cultural radicalism was not just an enlightenment project but also a "sanitary project." The detergent was a kind of utilitarianism that has been institutionalized in the Danish welfare state.

A critical term for this kind of political order is the "therapeutic state," working through large-scale social engineering; and a critical term for

9. Poul Vad, "Kulturradikalismen og modernitetens suppedas," in *KRITIK* 153 (Copenhagen: Gyldendal, 2001), pp. 1–9.

cultural radicalism is "the philosophy of good intentions." And as we know from history, good official intentions have often proven to be a cover for hidden and rather dubious motives. These hidden motives, in the case of cultural radicalism are—according to the conservative writer and politician of the Danish People's Party Søren Krarup—identified as the intention to perform suppressive guardianship, i.e., the intention to interfere with the private lives of the individual citizens through the use of state authority and cultural policy. In one of his most polemical books, from 1968, Krarup terms this phenomenon "democratism." Democratism is the democracy concept of cultural radicalism, which no longer regards democracy as a neutral concept but as a certain value concept. Again, democracy is regarded as a lifestyle.

In his book Krarup states that

> what was once, in the constitutional struggle [when Denmark became a constitutional democracy], a demand for civil legal capacity and political rights has in the recent years become a question of a qualified human attitude. To be democratic is today a question of *behaving* in a certain way. Democracy has been joined together with certain value concepts, and the most important of these are harmony, tolerance, openness, open-mindedness, and humanity. As a result democracy itself has become *the* value concept. It must be practiced in the school, in the workplace, and in the family, and it also necessarily follows that it must be practiced in the human soul. The realization of democracy must therefore be united with a democratic therapy.[10]

The philosophers of democratism, i.e., the cultural radicals, use a moralistic rhetoric concerning democracy and humanism when they argue in favor of their specific cultural policy, a policy which postulates that it is in the common interest of the public. But this kind of argumentation is, according to Krarup, pure hypocrisy and disguises an ideological justification of political special interests, i.e., the interests of cultural radicals. Thus, the official purpose of the cultural radical cultural policy is revealed by different conservative intellectuals[11] as a tactical disguise of the will to power. The moralistic rhetoric is, in the end, a matter of legitimating

---

10. Søren Krarup, *Demokratisme: en kritik* (Copenhagen: Gyldendal, 1968), p. 11.

11. Krarup, *Demokratisme*; Søren Krarup, *Kristendom og danskhed: prædikener og foredrag* (Højbjerg: Hovedland, 2001); Henning Fonsmark, *Historien om den danske utopi: et idépolitisk essay om danskernes velfærdsdemokrati* (Copenhagen: Gyldendal, 1990).

potential violations of the individual: when democracy becomes therapeutic and when the cultural radicals presume to know the determination of the individual, i.e., a good life and social harmony, they also see themselves as justified in insisting the dissenters (i.e., conservatives) become as they intend them to be—according to the democratic philosophy of cultural radicalism.

As Krarup and others have shown, the cultural policy of cultural radicalism is, therefore, grounded in totalitarian guardianship and self interest. Democratism, in other words, is a useful means for an intellectual elite to consolidate their cultural radical hegemony.

The Elite and Democratic Modernization

Conservatives have thus articulated a dual critique of cultural radicalism: that it destroys the national identity in the name of democracy, and that it is a project of the intellectual elite, representing a particular class of society that forces their values on all people. What is the relationship between democratic modernization and this elitist project?

There is a direct relationship to the extent that the therapeutic state is simply the modern managerial state, which was founded in the twentieth century. This is an elite government that radically intervenes in people's lives. Its raison d'être is based on the ideology that science will solve not only the practical problems of society but also the citizen's psychological problems. Not only law and social science but psychoanalytic and pedagogic expertise as well are granted a central role in this kind of government. This is true not only in Denmark and the Scandinavian countries but throughout the West.[12] But let me try to elaborate on what I have written in connection with Krarup and others.

The problem with cultural radicalism is that it sees democracy not only as a neutral parliamentary program. Democracy is also something more substantial, namely, a way of life. Being a democrat does not merely entail casting a vote in elections, but having a qualified attitude and an ideal worldview; it is not just to act, but to *be* in a certain way. Democracy in this sense is indeed a potent value concept that is to be practiced not only in the voting booth but also in spiritual life, through a governmental

---

12. See James L. Nolan, *The Therapeutic State: Justifying Government at Century's End* (New York: New York University, 1998); Paul Gottfried, *After Liberalism: Mass Democracy in the Managerial State* (Princeton, NJ: Princeton UP, 1999); and Christopher Lasch, *The True and Only Heaven: Progress and its Critics* (New York: Norton, 1991).

therapy. Democracy is founded, according to this elitist idea, on specific progressive values such as progressiveness, openness, and open-mindedness. If you are diagnosed as reactionary, introverted, and biased, you become subject to treatment. Therefore, the actual realization of democracy is based on a democratic therapy. The state must, in other words, take the citizens under treatment and educate them according to elite values so that they can become good democrats. It goes without saying that this implies a risk that the state infringes upon the rights of individual people to be left in peace, to freely choose their national identity, and to live according to their national culture.

Another relationship between democratization and the elite project is to be found in so-called constitutional patriotism, a theory that has been promoted by, among others, the German sociologist Jürgen Habermas, but which also forms a part of the heritage of cultural radicalism. Here, the national culture is also dismantled. According to this theory, it no longer makes sense to talk about a national identity as something organic, something that, so to speak, is "given" in advance. On the contrary, it is the result of a free and deliberate choice; it is a political choice of a constructed post-traditional identity. The cultural radical elite want the citizens to be consciously selective in their choice of membership. This is only possible if the nation is not "naturally grown," that is, if it follows a necessary path that cannot be tampered with by virtue of an act of will. According to post-national theory, any membership can thus be rationally defended or refuted by using a critically informed argument.

What citizens according to cultural radicalism should identify with in a modern, multicultural society is not the romantic culture nation. It should instead be the political order and the principles of the democratic constitution. So the advocates of the post-national and post-traditional perspective are in reality taking leave of the idea of the particular and concrete nation. What will replace it are exactly the universal and abstract ideas of liberal democracy, rule of law, and human rights.

Clearly, it is the elite's own class position, which is extrapolated and projected over the whole society. The cultural radical elite is cosmopolitan, and its representatives create their own identity from a theory of hybrid identities in the so-called liquid modernity. The conservative critique is related to a broader Western criticism. The elite is living in the illusion of a global world without borders, shopping in the multicultural bazaar, according to the French conservative philosopher Alain Finkielkraut. A similar criticism is found in Christopher Lasch's *The Revolt of the Elites.*[13] Here, the elite is criticized for living in a world of abstractions: they are advocates of a universal civilization, but they belong to a small elite, far removed from ordinary people's values. They are, in Samuel P. Huntington's words, "dead souls" belonging to "the Davos culture."[14] The term refers to the Swiss city of Davos, where intellectuals, business people, and politicians meet and form idealistic opinions as to how the world and its citizens should be: cosmopolitan, emancipated, liberal, and individualistic—in short, civilized. Not to be civilized means to be morally reprehensible: intolerant, reactionary, chauvinistic, and nationalistic.

Finally, in Germany one finds a critique of constitutional patriotism presented by writers such as Karl Heinz Bohrer,[15] which is comparable to the Danish conservative critique. Constitutional patriotism is cold, abstract, universalistic, theoretical, and rational. It rests on fragile, constructed identities, which are not grown out of concrete human interaction and cooperation: i.e., from culture. Reason itself does not create social cohesion and valuable connections between the state and its subjects, the people. There is also a need for "Sittlichkeit," a moral sense of loyalty between citizens, which again requires a national culture.

From Cultural Radicalism to National Conservatism

The turn from radical cultural policy to national conservative cultural policy happens at two stages. First, a critical conservative corrective to cultural radicalism is articulated. Second, a positive national project is articulated on its own terms.

In the current public debate in Denmark, the criticism of conservatives is directed toward cultural radicalism's lack of self-correction as an emancipatory ideology. Conservatives are also advocates of enlightenment, but they advocate for an enlightenment project that, so to speak, enlightens itself and its own limits as well. Or to put it another way: conservatism is rooted in a realistic recognition of the individual person's potential for better and worse. One might characterize this realism as an

---

13. Christopher Lasch, *The Revolt of the Elites and the Betrayal of Democracy* (New York: Norton, 1995).

14. Samuel P. Huntington, *The Clash of Civilizations and the Remaking of World Order* (New York: Simon & Schuster, 1996).

15. Karl Heinz Bohrer, *Ekstasen der Zeit: Augenblick, Gegenwart, Erinnerung* (Munich: Carl Hanser Verlag, 2003).

intellectual honesty that breaks with the rational constructiveness of cultural radicalism.

The conservative diagnosis of the breakdown of cultural radicalism points to the fact that cultural radicalism suppresses the pessimistic insights into, and the realistic experiences of, for instance, the basic human tendency to live by cultural traditions and under the influence of cultural—e.g., national, ethnic, or religious—prejudices.[16] Moreover, the elitist shaping of cultural radicalism is exposed by conservative criticism. For who is to decide when the citizen is free if not the well-educated, emancipated, and open-minded few who know better than the rest?

In a more positive light, one could say that cultural radicalism actually defined the function of art and the purpose of cultural policy quite clearly, and thus it put forward a clear criterion of valuable art. But the first conservative Minister of Cultural Affairs in the current Danish right-wing government, Brian Mikkelsen, did the same, and as a result he came under attack from cultural radicals. But his project is precisely undisguised. In the late months of 2004, Mikkelsen defined an initiative to articulate and present what he termed a "national cultural canon," including the best works of art ever created in Danish culture. On the official website of the Ministry of Cultural Affairs, the cultural canon is explained in the following way:

> A group of Denmark's best artists and most knowledgeable art experts has been looking at hundreds of works of art, discussing them, choosing and rejecting them over and over again.... [A] canon contains the most important and most distinguished elements within its designated area. Here you can read about a Danish cultural canon—a collection and presentation of the greatest, most important works of Denmark's cultural heritage. The cultural canon is intended to serve as a compass showing the directions and milestones in Denmark's long and complex cultural history. At the same time, the cultural canon is intended as a platform for discussion and debate.[17]

Such a canon, which is written down, openly invites all citizens to evaluate and criticize its content. It is, however, more difficult to evaluate and

---

16. This is something that hermeneutic philosophy has always been aware of. Cf. Hans-Georg Gadamer, *Truth and Method* (London: Sheed and Ward, 1993).

17. For more information, see the "Cultural Canon" page on the website of the Danish Ministry of Culture, available online at http://www.kum.dk/sw37439.asp.

criticize the non-transparent power hierarchies in the cultural and artistic environment, an environment that, in Denmark at least, often has a cultural radical bias directed against cultural conservatism. One could just point to the fact that several artists frequently gather together and criticize the Danish right-wing government.

The Cultural Unity of the Nation

Due to the aforementioned reasons, the cultural radical cultural policy is losing legitimacy in Denmark, and instead we are witnessing the breakthrough of a national conservative cultural policy. The debate about the national cultural canon is only one symptom of this break with the long-standing consensus in Danish cultural policy.

The national conservative cultural policy which Mikkelsen, among others, has articulated, shifts focus from the individual to the community. Cultural radicalism was engaged in the problem of individual authority: how can the state educate the citizen to become a good democrat? National conservatism sees the conservation of social cohesion as the most urgent problem today, not least because the solidarity between citizens in the modern "multicultural state" is beginning to fade, according to national conservatives.

National conservatism is in some ways more democratic than cultural radicalism because it takes account of the people and its popular culture and because it wants to preserve the identity of the people. Cultural radicalism, by contrast, is an elite project. What does this mean in the Danish context? The Danes constitute a people that is deeply rooted in a national culture; they have for generations lived together in certain ways, on a particular territory, and within the same state. The shared history has marked the people with some unifying moral values, social experiences, and implied modes of communication, and this culture has fostered a loyalty that is the foundation of a strong liberal citizenship and culture of trust. (In the World Values Surveys, Denmark comes in first on the area of mutual trust.) That the mutual ties between the Danes have been civilian in nature has created the basis for a voluntarily community life that to a large extent has had an informal and non-assertive character.

In Denmark, this civil commitment has historically been expressed in a well-organized and self-conscious popular community. It has, for example, been focused on populist movements, cooperative, sports, peasant and labor movements, and free church and free school associations.

The forming of various networks of freely chosen civil associations occurs in a very active manner, and there is an explicit cultural self-confidence. Danes are proud of their country, and civil society is a vibrant and concrete reality. Neighborhoods, local life, charitable and educational associations, and the many socially inclusive citizen initiatives all play a pivotal role in the national community. The loyalty in local communities contributes to the overarching national loyalty, upon which the political order also depends.

Thus, conservatives argue, it is neither possible nor advisable to try to construct a common social loyalty in top-down manner, i.e., from above. A strong sense of community has grown out of a long, historic tradition and is based on tangible and immediate things, such as a common language and the sense of belonging to a homeland. Democratic, universalist principles alone do not create social cohesion or trust between the state and the people. Here we are faced with the main objection to the post-national theory of the elite: a democracy must be anchored in a culture with shared norms. This is an intellectual observation that has also characterized the national conservative cultural policy in Denmark since 2001.

The Purpose of National Conservative Cultural Policy

The main purpose of national conservative cultural policy is to unite the many different individuals and subcultural groups within a social community, i.e., the nation. The nation creates a unifying value system upon which modern democracy depends. Conservative intellectuals have traditionally articulated a thorough conception of the valuable aspects of the nation-state, regarded as a liberal democratic state, i.e., a state whose boundaries coincide with the boundaries of the nation. It is characteristic of national conservatives that they consistently argue for a pre-political source of unity, which underpins the state and makes it legitimate. This means that the unity of the state is grounded in the unity of the nation. Generally, the point of view of national conservatives is that unity (i.e., national unity) is to be understood in social and cultural terms, not in political terms. According to national conservatives, it is therefore crucial that we preserve the national loyalty and national sovereignty that characterizes the nation-state.

A common criticism of national conservative cultural policy is that, contrary to the official conservative rhetoric, it follows a *political* dictate regarding what kind of culture is to be promoted: what is termed national culture is in fact quite arbitrary. But the critics thereby overlook what is characteristic of the nation-state: namely, that its democratic institutions, including its cultural policy, is grounded in a thick popular community consisting of pre-political norms and values. Or to put it another way, the state is grounded in a national culture, which implies common territory, language, history, and customs. The benefit of this foundation is that the public and the political system are bound together in a very stable manner, which also promotes a culture of trust necessary for liberal democracy to work effectively.[18]

In his book *The Need for Nations*, the British philosopher Roger Scruton explains the idea of nationality and national art in the following way:

> Nations are defined not by kinship or religion but by a homeland. National loyalty is founded in the love of place, of the customs and traditions that have been inscribed in the landscape and of the desire to protect these good things through a common law and a common loyalty. The art and literature of the nation is an art and literature of settlement, a celebration of all that attaches the place to the people and the people to the place. This you find in...the art and literature of every nation that has defined itself as a nation. Listen to Sibelius and an imaginative vision of Finland unfolds before your inner ear; read Mickiewicz's *Pan Tadeusz* and old Lithuania welcomes you home; look at the paintings of Corot and Cézanne, and it is France that invites your eye.[19]

To resume: according to national conservatives the democratic institutions and civil rights are, in the nation state, deeply rooted in a unified community, which is based upon a pre-political code of practice, mores, moral norms, and values—i.e., a national culture. The fact that the state is rooted in a national unity has numerous positive consequences, not the least of which is that the population and the political system are related in a very stable manner.

The turn toward a more conservative cultural policy, in a broad sense, is not just a Danish phenomenon. Several European nations, such as Germany and France, have in recent years elected right-wing governments,

---

18. Cf. Francis Fukuyama, "Social Capital," in Lawrence E. Harrison and Samuel P. Huntington, eds., *Culture Matters: How Values Shape Human Progress* (New York: Basic Books, 2000), pp. 98–112; and Francis Fukuyama, *The Great Disruption: Human Nature and the Reconstitution of Social Order* (London: Profile, 1999).

19. Roger Scruton, *The Need for Nations* (London: Civitas, 2004), p. 16.

and, just as in Holland, the result has been a stricter policy—or at least a rhetoric—against multiculturalism in the wake of the riots in the suburbs of Paris and the assassination of the Dutch politician Pim Fortuyn and the filmmaker Theo van Gogh. Moreover, in several European countries alongside Denmark, national conservative movements have developed, whose activities have intellectually prepared the way for political developments. Germany is an interesting case.

Experience with right-wing nationalism in the interwar period has created a strong anti-national sentiment in public opinion in Germany since 1945. But throughout the 1990s, intellectuals in the so-called "new right" began to defend a national identity. The German intellectual right can thus be characterized as a kind of cultural seismographer, which early registered the emergence of a new national self-confidence. It resulted in the 1994 book *Die selbstbewusste Nation*, edited by Heimo Schwilk and Ulrich Schacht,[20] which was centered on Botho Strauss's essay "Anschwellender Bocksgesang," published the year before. Although national identity has not yet become mainstream in Germany, it is today defended among an increasing number of opinion makers, and even among intellectuals in the established media—for example, Matthias Matussek, the editor of *Der Spiegel*, who in 2006 published the book *Wir Deutschen*, which carries the subtitle *Warum die anderen uns gern haben können*. The title of one of the most recent books (also from 2006) by Karlheinz Weissmann, a leading figure of the new right, may also be interpreted as a kind of seismic warning: *Unsere Zeit kommt*.

In Germany, national conservatism has not had as much political significance as it has had in Denmark. There are, of course, obvious historical reasons for this. Historically, Danish national identity has also been less affected by "Blut-und-Boden" ideology, and it has been more civil and informal, less authoritarian, less aggressive, and less politically mobilized than in Germany, France, or even Great Britain. The image of the ideal model of integration, which has been formulated by conservatives and gained ground in Danish cultural policy, has been put forward by Samuel Huntington in *Who are We?* It is the image of a bowl of tomato soup in which the various minority cultures are the salad, croutons, and spices, while the main national ingredient (the Danish core culture) is

20. Heimo Schwilk and Ulrich Schacht, eds., *Die selbstbewusste Nation: "Anschwellender Bocksgesang" und weitere Beiträge zu einer deutschen Debatte* (Berlin: Ullstein, 1994).

the tomatoes. The intention has been to maintain Denmark as a culturally homogeneous society.

Elements in the Cultural Policy

There is a delicate relationship inherent in the right-wing ideology between the liberal position that government should not interfere in the culture and the conservative idea of state support in order to preserve the national culture. Liberals argue that the experience of membership is not a political experience but a social experience. It occurs independently of the state, which should not impose or prohibit particular forms of membership, but should only guarantee the universal rights of the individual.

Conservatives partially agree with this reasoning: you cannot create social unity through policy directives. This is something that both liberal and conservative commentators have often stated. One could mention, for instance, the critiques of Soviet Communism, the cultural radical therapeutic state, the politicizing welfare state, and the European Union bureaucracy. Cohesion cannot be enforced—or constructed—from the top down by political initiatives, even if by means of good intentions. It is precisely *totalitarian* to impose loyalty upon citizens. The right-wing liberal and conservative thought has again and again emphasized that the national community grows organically or spontaneously out of a long historical development and is based upon concrete human relationships. (In Denmark, the idea of the nation as organically grown is articulated by Krarup).[21]

But liberals and conservatives disagree as to whether and how the established social unity must be *preserved*. Conservatives, who have gathered momentum in the current cultural policy, go further than the liberal position and rely on an idea of the sort of culture that the government regards as desirable and that it therefore ought to support with political and economical means. When a legitimate political order depends upon a pre-political and pre-contractual idea of membership of a national community, it will not simply have the consequence that government initiatives affect the private values of citizens, but also that the state is largely determined by these values and thus the national culture as well. That is why conservatives demand that the foundation of civic loyalty is pre-political, i.e., national.

So, according to conservatives the national unity is to be preserved by means of an active cultural policy carried out by the state. Given the

---

21. See Krarup, *Kristendom og danskhed.*

fact that the nation-state gains authority and legitimacy from the nation, it must also in a substantial manner recognize the public institutions through which the nation expresses itself. These institutions are labeled under the concept of the "establishment," which is a concept that has been put forward by Scruton in *The Meaning of Conservatism*. According to Scruton,

> the powers that flow through civil life can seek and achieve establishment in a constituted state. Establishment is the great internal aim of politics: the aim of government. It is through this that the forces of society become subject to the power of the state, by finding authority through the authority of the state. The conservative belief is that the order of the state must be objective, comprehensive, and felt to be legitimate, so that the contrasting conditions of society can achieve their ideological fulfilment by being subject to a common sovereign power. Without this completion in establishment civil society remains always on the brink of fragmentation.[22]

Modern national conservatives such as Scruton articulate a positive concept of national identity, national unity, and cultural community that gives way to numerous more or less controversial political prescriptions. These prescriptions obviously imply that the state gives support to traditional cultural institutions (such as museums, archives, libraries, etc.) whose purpose is to preserve the national cultural heritage. But the political prescriptions may also imply a certain media policy. The community in the media, which national conservatives regard as valuable, is not dictated from above, i.e., by the broadcasting media—in a Danish context, by "Denmark's Radio," which enjoyed a monopoly until the late 1980s. This was true under the old cultural radical hegemony. But the national community is a value-based community, which grows from below. In the popular Danish television serials, such as *Krøniken* ("The Chronicle"), a history-based serial about Danish culture in the postwar period, the public is united in collective contemplation of its own historical experiences, which thus confirms its own national identity.

Other political prescriptions, which do not necessarily belong to the cultural sector in a strict sense, may imply an active support of an established church or a restrictive immigration policy. They may also imply a certain language policy and a more head-on approach to the shaping of educational institutions. The purpose of these prescriptions is partly to hand

22. Roger Scruton, *The Meaning of Conservatism* (Hampshire: Palgrave, 2001), p. 172.

down the established common cultural identity to the future generations. This policy calls to mind the "founding father" of modern conservatism, Edmund Burke, and his famous concept of a "contract between the generations," which was expressed in *Reflections on the Revolution in France* from 1790.[23] The policy thus serves to make the citizens even more familiar with their common national culture. For modern conservatives it is important to preserve a core national culture as opposed to a multicultural agenda. This could be done by applying a binding canonical curriculum in the schools.

It is also in light of this context that the national cultural canon is to be interpreted. The official purpose of the canon is to illuminate the national masterpieces of Danish art and culture. This follows from a dominant aspect of the national conservative cultural policy, whose main purpose is to conserve a core national culture in the age of globalization. (In this sense, it is not so crucial what content is put in the canon, but *that* a canon of traditional cultural values is made to resist cultural relativism and levelling.) Among the official reasons for a national cultural canon are that a canon will:

- contribute to a lively cultural debate by acting as a yardstick for quality—a yardstick that will obviously be constantly challenged and discussed

- give citizens an easy introduction to Danish art and culture and hopefully also inspire them to immerse themselves further in the individual art forms

- present a competent, qualified suggestion of the elements of Denmark's cultural heritage that are valuable, of good quality, and worth preserving for our descendants

- make us more aware of who we are and give us more information on the cultural history of which we are a part

- give us reference points and awareness of what is special about Danes and Denmark in an ever more globalised world

- strengthen the sense of community by showing key parts of our common historical possessions.[24]

23. Edmund Burke, *Reflections on the Revolution in France* (London: Penguin Books, 1986).

24. Quoted from Danish Ministry of Culture website, online at http://www.kum.dk/sw37439.asp.

Again, the national conservative cultural policy is not only opposed to a cultural radical cultural policy, but it is also opposed to a multicultural and liberal policy. According to the multicultural policy, the state must give equal recognition to the plurality of cultures in society. According to the liberal policy, the state must refrain from giving support to art and culture with political and economical means. According to the national conservatism, the state must, on the contrary, be neither neutral nor passive; it must actively support the national culture by means of a cultural policy.

But if it is the task of the state to conserve the national unity and give substantial support to the national community, then the following questions arise: To what conception of the nation must the cultural policy give special attention? How do we define the nation? And what about the practical policies? These questions are not at all easy to answer. But that is not a reason to refrain from giving a try.

Lifestyle Welfare: How the New Class has Transformed the Scandinavian Welfare State

Klaus Solberg Søilen

Three hypotheses are presented in this article, each supported by observations and theory. The first is that party distinctions in Scandinavian politics no longer involve coherent ideas related to political ideologies, but that parties instead have become machines to maintain power and keep supporters employed. The second is that the tradition among political parties in Scandinavia, and especially in Sweden, for accepting federalist measures as a response to central state inefficiencies has been checked by the development of the welfare state; it can only regain momentum through external pressure, in the form of increased competition through the phenomenon known as globalization. The third is that the Scandinavian welfare state model has shifted from providing support to the poor to guaranteeing the middle class a certain lifestyle.

The main model for the Scandinavian cooperative society was the Weimar Republic, and the main ideologists were Ernst Wigforss and Alva and Gunnar Myrdal. Wigforss was much inspired by Rudolf Kjellén, a right-wing political scientist and politician and the father of the study of Geopolitics. The idea of "folkhemmet," the people's home, was borrowed from lectures Kjellén gave in 1910 about the state as an organism. It was a model of an all-encompassing state, independent of any left- or right-wing political affiliation.

Both Norway and Denmark largely adopted the Swedish theories of Social Democracy. In the Norwegian model today, it is the state itself that is the owner of most of the key industries. There is no significant interplay between the public and private sectors when it comes to the common good, as there is in Sweden, which is very much the example of the corporate state, the Japan of Europe.[1] Instead, there are organized conflicts. In contrast, the Danish state is an organic community of small merchants and traders closely organized around the capital. Problems are solved though flexibility and a system of high turnover in the general workforce.

The Emergence of the New Class

Democratic Socialism in Europe, and particularly in the Scandinavian countries, systematically uses the welfare state as a redistribution machine to stay in power. Workers receive social security in return for political support. The development must be seen in an historical context. The welfare system started as a way to assist workers who became ill and needed income security. As the salaries of the workers increased and the prices of products decreased, they entered the middle class. The welfare state adapted to this change and slowly directed its policies away from the neediest groups in order to follow its electoral base. The bipolar order of industrialism—along the whole spectrum from social democrats, socialists, and communists, on one side, to capitalists, on the other—slowly disappeared in the Western world. Or, more correctly it was transferred to developing countries where it has taken root, while the ruling elites in the West started to talk about a classless society. Meanwhile, a new class was emerging in a single polar world, which came to control the political and democratic process.[2] This is characteristic of the process that Carl Schmitt calls "the turn to the total state," omnipresent and all-powerful, both in a technical sense (qualitatively) and because it is present everywhere (quantitatively).[3] In the nineteenth century, the state was still separable from society. In the twentieth century, the state became the self-organization of society.[4] The New Class enforced its position by increasing the population

---

1. See Nikolaj-Klaus von Kreitor, "The Political Idea of the People's Home: Reply to Goran Dahl," *Telos* 100 (1994): 243. Kreitor argues that "it is the Prussian sense of service and loyalty that suits the Swedes best." See also Nikolaj-Klaus von Kreitor, "The 'conservative revolution' in Sweden," *Telos* 98–99 (1993–94): p. 249.

2. The hypothesis of the New Class was introduced by Milovan Dilas, in *The New Class: An Analysis of the Communist System* (San Diego, CA: Harcourt Brace Jovanovich, 1983), and has been confirmed in research by others, including John McAdams, "Testing the Theory of the New Class," *Sociological Quarterly* 28 (1987): 23–49. According to McAdams, "a post-industrial economic order gives rise to an elite which has a class interest in the expansion of government: the New Class."

3. Carl Schmitt, *Legalität und Legitimität* (Berlin: Duncker & Humblot, 1932), p. 10.

4. Carl Schmitt, *Positionen und Begriffe im Kampf mit Weimar* (Berlin: Genf, 1988), p. 151.

of eligible voters, by inviting new groups to vote, and by decreasing the voting age. Step by step, society came to be governed by a new and much larger group of civil servants, and today it matters little which political party rules; the room for political maneuvers is so small that any major alteration means the loss of the next election.

More remarkably, this has been a transformation without any single significant social thinker or ideologist—or, phrased differently, it has by and large been an unforeseen consequence of socialist thinking. In retrospect, this lack of an intellectual father has been advantageous for New Class ideology and has guaranteed its resistance against much social critique because there is no clear target to criticize. Nonetheless there are genuine losers in this new class system: the younger generation, the elderly, those striving for private initiatives against bureaucratization, and anyone outside of the establishment.

The welfare state, the product of the increased strength of the labor movements at the start of the twentieth century and the formation of Social Democratic parties, is the primary mechanism whereby the have-not's allocated wealth to themselves and built the base of supporters that would reelect them. The New Class intuitively understood that to have a large dependent population would guarantee electoral victories, even if it meant turning a large part of the population into passive recipients of government largesse. In times of Social Democratic rule, politicians and bureaucrats govern in harmony. In times of conservative rule, the politicians largely have to adapt to the logic of the bureaucracy.

The welfare state was built through the support of two political blocs, the Socialists and the Social Democrats. The Communists quickly marginalized themselves by hoisting the anti-democratic flag, by supporting Stalin, and by favoring the policies of the Soviet Union. In Denmark, it was the Socialist People's Party and the Social Democratic Party; in Norway, the Socialist People's Party and the Norwegian Labor Party (Social Democrats); in Sweden, the Left Communist Party and the Social Democratic Labor Party; and in Finland, it was the Left Alliance and the Social Democratic Party. The political and ideological structure in these countries is much the same. It is a machine whereby Social Democrats and their allies can win elections and secure political power.

The major types of programs in the welfare state are transfer programs, such as welfare, social security, and unemployment insurance, and, on the other side, service programs, such as hospitals, day-care centers, and schools. Pensions and health-care services account for as much as eighty percent of these states' welfare expenses. Now, lower birth rates and higher life expectancy have led to gloomy predictions for future decades. Consequently a shift toward capital taxation will become more important.

Experience has shown that pensions and medical services are areas in which the state has little competence in managing efficiently; bureaucrats are neither financial experts nor medical practitioners. Fearful of the alternatives, the state argues that privatization will lead to "American conditions." In reality, services to the poorest could be guaranteed by allowing for some state-run alternatives.

Mismanaged pension funds are the number one financial threat in most Western European countries today. It has in turn become the number one argument to allow for massive immigration into Europe, as is even advocated by the Organisation for Economic Co-operation and Development. However, due to their welfare system, the Scandinavian countries have attracted the most unskilled immigrants, while the United States tends to attract the more skilled, who are more confident that they will make it on their own. This suggests that Scandinavian immigration by itself is not going to solve the old-age dependency ratio, and risks instead leading to increased ethnic conflicts in periods of recession.[5]

The public services included in the welfare program, together with major state institutions like the police and the military, have provided examples of inefficiencies and bureaucracy in Scandinavia for decades,[6] but the support of these groups is so important for winning any election that any major retrenchments have become politically impossible. Any major political party aspiring to power understands and respects this reality, as is particularly apparent in the Scandinavian countries. The United States is an exception: the country never built and never accepted the accelerated versions of these welfare systems in the first place. Once these welfare systems are established, they are difficult, almost impossible, to dismantle within the democratic system itself, as they become an important factor in the modern electoral mechanism.

---

5. Assaf Razin and Efraim Sadka, *The Decline of the Welfare State: Demography and Globalization* (Cambridge, MA: MIT Press, 2005).

6. For example, Scandinavian police are known to prefer desk jobs before patrolling the streets, and when they go out they leave in groups. Compare this to the U.S. model, where one man can be on patrol the whole day while communicating with colleagues over the radio.

The welfare state has turned a large part of the population into financially dependent individuals. It has made many citizens less inclined to work and less able to take care of themselves. Sickness-related absence has for decades been far greater in Sweden than in most other European countries, to the extent that it has become a threat to the financing of the welfare state.[7] When they are sick, Scandinavians stay at home for a longer period of time than most other Europeans, using the occasion to do some work around the house. This obviously indicates some noteworthy lack of virtue. As Yuichi Shionoya argues, the absence of virtue from Euro-American civilization has produced the current crisis of the welfare state.[8]

Nowhere else is mass government and bureaucracy found in greater plenty. Sweden has the highest general government expenditure of any country, with 58.5% of GDP (according to 2002 figures).[9] Both Denmark and Finland are among the highest in government expenditure, with over 50%.[10] Sweden also has the highest general government taxation as a percentage of GDP of any country, with 53.6%, closely followed by Denmark, with 49.5% (2001). Two other key indicators that measure the size of government are social protection as a percentage of GDP and the percentage of employees in public administration. Sweden also tops the list of these indicators with social protection at 30.9% of GDP (2002), and this figure rose to 33.5% in 2003 in another study. Employment in the public sector is missing for Sweden in the same study, but Denmark is at 7.1%. The list is topped by Belgium and France, both with just over 10%.[11] Belgium, France, and the Netherlands also provide striking examples of New Class ideology. Still, no other country has a higher total taxation rate, a higher public expenditure rate, and a higher public consumption expenditure rate than Sweden. In Europe, only Slovenia has a lower inequality of income

7. Jan Sundquist, Ahmad Al-Windi, Sven-Erik Johansson, and Kristina Sundquist, "Sickness Absence Poses a Threat to the Swedish Welfare State: A Cross-sectional Study of Sickness Absence and Self-reported Illness," *BMC Public Health* 7 (2007).

8. Yuichi Shionoya, *Economy and Morality: The Philosophy of the Welfare State* (Cheltenham: Edward Elgar Publishing, 2005), pp. 271–73.

9. Lucien Peters and John Verrinder, "The Size of the Government Sector from Different Perspectives," paper from 24th CEIES seminar, *The Size of the Government Sector–How to Measure*, Eurostat (October 2003), p. 77.

10. We found no comparable figures for Norway and Iceland. As they are not EU countries, they are often omitted from similar studies. However, their figures are probably at least just as high.

11. Peters and Verrinder, "The Size of the Government Sector," pp. 77–80.

distribution for 2004.[12] Of all welfare states, the Scandinavian countries offer the most developed example of New Class ideology, confirming our first hypothesis.

New Class ideology is an expensive political system. The more that employees are financed through the state budget, the more dependent the state becomes on annual increases in GDP—or "sustainable development," as Social Democrats prefer to say in order to avoid any mention of money. Due to increased global competition, the New Class is being forced into a rhetoric of efficiency very much against its own will. This competition is likely to increase as we enter what the World Bank calls the "next globalization," in which developing countries (China, India, and Brazil) will take a larger part of the economic growth through increased productivity in global production chains and the accelerated diffusion of new technologies.[13]

Experience has shown that political elites will sacrifice their own voters. In the final analysis, the welfare state today is less about solidarity than it is about self-interest.[14] New groups will be cast out of their protected environments, even under Social Democrat rule. Such changes are possible in the context of an economic recession and high unemployment rates, as well as through a political focus on deservingness.[15] Thus, Denmark was the first Scandinavian state to make major changes to its welfare system, during an economic recession in the mid-1980s. In 1990, the limit on unemployment benefits was lowered from nine to four years, the unemployed were required to participate in job-training programs and to be available for work anywhere in the country, and the pension system was gradually transformed from a universalistic system into a more contributory one.[16]

---

12. Eurostat, *Europe in Figures: Eurostat Yearbook 2006–07* (Luxembourg: Office for Official Publications of the European Communities, 2007), p. 116.

13. The World Bank, *Global Economic Prospects: Managing the Next Wave of Globalization* (Washington, DC: The World Bank, 2007).

14. Daniel Beland and Andre Lecours, "Sub-state Nationalism and the Welfare State: Quebec and Canadian Federalism," *Nations and Nationalism* 12 (2006): 77–96. Beland and Lecours argue that nationalism and the welfare state revolve around the notion of solidarity. This experience does not seem applicable to the Scandinavian countries.

15. On the effects of deservingness argument, see Rune Slothuus, "Framing Deservingness to Win Support for Welfare State Retrenchment," *Scandinavian Political Studies* 30 (2007).

16. R. H. Cox, "The Social Construction of an Imperative: Why Welfare Reform Happened in Denmark and the Netherlands but not in Germany," *World Politics* 53 (2001): 477–83.

Moving into the Middle

Politicians want to rule. They are mostly people who pursue careers in a sphere where loyalty goes before competence. Modern politics is less about defending certain values, and it has increasingly little to do with honor. When politicians make fools of themselves in the eyes of the public, they simply "do a poodle," i.e., they admit fault in public. It is institutionalized humiliation. And as more people are given the right to vote, there is only one position from which to obtain that power: the middle. It matters little which side you come from. We saw this in the shift in the United Kingdom with New Labor moving to the right, and we have seen it in Sweden with the Moderate Party moving to the left.

New Labor in England was the first of the great parties to move into the middle when it broke with tradition and said that the welfare state should no longer extend opportunities for selflessness, enhance social solidarity, or deliver greater equality of outcome.[17] That was in May 1997. But right-wing parties have also moved to the middle. In 2006, the Swedish Conservative Party called themselves the "nya moderaterna," literally "new moderates," and they practically adopted a large part of the social democratic agenda. They made unemployment their major cause and joined with the Centre Party and the Liberal Party to form "the Alliance."

The political scenery today is hardly differentiable anymore. In Sweden, it is now the Moderate Coalition Party that speaks about full employment, improvements in the schools and in health care, and the importance of a multicultural society. This intrusion is frustrating for the Social Democrats because they do not know what else to disagree about. So they end up just saying that they want a more equal society. The irony is that they can win the election simply by keeping the same political position and exploiting minor faults committed by the ruling coalition parties. This has turned political life into more of a soap opera where the media plays the role of the witch-hunter. Consequently, it is difficult to get well-educated citizens to run for election, which further weakens our democracies.

The voting masses always love change, and the political parties in the middle never get embarrassed when presenting themselves as new and different. The actual politics does not change much, only the faces of the politicians who defend it. Voters who see that there are no major differences between political parties start to lose interest in politics altogether

---

17. Robert M. Page, "Without a Song in their Heart: New Labour, the Welfare State and the Retreat from Democratic Socialism," *Journal of Social Policy* 36 (2007): 19–37.

or they vote radically, maybe as a protest, maybe just out of frustration. In Norway, for example, the right-wing Progress Party is the second largest party with 38 out of 169 seats in Parliament.

Lifestyle Welfare

The Scandinavian welfare states today have less and less to do with the original idea of social security for the poor, as once developed in the labor movements. It is less about putting food on the table and getting medicine to cure illnesses and more about guaranteeing a certain standard of living. (Welfare theorists nostalgically refer to the first period as "the golden age of the welfare state.") It resembles the socialist idea that everyone is assumed to have the right to a certain way and quality of life, independent of one's contribution to the common good. In short, it is a system of rights, not of duties.

When the Social Democratic parties govern, they make it easy for people to enter early retirement and receive other social security benefits and financial advantages. They also make it a taboo to criticize the misuse of the system, especially any mentioning of a fraudulent state, when in reality, as has been disclosed over the past few years, fraud and economic inactivity are quite common. A recent unpublished study based on an opinion poll in Sweden found that sixteen percent of the population admitted to having cheated the welfare system. What the real figures are will never be known. As long as the Social Democrats ruled, there were no "cheaters" and no one was allowed to assume otherwise. When the conservative party took over in September 2006, it could suddenly finance apparently unlimited numbers of special investigations into social system frauds simply by utilizing the extra money that these investigations brought back to the state. The Conservative Party and what is called the center-right Alliance in Sweden now ask not whether people are ill but how much they are able to work, since everyone is assumed to be able to perform some work. But the government also knows that too much control and too much interference with welfare state policies will cause them to lose the next election. They can close one or two Social Democrat institutions, as they did with the National Institute for Working Life, but the Alliance does not dare touch the hospitals or the universities, even though they suffer from many of the same problems of political bias and inefficiency.

The Scandinavian Social Democrats today do not have to do very much to win elections. They can afford to be both incompetent and uninterested.

Through decades of a jobs-for-votes policy, where the welfare state jobs account for the major part, the parties conquering the political middle have made sure that they will obtain majority. The old bipolar system of workers and capitalists has been replaced by a new unipolar order: the New Class, consisting of a new culture of bureaucrats who rule over their own state employees. This is no longer the *Beamtenstaat* (bureaucratic state), or *ambetsmannastat* of the few, the selected class of civil servants recruited early on from the nobility during the reign of Gustav Vasa, but a locked mechanism of organized voters and individualist interests. The tradition among political parties in Scandinavia, and especially in Sweden, for accepting federalist measures as a response to central state inefficiencies, well described by Rune Premfors,[18] has been challenged by the development of the welfare state. Changes seem only to be possible through outside pressure, first of all through increased demands on efficiency through the globalization process, fueled primarily by China's economic strength. It may be that such processes will help to take the Scandinavian countries out of their welfare state stalemate and to revitalize the federalist tradition, but the mere size of the public sector suggests that the meritocratic model can only be reimplemented in certain parts at best.

To anticipate some of my critics, New Class society has many positive effects. If you can live with the inefficiencies, the failed dream of a meritocracy, the over-politicized institutions, and the heavy burdens of taxation and social control, Scandinavia offers a better life for most people than anywhere else in the world. All of the Scandinavian countries have employment rates of around 75%. Only Iceland's is higher, with above 80%.[19] The Scandinavian countries have the lowest at-risk-of-poverty rates, with 11% for Finland and Norway, and 12% for Denmark (2003 figures). In comparison, countries such as Greece, Ireland, and Slovakia have poverty rates almost twice as high.

It is also true that any alternative political system would have its own power structure, and would therefore also be susceptible to criticism. The point here, however, is that "democracy," with its support by modern science, does not provide any critical explanation for the nature of our

---

18. Rune Premfors, "Reshaping the Democratic State: Swedish Experience in a Comparative Perspective," *Public Administration* 76 (1998): 156.

19. Ibid., p. 132.

existing political system. It does not ask "what" political system we should have, only "how" it should work.[20]

Besides, what looks like positive effects includes a number of negative consequences related to financial and social dependence. On such points, the Scandinavian countries come out among the worst. The at-risk-of-poverty rates before social transfers are 32% for Denmark and 28% for Finland (with no figures for Sweden). This suggests that poorer citizens in the Scandinavian countries are better off thanks to the welfare system, but also that Scandinavian citizens are highly dependent upon the welfare system and that they are less able to take care of themselves. Most other countries in the EU, such as Slovenia, Hungary, and Bulgaria, have a far lower risk of poverty before social transfers than Scandinavia.[21] There is yet another negative consequence: dependence on the welfare state has reduced private financial support.[22] This has weakened family ties, and most Scandinavians now live in single households.

Given such criticisms, one would think there would be more opposition to the welfare state system. However this is not the case. There is no real disagreement about the existence of the welfare state among established political parties in the Scandinavian countries. Its political importance is too overwhelming. The majority of middle-class voters continue to support the welfare state. This also explains why most welfare programs are highly popular among citizens. The welfare state is here to stay, and "contrary to what institutionalists think, the welfare state is not necessarily stagnant."[23]

The welfare state in its second stage has been transformed into a political tool for winning elections, for taking resources from the haves and giving it to the have-not's. It is a modern version of Robin Hood. Unlike in Sherwood Forest, however, most of the funds today go to the middle class, not to the poor. The welfare state is more about assuring citizens a certain

---

20. The point is made in Hannah Arendt, *Between Past and Future* (New York: Penguin, 1977), p. 57: "modern science was born when attention shifted from the search after the 'what' to the investigation of 'how.'"

21. Eurostat, *Europe in Figures*, p. 117.

22. On private financial support in Sweden, see also Ulla Björnberg and Mia Latta, "The Roles of the Family and the Welfare State," *Current Sociology* 55 (2007): 415–45.

23. Duco Bannink and Marcel Hoogenboom, "Hidden Change: Disaggregation of Welfare State Regimes for Greater Insight into Welfare State Change," *Journal of European Social Policy* 17 (2007): 31.

lifestyle than about subsistence levels of food and shelter. This should, one would think, make it harder to defend morally if not politically, but this is not the case. It may instead be a question of habit.

The New Class basically consists of a ruling bureaucracy of civil servants with support from a broad middle class, most of which is employed by the state or local government or receive funds directly from them, including most artists and culture workers. It is the New Class, not the poor and needy, who profit most from the welfare system. The results include systemic discrimination against the young and the elderly. In the eyes of the New Class, in times of economic recession, the young threaten their jobs and the elderly are of little concern to them because they have not been able to organize themselves politically, at least not yet. The New Class bureaucrat would much rather defend an incompetent colleague than admit a young, competent co-worker whose loyalty is uncertain. This is the same New Class bureaucrat who has demanded of private business that anyone working in private organizations for longer than six months cannot be legally regarded as a temporary worker, while they themselves extort political obedience by keeping employees on temporary arrangements for years, often decades. Again, what looks like security and solidarity is mostly about jobs and votes. For the political elites, it is about power.

The struggle for a classless society has therefore led to the creation of a new class system under our modern democratic political system. This has been largely unforeseen, and may be considered more of a biological consequence of previous political and ideological engagements than the product of any written political program or theorist.

All of this seems to support the hypothesis that the Scandinavian welfare state model now provides the middle class with a certain lifestyle.[24] Support for this hypothesis can also be found in research by Duco Bannik and Marcel Hoogenboom, who conclude that much of the pressure and the change of the welfare state is due to citizens' demand for arrangements that correspond to their postmodern lifestyle.[25] Important, too, is the realization that this seems to be an ideologically grounded political system that is here to stay. This system is even gaining popularity in the Western world and has no serious competitor within the democratic system.

24. See Andreas Bergh, "The Middle Class and the Swedish Welfare State: How Not to Measure Redistribution" *The Independent Review* 11 (2007): 533–46.

25. Bannink and Hoogenboom, "Hidden Change."

The Romantic Image of the Welfare State

Despite these realities, a vague romanticism about the Scandinavian welfare model abounds.[26] Some authors treat the topic as if the welfare state were something that has to be saved at all costs, without consideration of the system's transformation over the past few decades.

It is frequently assumed that the welfare state model is the cause of the prosperity and high standard of living found in Scandinavia. In commentary by Isabela Mares and others, there is often talk about "important economic externalities" that are supposed to outweigh higher taxes, but these are never defined. In general, the assumption that the welfare system is the major cause of Scandinavian prosperity is rarely scrutinized. Few researchers investigate the causes of geography, national character, and common history, perhaps because authors too often are specialists in the social sciences and lack deeper cultural knowledge. The Scandinavian countries are located in a well-tempered, peaceful, and historically prosperous corner of the world. The climate has turned them into a skilled people who have had to avoid inactivity in order to survive. Besides, this is a corner of the world that is rich in natural resources and that has experienced relatively few wars and even fewer foreign invasions. With these factors in mind, it is almost difficult not to prosper, welfare state or not.

The welfare state must be understood in its historical context. It is less the result of rational decisions made by prescient statesmen than a consequence of a certain chain of events, starting with industrialization and moving through the rise of the labor movements and socialist and social democratic theories. In Norway, it represented the opportunity of a newly independent state, while in Denmark and Sweden it involved the new power given to new groups of voters, especially women. As these new groups were invited to join the political arena, they also wanted a share of the political power. This development has been stronger in the Scandinavian countries than in Finland, whose military and political leaders and leading civil servants have always been concerned with the Russian threat. Ironically enough, this refusal to share power has become one of the strengths of the Finnish civil service. The example of the Nordic school systems is well known. While the achievement levels in math and the natural sciences have decreased alarmingly across the Scandinavian countries, the level has improved in Finland. This has given raise to

26. Isabela Mares, "The Economic Consequences of the Welfare State," *International Social Security Review* 60 (2006): 65–81.

numerous visits to Finland by school representatives. When asked what they "have done" to make the schools so good, the Finns answer "nothing," which is exactly the point. Instead of staying with an established system that worked well, the Scandinavian countries let new groups of less competent teachers into their system, thereby creating an intellectual inflation. This process has been led on the inside largely by supporters of the modern study of "pedagogy" and defended theoretically in the social sciences by the postmodernist ideas of Jacques Derrida and others.

To be fair, the Social Democratic Party in Sweden itself acknowledged the problem of intellectual inflation in the late 1990s, when it considered the possibility of starting private schools, even though this meant sacrificing a large group of their own voters. They could not reform the system from within, so they tried to let it destroy itself. The speed by which these private schools are now taking over elementary education is astonishing, regardless of one's political sympathies. It is rapidly forcing a whole class of teachers into the new performance logic of the private sector. This transformation was largely the result of outside pressure (globalization).

Other welfare supporters talk about how investment in public education and human capital will enhance growth.[27] Norway followed this path very strongly in the 1970s and 1980s. The result is that Norway seriously diminished its population of skilled craftsmen. For a decade now, there has been an overload of academics, and it is very difficult to get hold of a qualified carpenter or electrician. This has again led to higher salaries for skilled craftsmen. It is now hardly economical to undertake a longer academic education in the social sciences or the humanities. Sweden is currently experiencing the same phenomenon. Both countries have only been able to cope with the demand for skilled craftsmen through the importation of foreign workers, most coming from former East European Communist countries, above all from Poland and the Baltic States, but recently also from Romania. Without these workers Scandinavia would probably have entered an economic recession much earlier.

27. Costas Azariadis and Allan Drazen, "Threshold Externalities in Development Economics," *Quarterly Journal of Economics* 105 (1990): 501–26.

Philosophy and the Transition from Theory to Practice: A Response to Recent Concerns for Critical Thinking

Rossen I. Roussev

A recent *New York Times* article[1] has focused attention on Charles Miller's Commission on the Future of Higher Education and its interest in addressing the quality of student learning and its adequacy to the demands of practice. The commission has initiated a debate on the possibility of using "standardized testing" in universities and colleges in order "to prove that students are learning and to allow easier comparisons on quality."[2] Miller is quoted as saying, on the one hand, that "what is clearly lacking is a nationwide system for comparative performance purposes, using standard formats," and, on the other, that "there is no way you can mandate a single set of tests, to have a federalist higher education system."[3]

While these two statements may initially appear to be at odds, they actually mirror the different positions of the officials involved in the debate. Some of them[4] have been critical of the idea of a nationwide standardized test, noting "outside" interference in the academic evaluation, while others[5] have expressed concern about the manner in which students would

---

1. Karen W. Arenson's "Panel Explores Standard Tests for Colleges," *New York Times*, February 9, 2006. I am indebted to May Webber for drawing my attention to this article and for initiating the conversation out of which the present article grew.

2. Ibid.

3. Ibid.

4. Notably, Leon Botstein from Bard College, David L. Warren from the National Association of Independent Colleges, and John T. Durbin from the University of Texas in Austin. Ibid.

5. Kati Haycock from the Education Trust in Washington, Jonathan Grayer from the Kaplan, Inc., and Peter T. Ewell from the National Center for Higher Education Management Systems in Colorado. Ibid.

be evaluated. On the whole, there appears to be a consensus on the need for an adequate assessment of student learning and a reliable database for comparisons, but a national examination test is not yet feasible. Instead, the institutions are encouraged to evaluate their students locally and to supply their findings to the database in question. It is also mentioned that certain tests have already been developed and used, but their efficiency is not indicated. Thus, the suggestion appears to be that the institutions, or entities within institutions, should develop the methods for such an evaluation on their own as well.

To be sure, the concern raised by Miller's commission is not new, and the comments made by different officials fall very much within the range of what has been said and done in the past. Likewise, the general issue of the quality of student learning in higher education has been tied with specific well-known concerns about: (1) writing, analytical skills, critical thinking, and problem solving; (2) college dropout rates; (3) poor performance in the workplace and on literacy tests; and (4) the ability to read complex texts and to draw inferences.[6] All of these have been subject to much debate and research in recent decades, but addressing them from the position of policy-making will clearly demand answers relevant to practice. Yet, what kind of answers these will be remains to be seen.

A Philosophical Perspective

In this essay, I shall discuss the extent to which we can address such concerns in our philosophy classes, and apropos—within the field of philosophy.[7] I shall endeavor to show that much of the debate is in its substance *philosophical* (with all the semantic imports of this word) and that, in this sense, sophisticated philosophical discussions on the issue at stake may well provide the most decisive insights for its particular settlements in other areas of culture as well.

As regards the particular concerns listed above, it is immediately understandable that "poor performance in the workplace and on literacy tests" can be due either to the lack of certain specialized knowledge or to the inability to apply it in a particular problematic situation. Obviously, owing

6. Ibid.
7. One should not be led on by this way of setting the task to think that I will be trying to recapitulate the issue under debate in a certain particular field of inquiry. For I shall afford myself this reminder, despite all the compartmentalization and departmentalization of human knowledge, philosophy is nonetheless *not* just a particular discipline. It is actually the *most general* of all disciplines, at least insofar as its subject matter is concerned.

to the specificity of philosophy as a discipline, we can not compensate for students' lack of specialized knowledge, and at least on that account we cannot prevent their eventually dropping out of academic institutions. We can focus only on the *ability* to acquire and to use such knowledge, which also involves the employment of certain analytical skills and, more generally, the entire problem-solving capacity of the intellect, including critical thinking, the ability to draw conclusions, creativity, and writing.

Yet, similarly to suggestions made by some of the officials quoted in the above mentioned article, I will also bring points on behalf of the view that our evaluative findings about students' thinking abilities can be valid at most within the framework of the particular examinations we give. Indeed, such a position will not eliminate the need of evaluation and of data for comparisons in general, but it will pose once again the issue of the adequate understanding of these findings. Whereas the problematicity of such an evaluation will prop up my contention that while the contribution of philosophy to tackling the problem can be substantial, the dimensions of its solution are far-reaching. For the nature of the issue is such that it defies its articulation and proper treatment in a singular academic field—be it specialized or philosophical—but demands a *broader humanistic background*, comprising a sophisticated knowledge most of all from the humanities, social sciences, and arts, as well as the humanistic knowledge of the natural sciences.

Thinking and Metacognition

Traditionally, the concern for adequate thinking skills has been addressed by educational scientists, cognitive psychologists, and some philosophers. The so-called "critical thinking movement," which reemerged within the last several decades in response to precisely this concern, consists mainly of these types of scholars. In my previous work,[8] I have found that many of these investigators[9]—in a bid to come up with ways to foster one's

---

8. Rossen I. Roussev, *Philosophy and the Structure of Modernity: Fragments of Actualization* (Sofia: East West Publishers, 2005, in Bulgarian).

9. See Judith W. Segal, Susan F. Chipman, and Robert Glaser, eds., *Thinking and Learning Skills* (Hillsdale, NJ: L. Erlbaum, 1985), especially Martin V. Covington, "Strategic Thinking and the Fear of Failure," Jack Lochhead, "Teaching Analytic Reasoning Skills Through Pair Problem Solving," and Matthew Lipman, "Thinking Skills Fostered by Philosophy for Children"; Richard Paul, *Critical Thinking: What Every Person Needs to Survive in a Rapidly Changing World*, (Rohnert Park, CA: Sonoma State Univ., 1990); Margaret W. Matlin, *Cognition* (Fort Worth, TX: Harcourt Brace Publishers, 1994).

thinking abilities—prescribe techniques that have to do with self-monitoring, self-reflection, and ultimately self-correction. These techniques are generally associated with *metacognition*, a concept advanced by cognitive science, where it is typically understood as the knowledge of how our own cognitive abilities work and, at the same time, as an application of that knowledge toward self-correction.[10] This "knowledge of how our own cognitive abilities work" is a kind of personal or "own epistemology,"[11] which points to a fundamental *philosophical aspect* of our thinking in problem solving. Moreover, the metacognitive aspect of thought, as addressed by these investigators, is decisively involved in the *acquisition* and *application* of specialized knowledge, particularly in tackling any problems of a non-specialized character that may interfere with the work of our cognitive abilities in actual problematic situations. For their part, these problems can be called *cognitive problems*, since they arise in the invocation and use of knowledge regardless of its specialization, whereas their consistent overcoming is to be related to a reliable philosophical background, which suitably supports the philosophical aspect of thought.

As most of these investigators recognize the metacognitive aspect of mind's problem-solving activity, they do not do away with the need for its reliable evaluation. Yet in the absence of scientific certainty, they frequently resort to philosophical explanations. For instance, Martin V. Covington, while championing his notion of "strategic thinking" in problem solving, finds it necessary to make the philosophical concession that

> [a]lthough the fundamental nature of intelligence will likely remain as elusive as ever, this newer approach should lead us to *a more sophisticated understanding, largely through the recognition that intelligence can be defined only in terms of the context in which it is required.*[12]

To be sure, Covington maintains that the "standards for intelligent behavior" must be "well-defined" and "absolute," but he warns that the outcomes of their application are not immediately determinative of one's thinking abilities or cognitive problems.[13] Nevertheless, in his view, the latter result from what he calls "mind's strategic mismanagement,"[14] which he relates

10. Matlin, *Cognition*, p. 248.
11. Lochhead, "Teaching Analytic Reasoning Skills," pp. 110–11.
12. Covington, "Strategic Thinking," p. 409 (emphasis added).
13. Ibid., p. 398.
14. Ibid., p. 403.

specifically to the ability to handle—and *not* to the lack of—specialized knowledge.[15] Whereas he sees the improvement of students' "strategic thinking" in the cultivation of a specific responsiveness to "the more subtle nuances" of the functions of intelligence, as found in "metacognitively more sophisticated individuals."[16]

We need to note here that, so understood, the metacognitive aspect of thinking ensures the adequate unity of specialized knowledge utilized in a particular problematic situation, where, in the solving of a concrete problem, metacognition effectively dissolves all cognitive problems.[17] In this sense, the philosophical aspect of thought manifests itself as the permanent condition for the possibility of our thinking and indicates that in problem solving the intellect always deploys certain epistemological knowledge, which is thus indispensable for any transfer of specialized knowledge from theory to practice.

Philosophy and the "Problems of Mediation"

For its part, the philosophical aspect of our thinking, which utilizes our "own epistemology" in metacognition, leads us to the philosophical tradition, whose knowledge and problems are in substance *epistemological*. One can immediately make a parallel here between the ways in which the philosophical aspect of thought has been addressed by the investigators of mind's thinking abilities and the discussions of traditional philosophical

---

15. Covington mentions a number of factors that condition "mind's strategic mismanagement" in an educational environment, including professors' use of the existing "classroom reward system" (ibid., p. 390), students' inadequate setting of the problem-solving tasks (ibid., p. 392), flaws in the "ability to retrieve material from semantic memory" as well as in the "knowledge of procedures for transforming this material (inferences, generalizations)" (ibid., p. 403). But none of these points to a lack of specialized knowledge.

16. Ibid., p. 404.

17. In a more detailed fashion, Covington suggests that students follow three steps in solving particular problems: (1) *problem formulation*, which is basically an explanation, "a well-developed sense of the problem, or an understanding of what makes it a problem in the first place and how it might be reformulated to reduce its difficulty"; (2) *selecting of the most effective strategy* after considering a few possible; and (3) *self-monitoring*, a metacognitive requirement, which involves, on the one hand, "knowledge of one's own capacities, limitations, and idiosyncrasies" and, on the other, the permanent utilization of this knowledge along the acquisition of specialized knowledge through balancing among "hard and easy-to-learn-materials" within the "time constraints" and "teacher standards" (ibid., pp. 401–2). One may notice here that only the first of these steps involves the immediate necessity of specialized knowledge, while the last is never really last, since the first two cannot dispense with it.

problems. Indeed, the latter, in their generality, still remain open-ended—even if the tradition, led on by a demand for scientificity, has sometimes provided them with dogmatic solutions—as do the evaluations of mind's thinking abilities from the viewpoint of their investigators. In this sense, it does not come as a surprise to philosophers that investigators like Covington, who have ventured to seek depth and precision in determining the nature of the cognitive problems, ultimately relegate the manifestation and value of one's thinking skills to concrete and always unique problematic situations. The later Wittgenstein had similarly seen the dissolution of the epistemological problem of his early philosophy ("the correct use of language")[18] in the multiplicity of particular language uses.[19]

Drawing on the same parallel, one can go even further and investigate the relation of the knowledge of the philosophical tradition to our thinking skills,[20] even when the latter are employed in the most trivial problem-solving situations. Since both of these types of problems are *epistemological* in nature, it is possible that their persistence is due to a failure to come up with and utilize the *philosophical* knowledge necessary for overcoming such problems. Our conjecture is that this knowledge would first be sought within the field of philosophy, then acquired by studying philosophy (including in the higher education), and, subsequently, utilized in problem solving by way of metacognition.

We will need to see what kind of knowledge we can get from the philosophical tradition, but we will also need to see if there is anything that could interfere with its acquisition and application, that is, with its *transition from theory to practice*. Jürgen Habermas has discussed the latter question and has suggested that the exchange of specialized knowledge in modernity, both among the expert fields "on the level of culture" and between the "level of culture" and that of "everyday communication," faces "problems of mediation" that remain outside the scope of "the expert cultures" (i.e., "science, technology, law and morality") and thus fall within that of philosophy, which, as a non-expert field, can most legitimately take on the role of their "interpreter."[21] In this sense, we can

18. Ludwig Wittgenstein, *Tractatus Logico-Philosophicus*, trans. D. F. Pears and B. F. McGuiness (London: Routledge & Keagan Paul, 1963).

19. Ludwig Wittgenstein, *Philosophical Investigations*, trans. G. E. M. Anscombe, (Oxford: B. Blackwell & Mott, Ltd., 1967).

20. See Roussev, *Philosophy and the Structure of Modernity*.

21. Jürgen Habermas, "Philosophy as Stand-In and Interpreter," in *Moral Consciousness and Communicative Action*, trans. Christian Lenhardt and Shierry Weber Nicholsen

think of them as "philosophical problems" that persist—in a variety of forms—in the work of all problem solvers who ensure the exchange of expertise throughout the levels of theory and practice of modernity. For instance, they may persist in the form of cognitive problems in the work of professionals and students who utilize their expert knowledge in particular problematic situations, that is, *practically*; in the form of communication problems in the work of those researches who, bridging different fields and areas of specialization, theoretically address—within their research, again, *practically*[22]—the adequacy of problem solvers' thinking; or in the form of political or policy problems in the work of those policy-makers who seek a reliable expertise to *practically* address such problems within the jurisdiction of their institutions.[23]

Accordingly, in order to properly cope with the problems of mediation and to ensure the transfer of expert knowledge from theory to practice, the problems solvers need some "extra" knowledge that only philosophy can provide. At the same time, there should be nothing to interfere with the transfer of this knowledge from theory to practice except for its own inadequacy, since the problems of mediation that it can face fall exclusively within its own scope. For their effective overcoming, that knowledge itself, supplied only with a good will, must be sufficient. Hence, in problem solving we are all—always and inevitably—also philosophers, and this means that if we do not want to compromise the sophistication of our thinking, we cannot dispense with the background of the philosophical tradition. For, if any field has ever treated of philosophical problems, it is precisely that of philosophy (and not just the Western one).

(Cambridge, MA: MIT Press 1990), pp. 17–18; and Habermas, *Postmetaphysical Thinking: Philosophical Essays*, trans. William Mark Hohengarten (Cambridge, MA: MIT Press, 1992), p. 39. Cf. Habermas, "Die Philosophie als Platzhalter und Interpret," in *Moralbewusstsein und kommunikatives Handeln* (Frankfurt am Main: Suhrkamp Verlag, 1983), p. 26; and Habermas, *Nachmetaphysisches Denken: Philosophische Aufsätze* (Frankfurt am Main: Suhrkamp Verlag, 1988), pp. 45–47.

22. We realize that such is the paradox of our profession: what is theory for others is also practice for us. That is, there is a fundamental overlapping between theory and practice in both research and teaching. As Jens Høyrup has put it, "science is a practice concerned with knowledge." Høyrup, *Human Sciences: Reappraising the Humanities through History and Philosophy* (Albany: SUNY Press, 2000), p. 1.

23. W. T. Jones has expressed a similar view of the "immensely important social function" of philosophy while pointing that "all policy problems...are at the same time cognitive problems." See Jones, *The Sciences and the Humanities: Conflict and Reconciliation* (Berkeley: Univ. of California Press, 1967), pp. 3–5.

Philosophy as Competence

Now we need to address the decisive question: What is this vital and indispensable knowledge that comes from the area of philosophy, this knowledge that will be utilized in problem solving in order to overcome the recurrent problems of our thinking—that is, the cognitive problems, the problems of mediation or the philosophical problems, which we face in various forms even in the most trivial problematic situations? Decisive as this question may be, it will have to settle for an indecisive answer. Moreover, its proper understanding will have to remain philosophical, since the sense of this indecisive answer is what nonetheless provides the decisive philosophical momentum that ultimately makes us think and makes us good thinkers.

In its long history, philosophy has not been able to establish itself as an expert field in the same sense that sciences are taken as expert. Quite the opposite, most of its major representatives have consistently denied it such status and have discarded its ambitious metaphysical (that is, strictly scientific) projects. This means that if an adequate knowledge of the philosophical aspect of our thinking is to be sought in the tradition of philosophy, we emphasize, *this knowledge will not be an expert one.* It will not have the binding force that Kant conceived of as ensuing from the universal and absolutely necessary conditions for its possibility. It will not consist of a narrowly defined set of issues and solutions, isolated by proclaimed geniuses and ready to be applied in practice. It will not be a unique course to be designed and introduced in the academic curricula. It will not be a simplistic or technological solution. Instead, at its best, it will be a *philosophical competence,* understood in opposition to "expertise," and it will utilize precisely a sense of the impossibility for philosophical knowledge to become an expert one. That is, it will be a version of the Socratic wisdom of "I know nothing," a sense of the limits of our reason and language, a "throwing away of the ladder after climbing up it,"[24] a deconstruction of our metaphysical constructions.

As a matter of course, this competence will be utilized through thinking—that is, reflectively—as a specific ability of invoking it and entertaining it, while abandoning its metaphysical dimension, even if still having it at one's disposal, ready for a live application in the actual solving of a problem. In this manner, the philosophical competence utilized in problem solving is reduced to the efficient exercise of certain thinking skills

24. Wittgenstein, *Tractatus Logico-Philosophicus*, 6.54.

or abilities. Indeed, the latter may thus appear to deploy only a "glimpse" of the vast resource of the tradition, but it is also clear that *practically* it cannot be otherwise. For, the philosophical aspect of our thinking is fundamentally qualitative, that is, substantially unquantifiable, "invisible," or unaccountable for in expert terms, and thus not always and immediately traceable to its resource. In this sense, it is practically immeasurable and, therefore, incommensurable with its putative quantitative attestations, which is why we think of it as *competence* rather than as "expertise."

Hence, we say with thinkers like Wittgenstein and Covington that one's thinking abilities are manifested best in the particular problematic situations in which they are invoked, and not in the performance of a "unique" test that would "measure" them "as such." This does not mean that we should abandon the idea of testing for purposes of comparisons beyond the level of a particular examination, course, or institution. However, this does mean that the validity of any such attestation cannot be immediately transferred beyond its own particularity and that in all events the proper understanding of any such transfer demands a specific competence that only philosophy can provide. Thus, we assert once more with Habermas that at any level of the transition between theory and practice, philosophy plays an indispensable role: the role of mediating interpreter.

Far-reaching Dimensions of the Solution

Even if it seems that only a "glimpse" of philosophical knowledge is utilized in practice, this should not suggest that no more than a "glimpse" of philosophy is needed for the cultivation of one's philosophical competence. For, as already stated, this knowledge cannot be quantified, and therefore the present talk about "glimpses" can have no quantificational meaning whatsoever; it can be only very conditional, metaphorical, or—otherwise—philosophical. In this sense, theorists who neglect this (essentially philosophical) conditionality can only mistakenly conclude that if a special course of critical thinking is designed in the "best" (or "expert") way and then introduced into the curricula, the problems of our thinking will be resolved.[25] To them we repeat with Habermas that philosophy is not an expert field and does not occupy as definite a place in the

---

25. Such a conclusion is bound to a dogmatic sense, in which sometimes the notion of "thinking skill" is apprehended, when the non-expert character of its philosophical aspect has been neglected. Richard Rorty has drawn attention to its misunderstanding in recent times, as a result of ignoring the historical aspect of its philosophical treatment: "The notion of 'analytic skills' is...a relic of the earlier idea of a special 'method of philosophical

compartmentalization of human knowledge, as sciences do. In fact, philosophy has long been the most diverse intellectual venture, as regards both its matters and its methodologies of investigation. Even today (and perhaps today more than ever), philosophy cannot be confined to specific places, set by either cultural compartmentalization or institutional departmentalization of human knowledge. It traverses the borders of the well-known disciplines and practices, while its so-called "areas of specialization" vary, with degrees of generality, across the whole spectrum of both theory and practice: from philosophy of art to philosophy of literature, from philosophy of science to philosophy of biology, from environmental philosophy to political philosophy, from philosophy of mathematics to philosophy of technology, from ethics to bioethics, from normative ethics to ethics of engineering, and so forth.

In this sense, if we were to try to form an idea of its entirety, we could only think of it as an indefinite extract of all areas of life and culture, that is, as a certain sense of the overall situation of humanity, or as an eventually profound understanding of the human condition as a whole. Such characterizations are indeed too general to have an expert value by current standards, but they do indicate the nature and the extent of the problem of cultivating one's thinking abilities. It is a philosophical problem, while the scope of its aspects is such that no expert field could sufficiently treat of it. For its part, philosophy could offer only a certain competence for its treatment, but clearly it cannot do it all unassisted.

In this relation, Ciriaco Morón Arroyo has recently reminded us that philosophy is not just "another discipline" but "a number of humanistic disciplines," and he has pointed once again to the interconnections among its traditional areas, as well as to its relation to the sciences and other humanities.[26] In a similar fashion and in view of what was said in the preceding paragraph, we can maintain that the philosophical competence to be utilized in problem solving is to come not just from the well-known philosophical disciplines but also from all other disciplines that contribute to our understanding of the human condition as a whole, that is, those that have been traditionally called *humanities*, plus the humanistic knowledge that comes from the arts, social sciences, and natural sciences.

analysis'." Rorty, *Essays on Heidegger and Others: Philosophical Papers*, vol. 2 (Cambridge: Cambridge UP, 1991), p. 23.

26. Ciriaco Morón Arroyo, *The Humanities in the Age of Technology* (Washington, DC: Catholic Univ. of America Press, 2002), p. 64.

To be sure, we realize that these disciplines are as diverse as their methodologies and matters of exploration. But most of all we realize that they are not just a single discipline. And so, we also realize that in their use for the cultivation of philosophical competence their knowledges are *theoretically inseparable*, just as the proponents of the critical thinking movement have realized that in problem solving critical and creative thinking are *practically inseparable*.

Thus, we arrive at our main point as regards the concerns for critical thinking: the effective use of our thinking abilities for the overcoming of its most immediate "problems of mediation" (the cognitive problems) demands a *broader humanistic background*. Only the latter can ensure the adequacy of one's thinking in the transfer of one's expertise from theory and practice. A mere set of instrumentalized techniques handed down to us in the form of a course or "expert" theory will not do. What is needed is a *diverse and sophisticated humanistic curriculum*. In this sense, we should properly think of the critical thinking movement only as an indicator of the problem and not as its long-awaited solution.

The educational establishments have long offered an array of subjects that serve to foster students' analytic and reflective skills, their critical and creative thinking. Traditionally, these have included the humanities, social sciences, natural sciences, and the arts. Yet often the need for adequate thinking skills has proved pressing by the challenges of practice. Fair enough: we live in a dynamic age, and it is precisely the incessant pulse of that age that bears the indicator of the critical thinking movement.[27] But it will ultimately be the responsibility of the respective problem solvers who cope with the demands of our age, including the demand for an adequate philosophical competence, to ensure the successful tackling of the problems of mediation of the exchange between theory and practice, including at the level of policy-making.

Quantitative Attestations

The root of the problem is the diminishing academic influence of the humanities, the arts, and most social sciences, as generally indicated by lower student enrollment, underfunding, and reduction or exclusion from the curriculum. Much has been written and said about the "crisis" or "decline" of the humanities, as well as about their role and place in the university, including in the context of globalization. But in terms of the

27. See Paul, *Critical Thinking*.

well-established institutional practices of higher education, this is a *policy problem*, which is neither new nor immediately solvable and which has many ramifications. The current picture is bleak, primarily as a result of long-term negligence and inaction in the face of outstanding data. Here I simply cannot bring out all the facts that make it up, but I shall nonetheless try to illustrate its persistence in time, despite being recurrently addressed in research.

Thus, in Kurt Spellmeyer's very insightful book *Arts of Living*, from 2003, we find this very informative extract of data from the *Digest of Educational Statistics, 2000*:

> Since 1960, the number of bachelor's degrees has tripled nationally, increasing from 400,000 to about 1.2 million. Since 1970, the number of B.A.'s majoring in English has dropped from 64,342 (seven percent) to 49,708 (four percent). History and the social sciences, listed together in the *Digest*, have dropped by more than 20,000, from eighteen to ten percent of the total. Philosophy and religion, also aggregated, have never managed to rise to a single percent, but their fraction has also halved since 1970s.[28]

In addition, the number of doctoral degrees in these fields has followed similar trends. From 1970 to 2004, the doctoral degrees in English dropped from 1,650 (5.1 percent of the total) to 1,207 (2.5 percent), while the modest gains of the social sciences and history, from 3,660 (11.4 percent) to 3,811 (7.9 percent), of philosophy and religion, from 554 (1.7 percent) to 595 (1.2 percent), and of the foreign languages and literatures, from 988 (3.1 percent) to 1,031 (2.1 percent), have actually declined as a percentage of the total degrees awarded.[29]

Likewise, ten years ago, in the landmark publication *What's Happened to the Humanities*,[30] we find that in the period between 1966 and 1993, the percentage of bachelor's degrees in the humanities has dropped from 20.7 to 12.7 (a decline of 8 percent) of the total of all disciplines, while the percentage of doctoral degrees has dropped from 13.8 to 9.1 (a decline of

28. Kurt Spellmeyer, *Arts of Living: Reinventing the Humanities for the Twenty-first Century* (Albany: SUNY Press, 2003), p. 251n.

29. See National Center for Education Statistics, "Postsecondary Education," in *Digest of Education Statistics, 2005*, available online at the National Center for Education Statistics website, http://nces.ed.gov/pubsearch/pubsinfo.asp?pubid=2006030.

30. Alvin Kernan, ed., *What's Happened to the Humanities?* (Princeton, NJ: Princeton UP, 1997).

5 percent). For the same period, the liberal arts subjects (human, social, and natural sciences) have declined from 48 to 35 percent, with humanities in particular falling from 21 to 13 percent.[31]

Yet, the same concern was raised two decades earlier, when the National Endowment for the Humanities published Lynne V. Cheney's *Humanities in America: A Report to the President, the Congress, and the American People*, which includes the following unambiguous passages:

> Between 1966 and 1986, a period in which the number of bachelor's degrees awarded increased by 88 percent, the number of bachelor's degree awarded in humanities declined by 33 percent. Foreign language majors dropped by 29 percent; English majors, by 33 percent; philosophy majors, by 35 percent; and history majors by 43 percent.[32]

> ...as a 1988 survey funded by the National Endowment for the Humanities shows, it is possible to graduate now [1988], as it was five years ago, from almost 80 percent of the nation's four-year colleges and universities without taking a course in the history of the Western civilization. It is possible to graduate now, as it was five years ago, from *more* than 80 percent of our institutions of higher education without taking a course in American history. In 1988–89, it is possible to earn a bachelor's degree from:
>
> · 37 percent of the nation's colleges and universities without taking *any* course in history;
> · 45 percent without taking a course in American or English literature;
> · 62 percent without taking a course in philosophy;
> · 77 percent without studying a foreign language.[33]

So far as funding is concerned, those academic fields most directly related to what we identified as philosophical competence appear generally underappreciated. Faculty salaries are one important indicator. As a recently published survey by the College and University Professional Association for Human Resources demonstrates, there is a gap in the average faculty salaries between most human and social sciences, on the one hand, and

31. Ibid., pp. 245–58.
32. Lynne V. Cheney, *Humanities in America: A Report to the President, the Congress, and the American People* (Washington, DC: National Endowment for the Humanities, 1988), p. 4.
33. Ibid., p. 5.

the faculty of engineering, computer sciences, and business, on the other. At its highest (for theology and religious studies departments), this gap is between $25,000 and $33,000 at the level of assistant professor, and between $30,000 and $40,000 at the level of full professor. At its lowest (for the social sciences), the gap is between $16,000 and $25,000 at the level of assistant professor and between $21,000 and $30,000 at the level of full professor.[34]

The concern over such salary gaps is neither new nor recent. A decade ago, Lynn Hunt drew attention to it, as well as to the disturbing trend in the ratio of humanities to non-humanities degrees.[35] While based on a figure of the National Center of Educational Statistics,[36] in the academic year 1987–88, the average salary of the faculties in the humanities was over $4,300 less than in business and the natural sciences, about $8,000 less than in engineering, and over $18,000 less than in the health sciences. In the social sciences, it was over $3,400 less than in business and the natural sciences, over $6,000 less than in engineering, and over $16,000 less than in the health sciences. For the fine arts, the gap was even wider: over $8,000 less than in business and the natural sciences, nearly $12,000 less than in engineering, and nearly $22,000 less than in the health sciences.

Another sign of underfunding is the ever-increasing number of part-time faculty in the disciplines in question. According to the Bureau of Labor Statistics, "about 3 out of 10 college and university faculty worked part-time in 2004."[37] But according to a figure of the American Association of University Professors (AAUP), from 1973 to 2003 the fraction of part-time faculty in national totals for all institutions has doubled from 23 to 46 percent.[38] Within this picture, based on the *Digest for Education Statistics 2005*, the percentage of part-time faculty in the humanities and fine arts in 2003 was over 50 percent; it was much lower in engineering

34. "Faculty Salaries Rise by 3.4%; Law Professors Still Earn the Most," *The Chronicle of Higher Education*, March 10, 2006.

35. Lynn Hunt, "Democratization and Decline? The Consequences of Democratic Change in the Humanities," in Kernan, *What's Happened to the Humanities?* pp. 20–23.

36. See National Center for Education Statistics, "Postsecondary Education."

37. See Bureau of Labor Statistics, "Teachers—Postsecondary," in *Occupational Outlook Book*, available online at the U.S. Department of Labor website, http://www.bls.gov/oco/ocos066.htm.

38. See American Association of the University Professors, *The Devaluing of the Higher Education: The Annual Report on the Economic Status of the Profession 2005–06*, available online at the AAUP website, http://www.aaup.org/AAUP/pubsres/academe/2006/MA/sal/z06.htm.

(less than 30 percent) and the natural sciences (just over 33 percent); it was about 38 percent in the health sciences; and it was over 37 percent in the social sciences, including history.[39]

Yet, Spellmeyer has drawn attention to the Bureau of Labor Statistics report that, in 2000, part-time faculty accounted for about 33 percent of all faculty, noting that part-time faculty was mainly in the humanities (English, history, composition programs, math, and modern languages).[40] A decade ago Hunt also drew attention to the disturbing trends in the ratios of faculty to administration and faculty to students (with the ensuing preference for multiple choice tests).[41]

Still, the Bureau has recognized that various issues make the working condition of the part-time faculties difficult, as well as that "the hiring of more part-time faculty has put a greater administrative burden on full-time faculty."[42] The AAUP has made pressing comparisons between the earnings of part-time faculty and the "poverty level," and it has signaled that "the adequacy (or inadequacy) of part-time faculty salaries affects the quality of education our institutions can provide."[43]

Finally, some international comparisons on the academic research and development (R&D) expenditures for the humanities and social sciences, even if difficult due to limitations of data, can shed additional light on the situation. According to a statement from the National Science Foundation, in 1998 United States devoted a smaller percentage of its academic R&D expenditures to the humanities and social sciences than "most countries supporting substantial levels of academic R&D (defined at $1 billion in 1998)"—only 7.3 percent (of which only 1.3 percent go toward the humanities), compared to Japan's 33.9 percent, Germany's 21.5 percent (with 12.9 percent for the humanities), Australia's 27 percent (with 7.6 percent for the humanities) Spain's 22.1 percent (with 6.6 percent for the humanities), Sweden's 18.3 percent (with 6.1 percent for the humanities), or Russia's 11.7 percent (with 5.1 percent for the humanities).[44] But

39. National Center for Education Statistics, "Postsecondary Education."

40. Spellmeyer, *Arts of living*, p. 251n.

41. Hunt, "Democratization and Decline?" pp. 21–23.

42. See Bureau of Labor Statistics, "Teachers—Postsecondary."

43. See American Association of the University Professors, *The Devaluing of the Higher Education*.

44. National Science Foundation, "U.S. and International Research and Development funds: Funds and Alliances," *Science and Engineering Indicators, 2002*, available online at the NSF website, http://www.nsf.gov/statistics/seind02/c4/tt04-15.htm.

based on more recent data, the fraction of academic R&D expenditures for the humanities and social sciences in the United States has dropped further, to 4.3 percent (with 0.33 percent for the humanities) in 2003, and to 4.1 percent (with 0.35 percent for the humanities) in 2004,[45] while in most of the previously mentioned countries the percentages of academic R&D targeted for the humanities and social sciences have remained within nearly the same range over the years.[46]

Yet according to another international comparison on academic R&D from 1990, the United States in 1987 had also spent a relatively smaller portion of its funds on academically related research in the humanities (2.8 percent from the government budget, and $1.70 in expenditures per capita) than United Kingdom (6.3 percent, $3.10 per capita), West Germany (6.4 percent, $4.20 per capita), France (6.8 percent, $3.90 per capita), The Netherlands (8.5 percent, $5.60 per capita), and Japan (9.6 percent, $2.90 per capita).[47]

These quantitative indicators point only to some of the factors that constitute the so-called "crisis" or "decline" of the humanities and the other disciplines that play a role in the cultivation of effective thinking skills. Some researchers have also pointed to "demographic" factors that have posed various challenges to these fields, including the "baby boom" generation (1950–1970), the ensuing "trend to vocationalism,"[48] and the increase in the "multiethnic and feminine student population."[49] But it does not appear likely that demographic changes can explain the escalating economic strains on the humanities in a time of ever-increasing university

---

45. Ronda Britt, "Industrial Funding of Academic R&D Continues to Decline in FY 2004," National Science Foundation *InfoBrief*, April 2006, available online at the NSF website, http://www.nsf.gov/statistics/infbrief/nsf06315/; and John E. Jankowski, "Academic R&D Doubled During Past Decade, Reaching $40 Billion in FY 2003," National Science Foundation *InfoBrief*, July 2005, available online at the NSF website, http://www.nsf.gov/statistics/infbrief/nsf05315/.

46. National Science Foundation, "Research and Development: Funds and Technology Linkages," *Science and Engineering Indicators, 2006*, available online at the NSF website, http://www.nsf.gov/statistics/seind06/c4/tt04-14.htm.

47. Ton Langendorff, "Support for the Humanities: some international statistics," in Erik Zürchner and Ton Langendorff, eds., *The Humanities in the Nineties: A View from the Netherlands* (Amsterdam: Swets & Zeitlinger, 1990), p. 17.

48. Roger L. Geiger, "Demography and Curriculum: The Humanities in American Higher Education from the 1950s through the 1980s," in David A. Hollinger, ed., *The Humanities and the Dynamics of Inclusion since the World War II* (Baltimore: John Hopkins UP, 2006), pp. 51ff.

49. Hunt, "Democratization and Decline? pp. 17ff.

budgets,[50] nor the declining proportion of students with interest in these subjects. Nevertheless, amid the dark tones, there is good news. We are told that, after numerous alarming signals, the American Academy of Arts and Sciences has begun a "long-term data-collecting project, the Humanities Indicators," in order to assess and monitor the state of these disciplines in terms of "hard numbers."[51] We can only wish a good luck to this project, hoping that it is the long-awaited light at the end of the tunnel. But it should not take much for a critically thinking mind to draw the parallel between the growing concern for adequate thinking skills and the eclipse of these subjects within academic curricula, which—in a little too straight-forward a fashion—have been frequently regarded as occupying the space of much needed specialized subjects. At this point, though, it is clear that the eclipse of those academic subjects that support a broader humanistic knowledge has been to the detriment of students thinking skills.

A Global Concern

While more apparent in the United States, the concern for the future of the humanities has attained global dimensions. More recently it has reignited the debate on the status of knowledge and the future of the university, now far beyond the old debate of the "two cultures" initiated by C. P. Snow.[52] In a recent publication titled *Innovation and Tradition: The Arts, Humanities and the Knowledge Economy*,[53] we find a number of insightful articles on the current situation, status, funding concerns, and prospects of humanities in the context of globalization. The book begins with an ironic "provocation," a tirade by a self-proclaimed founding body with the unambiguous name "Committee for the Extermination of Arts and Humanities Funding in the Higher Education."[54] It covers a wide range of topics, including the place of the humanities and philosophy in the structure of the university; the roles of the state and the international institutions, such as the Organization for Economic Cooperation and Development (OECD) and UNESCO, in settling the humanities within the so-called "knowledge economy"; the

50. Spellmeyer has pointed that the increase of university budgets has been "more than eightfold" over three decades. Spellmeyer, *Arts of Living*, p. 3.

51. Jennifer Howard, "Reading and Writing get Arithmetic," *The Chronicle of Higher Education*, April 14, 2006.

52. C. P. Snow, *The Two Cultures and the Scientific Revolution*, (Cambridge: Cambridge UP, 1959).

53. Jane Kenway, Elizabeth Bullen, and Simon Robb, eds., *Innovation and Tradition: The Arts, Humanities and the Knowledge Economy* (New York: Peter Lang, 2004).

54. Simon Robb and Elizabeth Bullen, "A Provocation," in ibid., pp. 1–9.

calls for change for the humanities within the structure of education; and understanding the humanities from the perspective of current R&D policy. It also provides numerous international examples.[55]

Still, the concern for the overall condition of humanities on the international level was raised even earlier. In his 1991 address to UNESCO, Jacques Derrida stated that

> philosophy is everywhere suffering, in Europe and elsewhere, both in its teaching and in its research, from a limit that, even though it does not always take the explicit form of prohibition or censure, nonetheless amounts to that, for the simple reason that the means for supporting teaching and research in philosophy are limited.[56]

Derrida further observed that such funding restrictions have been generally "motivated by budgetary balances that give priority to research and training that is, often correctly, labeled useful, profitable, and urgent, to so-called end-oriented sciences, and to techno-economic, indeed scientifico-military, imperatives," but he has also insisted that "the more these imperatives impose themselves..., the more also the right to philosophy becomes increasingly urgent, irreducible, as does the call to philosophy in order precisely to think and discern, evaluate and criticize, philosophies."[57] These statements, which very clearly bring the concern for philosophy outside its own field, once again point to the indispensability of what we here call philosophical competence, attested to as the "right to philosophy."

This right, which is "increasingly urgent" and "irreducible," the right to "think and discern, evaluate and criticize, philosophies," is precisely the right that in problem solving becomes a necessity, the necessity for a critical and creative reinvention of one's expert knowledge in a particular problematic situation. Yet this right cannot but appear as *obligation*, since it cannot be justified in expert terms and set in motion along the transition

55. See Greg Hainge's insightful article "The Death of Education, A Sad Tale: Of Anti-Pragmatic Pragmatics and the Loss of the Absolute in Australian Tertiary Education," in ibid., pp. 35–45; Jane Kenway, Elizabeth Bullen, and Simon Robb, "Global Knowledge Politics and 'Exploitable Knowledge'," in ibid., pp. 135–49; Stuart Cunningham, "The Humanities, Creative Arts, and the International Innovation Agenda," in ibid., pp. 113–24.

56. Jacques Derrida, *Ethics, Institutions, and the Right to Philosophy*, trans. Peter Pericles Triffonas, (Lanham, MD: Rowman and Littlefield, 2002), pp. 14–15. This quotation and the next one also appear at the beginning of Greg Hainge's "The Death of Education, A Sad Tale."

57. Ibid., p. 15.

of expertise in the "usual way." For, the importance of the right to philosophy, or to philosophical competence, in the exchange of expertise remains
in a certain important (indeed philosophical) sense "unjustifiable," inex-
plicable, incomprehensible, "open-ended," just as humanity does, unlike
the essence of the machine or the nature of physical object.

The Broader Humanistic Background and the University

To those short-sighted policy-makers who do not see the connection
between studying literature and the performance of immediate duties in
professions like nursing, finance, engineering, management, dentistry, or
plumbing, we say that the sense of responsibility, which is much coveted in
all professions, cannot be instituted in an individual just because a higher
ranking executive demands it. Humans are humans, not machines; they are
not operated by buttons or mouse clicks. They need to know themselves
in order to be able to handle themselves and their occupations in the best
way. Yet people can know themselves adequately only through cultural
history, which opens up for them through the kinds of knowledge acquired
in the humanities. Today, we have forgotten and remain unaware of the
motto of the Delphic temple, even if it has been speaking to us for some
three millennia.

Similarly, art subjects, which appeal directly to one's sense of creativity
at its most uninhibited and thus at its most susceptible to cultivation, foster
an inventiveness that may prove useful even in the most trivial problematic situations. For, we already know, the successful thinking in problem
solving is not just critical but also creative. In this sense, it does not come
as a surprise that pioneering educators such as Dorothy Heathcote suc-
cessfully utilized drama for the purpose of cultivating efficient thinking
skills.[58] Indeed, it only reaffirms the importance of subjects in the arts and
the humanities and the need of their reassertion, with all the exigency of
policy-making. This may be a challenging proposition for some deans and
university presidents, but mere "common sense" or "scientific expertise"
(the philosophical competence is reducible to neither of them) will not
suffice to advance a rationale for these subjects' reduction or exclusion.
Instead, as leading academic establishments have shown, we need centers of humanities and research institutes that integrate the approaches

58. Dorothy Heathcote, *Collected Writings on Education and Drama*, ed. Liz Johnson
and Cecily O'Neil (Evanston, IL: Northwestern UP, 1991); Ken Robinson, ed., *Exploring
Theater and Education* (London: Heinemann, 1980).

of different disciplines and promote interdisciplinary knowledge and the broader humanistic background that comes with it, in order to open up perspectives for efficient thinking. Such an integrative approach has already been advocated by the American Council of Learned Societies[59] and by the Commission on the Humanities sponsored by the Rockefeller Foundation in 1978.[60] But before that, it found a comprehensive theoretical treatment in the pivotal work of Talcott Parsons and Gerald Platt, *The American University*.[61]

As Parsons and Platt explained, the integration of different kinds of knowledge was taking place through the fulfillment of four basic functions of the university.[62] On the one hand, the university incorporates both the function of conveying "knowledge for 'problem solving'" for preparation of "professional practitioners as 'specialists'" and the function to propagate "knowledge 'for its own sake'," which is intended "especially for undergraduates as 'generalists'."[63] On the other hand, the advancement of these two functions is institutionally enmeshed with the advancement of both the core function of the higher education toward "research and graduate training," which is conducted by the academic "specialists," and the "societal definitions of the situation," which in a great extent too is being done by academicians but now in the role of "generalists," contributing to a more sophisticated understanding of the culture as a whole.[64] Understood in this way, the role of the university in society and culture is to generate and propagate both specialized knowledge ("knowledge for 'problem solving'") and general knowledge ("knowledge 'for its own sake'"), which correspond precisely to what we associate here with, respectively, *expertise* and *philosophical competence*. Essentially, this role of the university is made possible by the institutional integration of teaching and research, which involves the academic community in an exchange with the larger community of the rest society and culture ("Two concepts, institutionalization and interpenetration, illuminate the relations between

---

59. See "Speaking of the Humanities," ACLS Occasional Paper, no. 7 (1989), pp. 7, 30ff.

60. See Commission on the Humanities, *The Humanities in American Life: Report of the Commission on the Humanities* (Berkeley: Univ. of California Press, 1980), pp. 99–100, 114–15.

61. Talcott Parsons and Gerald Platt, *The American University*, (Cambridge, MA: Harvard UP, 1973), pp. 90ff.

62. Ibid.

63. Ibid.

64. Ibid., pp. 90ff. and ch. 3.

culture and society").[65] In fact, as Habermas has observed, the principle of unity of teaching and research has been foundational for the modern university and has been repeatedly reasserted during the last two centuries, even if it has occasionally reinvented to meet external cultural pressures through different dynamics of communication.[66] For, via the integration of teaching and research, the university practically avails its expert and humanistic knowledge for an exchange with the rest of society and culture, an exchange that we generally call the transition between theory and practice.

But if the exchange (communication) between the levels of theory and practice cannot dispense with an adequate philosophical competence, it will be necessary to approach those academic subjects that enhance a broader humanistic background in their utmost sophistication, and to reassert their value in higher education on a par with the specialized subjects. What is more, it will be necessary to continually seek new venues for their closer integration, not only with expert theoretical knowledge but also with the ever-challenging dynamics of social practices. In a more general and less scientific sense, we need to support their active presence in our lives, as inseparable from the life of our society, culture, and civilization.

On the opposite side, simplification can produce only naïve claims and ultimately useless clichés. We have been through that already. And we have seen, through quantitative attestations, that in recent decades the exchange between the institution of higher education and the external world has brought a disproportionate economic strain to our teaching and research and to the humanities as disciplines.

Speaking at Stanford University in 1998, Jacques Derrida pointed to the political significance of this exchange, both for the university and for the humanities,

> This is today, in the United States and throughout the world, a major political stake: to what extent the organization of research and teaching have to be supported, that is, directly or indirectly controlled, let us euphemistically say "sponsored," by commercial and industrial interests? By this logic, as we know, the Humanities are often held hostage to the departments of pure and applied science in which are concentrated

65. Ibid., p. 33.
66. Jürgen Habermas, "The Idea of the University," in *The New Conservatism: Cultural Criticism and the Historians' Debate*, trans. Shierry Weber Nicholson (Cambridge, MA: Harvard UP, 1996), pp. 100–27.

the supposedly profitable investments of capital foreign to the academic world.[67]

For us, it is clear that this political situation of the accelerating external dependence of the university, and of the humanities within the university, is neither justified nor useful for the enhancement of one's thinking abilities (one's philosophical competence). In this situation, the so-called "knowledge economy" overtakes and marginalizes the university within its own sphere, the universal sphere of knowledge, by identifying it more and more—via a metonymical contraction—with only parts of itself, by transforming it into a mere department of "commercial and industrial interests." And since this marginalization of the university within itself is ultimately a marginalization of its traditional nucleus, the humanities, it signals to the university once again that it must come to terms with its own identity and revisit its traditional autonomy, its profession, and indeed the future of the humanities.

This falls perfectly within the jurisdiction of the university, which has the inherent right and "unconditional freedom" to pursue and propagate the "light" of "truth," even if the "status" and the "value" of the latter could be endlessly debated.[68] As Derrida reminds us, "these are discussed, precisely, in the university and in departments that belong to Humanities."[69] But when its autonomy is called into question, the university's professorial function alone will not suffice to advance its idea of itself. Instead, upholding its "sovereignty" will have to necessitate "not only a principle of resistance, but a force of resistance—and of dissidence."[70]

In this sense, we can think along with Derrida of the university profession as a "profession of faith" suspended between its indefinite theoretical goal and an ever more complex practical pursuit of it, between "performative and constative speech acts," in an endless application of the conditionality of its own work, of an "as if," which however is ultimately apperceived and inaugurated in and throughout the work of the humanities.[71] This means that the university profession is suspended

67. Jacques Derrida, "University without Condition," in *Without Alibi*, trans. Peggy Kamuf (Stanford, CA: Stanford UP, 2002), p. 206. Jacques Derrida, *L'université sans condition* (Paris: Editions Galilée, 2001), p. 19.

68. Ibid., p. 202; cf. Derrida, *L'université*, pp. 11–12.

69. Ibid., pp. 202–3; cf. Derrida, *L'université*, pp. 11–12.

70. Ibid., pp. 206–7; cf. Derrida, *L'université*, pp. 19–20.

71. Ibid., pp. 202–9, 230ff.; cf. Derrida, *L'université*, pp. 11–24, 64ff.

between theory and practice in more than one way: it is not just the practice of theory-making, which gladly bestows its products on the practices of problem solving; it also needs *political conditioning*, whose maintenance, unlike its proper apprehension, falls well outside the university's own province. Hence, our appeal to politics and policy-making for the reinstatement of the humanities in the higher education in their full scope.[72]

In Conclusion

It is obviously implausible to design a "unique" course (or limited set of courses) that can be sufficient for the particular purpose of cultivating adequate thinking skills or philosophical competence. For a sophisticated thinking is exercised within more, rather than fewer, concepts, and not in a single set of instrumentalized thinking techniques. The more sophisticated one's philosophical competence, i.e., humanistic background, the more promising one's thinking in problem solving. We philosophers (and now I mean everyone) can find a classic discussion of this understanding in Wittgenstein's *Philosophical Investigations*:

> Correct prognoses will generally issue from the judgments of those with better knowledge of mankind.
> Can one learn this knowledge? Yes; some can. Not, however, by taking a course in it, but through '*experience*'.—Can someone else be a man's teacher in this? Certainly. From time to time he gives him the right *tip*.—This is what 'learning' and 'teaching' are like here.—*What one acquires is not a technique; one learns correct judgments*. There are

---

72. In view of the above, it is not surprising that Derrida sees the uncompromised future work or "profession" of the humanities, as apperceiving itself, its proper meanings and value, throughout the *full scope* of its suspended history, faithfully involving: (1) "the history of man, the idea, the figure, and the notion of 'what is proper to man'"; (2) "the history of democracy and the idea of sovereignty"; (3) "the history of 'professing', of the 'profession' and of the professoriat"; (4) "the history of literature,... of the concept of literature, of the modern institution named 'literature'"; (5) "the history of the profession, the profession of faith, professionalization, and the professoriat"; (6) "the history of 'as if' and especially... the distinction between performative and constative acts"; (7) the "knowledge," "profession of faith," "mise en oeuvre,... the performative putting at work of the 'as if'," which provide the power, "the 'I can', 'I may' or 'I am empowered to...'" for the arrival of an 'event'" (ibid., pp. 230–37; cf. Derrida, *L'université*, pp. 68–79). Our rhetorical question here is: should any fields or power structures other than the humanities be left to legitimately decide on these matters?

also rules, but they do not form a system, and *only experienced people can apply them right.* Unlike calculating-rules.[73]

The "better knowledge" that we need for our philosophical competence will come through a multifaceted "experience" with the disciplines of the arts and humanities, and with the humanistic knowledge of the social and natural sciences. The best way to prepare the thinking skills of our students for the demands of practice is therefore to include these subjects as a vital component in the higher education and to support interdisciplinary incentives, in both teaching and research, that enhance their intra- and extra-institutional integration. The practical benefit of such integration would be that students would not perceive the different subject areas as distant and unrelated. Indeed, in a certain important sense knowledge is singular and unified; only its specializations make it different. And yet, its unity is established through thinking, which is in its nature *philosophical*, whereas "philosophical" in its all-encompassing sense means *humanistic*.

A too inert understanding of the unity of knowledge may lead some to erroneously conclude that it may be possible to invent a universal method of problem-solving to make up for what here has been termed philosophical competence. To them we say, philosophy is neither expertise nor technology; it can't be simplified for the sake of "good intentions." Instead, even when things are getting simple in there, their simplicity demands its proper understanding, which—in the limiting case—is always and exclusively within the background of the philosophical tradition, taken in its plurality and utmost sophistication. And we refer them to Wittgenstein once again: "There is no *a* philosophical method, though there are indeed methods, like different therapies."[74]

As we abandon the search for a universal method in problem solving, we need to affirm our understanding of philosophical competence as distinct from expertise, that is, as being no more and no less than a sophisticated theoretical conjecture whose value can be tested only in practice—as the therapy of actual "expert" problems. In this sense, we can say that when an expert problem has been solved, its therapy has been completed, and that only then have the "problems of mediation"—the non-expert problems, the cognitive problems, the problems of our critical and creative thinking,

73. Wittgenstein, *Philosophical Investigations*, p. 227, emphasis partly added. In the original passage only the words *experience* (in the fourth sentence) and *tip* (in the seventh sentence) are italicized.

74. Ibid., p. 133.

the traditional philosophical problems—been overcome. The solved expert problem is the only visible indication of the philosophical competence, which, like the "problems of mediation," is itself invisible; whereas "invisible" here also means "insusceptible to expertise." Indeed, one usually does not think of the plumber who has just fixed a faucet as having also demonstrated a "philosophical competence," that is, as having dealt with quite a few philosophical problems—"problems of mediation"—in the meantime. But this only speaks of how prone one is to neglect the human aspect in problem solving by reducing the problem solver to a *mere* expert. On the contrary, in plumbing, as in any other profession, the use of "expertise" never goes without philosophical competence—its proper mediator, the one that is needed where "problems of mediation" can arise, and this is precisely everywhere where problem solvers (as humans) mediate the transition of expert knowledge from theory to practice.

The practical value of this competence involves its use in preventing the inadequate transfer of any principle, method, technique, procedure, expertise, or theory of resolution to a particular problematic situation. Philosophical competence is thus a resistance to the too straightforward application of concepts, that is, to the lack of thinking, to the non-critical thinking, to the non-creativity, to the inability to invoke and play alternative solutions in one's mind in practice. Philosophical competence actualizes the humanistic aspect of our knowledge in a way that cannot be sufficiently accounted for in expert terms, which is why some experts may be inclined to neglect its importance. But despite its "expert insufficiency," it has no alternatives as the condition for utilizing expert knowledge in problem solving. For this humanistic aspect, this aspect of humanity, and of humanities, brings forward the radical difference between a human problem solver and a machine, a difference that demands from one's thinking to be always supplied with knowledge of oneself as human person, and not just with the knowledge of one's area of expertise.

Finally, since the cultivation of one's humanistic background is not a simple task and takes place most decisively, even if not exclusively, throughout one's education (which is at its most sophisticated in higher education), it can and must be promoted more determinedly through a diverse and sophisticated humanistic curriculum. If the maintenance of the latter presently faces challenges, these do not make it less indispensable. So be it, we can only advise the respective problem solvers on the level of policy-making to come up with solutions in a philosophically competent manner.

Art as a Social System: The Sociological Aesthetics of Niklas Luhmann

Matthew Rampley

The work of Niklas Luhmann represents perhaps the last major body of social theory of the twentieth century. Beginning with *Social Theory or Social Technology: What Does Systems Research Achieve?* jointly published with Jürgen Habermas in 1971, Luhmann spent the following three decades up until his death in 1998 laying out the basis for a comprehensive theory of social systems.[1] The author of some sixty books and three hundred and eighty essays and articles, Luhmann has had an enormous impact on social and cultural theory in the German-speaking world. In Britain and North America, however, he remains a relatively marginal figure.

This stands in inverse proportion to Luhmann's potential significance, not only for social theory but, more particularly, for the sociological understanding of art. Indeed, one of Luhmann's major achievements was the formulation of a sociological aesthetics that challenges many of the orthodoxies of current social theories of art. As with his general sociological theory, however, his work in this area has received little attention.[2]

One reason for this may be the success with which Habermas, for one, dismissed Luhmann's enterprise as an exemplar of counter-enlightenment thought, comparing it to the work of other conservative social theorists,

---

1. Niklas Luhmann and Jürgen Habermas, *Theorie der Gesellschaft oder Sozialtechnologie: Was leistet die Systemforschung?* (Frankfurt am Main: Suhrkamp, 1971).

2. Exceptions include: Erkki Sevänen, "Art as an Autopoietic Sub-System of Modern Society: A Critical Analysis of the Concepts of Art and Autopoietic Systems in Luhmann's Late Production," *Theory, Culture and Society* 18, no. 1 (2001): 75–103; Niels Albertsen and Bülent Dicken, "Artworks' Networks: Field, System of Mediators?" *Theory, Culture and Society* 21, no. 3 (2004): 35–58; Julian Stallabrass, *Art Incorporated: The Story of Contemporary Art* (Oxford: Oxford UP, 2004), pp. 114ff.

such as Arnold Gehlen.[3] It may also be due to the fact that works exploring art, culture, and literature through the lens of systems theory have often led to disappointing results.[4] Relying on the restatement of existing understandings in the abstracted vocabulary of Luhmann's thinking, they have often added little in terms of critical or historical insight. Such efforts do not do service to the range and depth of Luhmann's thought, which, I argue, merits deeper critical attention. In this article, I offer an analysis of his thought, addressing, in turn, salient aspects of his general systems theory, his account of art as a social system, and its significance for existing modes of interpreting art and cultural practice.

Systems Theory as Social Theory

While the systems theory of the 1960s was oriented primarily to the study of organizational, administrative, and technological processes, in the work of Luhmann it became the basis of a project that aimed to question the traditional bases of sociology. Drawing on a range of discourses mostly unfamiliar to social theory—from the biological theory of Humberto Maturana and Francisco Varela to the mathematical logic of George Spencer Brown—Luhmann argues that societies are to be conceived as systems, of which the basic element is communication, or, more properly, the communicative event.[5] This stems from the basic notion that "Society is a system for constituting meaning."[6] As such, social systems are located in the virtual space of communicative interaction. This might appear to be comparable to Habermas's concept of the speech community, except that where the latter places the *subject* at the center of communicative action, Luhmann insists that conscious subjects *cannot* be the basis of the social system.[7] The basis of this is the contention that consciousness—or, to use Luhmann's

3. Robert Holub, "Luhmann's Progeny: Systems Theory and Literary Studies in the Post-Wall Era," *New German Critique* 61 (1994): 143–59.

4. See, for example, Dietrich Schwanitz, *Systemtheorie und Literatur: Ein neues Paradigma* (Opladen: Westdeutscher Verlag, 1990); David J. Krieger, *Kommunikationssystem Kunst* (Vienna: Passagen Verlag, 1997); Stefan Weber, ed., *Was konstruiert Kunst?* (Vienna: Passagen Verlag, 1999).

5. See Humberto Maturana and Francisco Varela, *Autopoiesis and Cognition: The Realization of the Living* (Dordrecht: Reidel, 1980); George Spencer Brown, *The Laws of Form* (London: George Allen and Unwin, 1969).

6. Niklas Luhmann, *Die Gesellschaft der Gesellschaft* [*Society as a Social System*] (Frankfurt am Main: Suhrkamp, 1997), p. 50.

7. See Jürgen Habermas, *Communication and the Evolution of Society*, trans. Thomas McCarthy (London: Heinemann, 1979) and *Theory of Communicative Action*, trans. Thomas McCarthy (London: Heinemann, 1984).

terminology, the "psychic system"—is *closed* to others. Indeed, it is the closure of psychic systems that drives the impulse to communicate. As Luhmann states: "Because operative closure locks the door to the inner life, imagination, and thoughts of others, the other holds us captive as an eternal riddle. This is why the experience of other human beings is richer than any experience of nature....And it explains why lovers are capable of talking endlessly about themselves with no interest whatever in anything else."[8] Moreover, because psychic systems are closed, "humans cannot communicate; not even their brains can communicate; not even their conscious minds can communicate. Only communication can communicate."[9] As a psychic system, "I" respond not to other psychic systems, but to their communications, and they to mine. Consequently, communicative acts develop an autonomous logic. To cite Luhmann: "communications can only be produced in a recursive relation to other communications, thus only within a network."[10]

The basis of society is, therefore, not social subjects but rather the recursive network of communications *between* them. Moreover, since the psychic system is operationally closed to others—communication is never a window onto the inner self—such communications are always open to subversion, misunderstanding, and suspicion. This introduces a central theme: the failure or disruption of meaning:

> Once embroiled in communication, one can never return to the paradise of innocent souls....Sincerity is incommunicable because it becomes insincere by being communicated....One can easily utter something about oneself, about one's own state, moods, attitudes, and intentions; but one can do this only to present oneself as a context of information that could also be otherwise. Therefore communication unleashes a subversive, universal, irremediable suspicion...[11]

A further distinctive aspect of Luhmann's account is the emphasis on temporality and the dynamic nature of communication. The latter consists

8. Niklas Luhmann, *Art as a Social System*, trans. Eva M. Knodt (Stanford, CA: Stanford UP, 2000), p. 13. All subsequent references will be cited parenthetically within the article.

9. Niklas Luhmann, *Theories of Distinction: Redescribing the Descriptions of Modernity*, trans. Joseph O'Neil et al. (Stanford, CA: Stanford UP, 2002), p. 169.

10. Luhmann, *Die Gesellschaft der Gesellschaft*, pp. 82–83.

11. Niklas Luhmann, *Social Systems*, trans. John Bednarz, Jr. (Stanford, CA: Stanford UP, 1995), p. 150.

of ephemeral utterances, "system events [that] disappear from moment to moment."[12] Unless they are responded to, the communicative process comes to a halt. This produces an image of systems as radically contingent and unstable; their existence through time is completely dependent on there being continued communications. If communications cease, so does the system that they constitute.

Given the ephemeral basis of social systems, a key question concerns the means by which they maintain coherence. Luhmann argues that systems originate in a reflexive process.[13] A communication takes place, and it is either responded to or not. If it is not responded to, no recursion takes place and hence no system emerges. However, if it is responded to, it is reflected upon, and as soon as this occurs, an intermediary, third element is introduced—a *tertium comparationis*—which functions as the basic minimum condition for the "take off" of a social system. For this *tertium comparationis* provides the focus for the communication, and this introduces the fundamental idea, namely, that the coherence of social systems is produced *semantically*.[14] Social systems are identified by codes governing the communicative acts constituting them, and each code is based on a binary opposition (Luhmann terms this the "guiding difference"). Hence the legal system is based on the opposition legal/illegal, the economic system on the difference between payment and non-payment, and the art system on the opposition of the beautiful/ugly. These codes are not necessarily fixed and are subject to modulation and revision. Regarding art, Luhmann recognizes that this distinction was displaced by other guiding differences, such as that of beauty/sublimity or interesting/uninteresting (a particularly important distinction within Romantic aesthetics) or simply originality/derivativeness. It is also by means of such guiding differences that social systems draw a boundary between themselves and their environment. The environment is not a given but rather is produced and defined by the system, and social systems are marked by a continual movement between self-reference and hetero-reference (i.e., a differentiation from their environment).

A central role is also played by the concept of evolution, though not, as is commonly understood, the teleological progressive linear development

<hr />

12. Ibid., p. 177.

13. Niklas Luhmann, "Reflexive Mechanismen," *Soziale Welt* 17 (1966): 1–23.

14. See Niklas Luhmann, "Gesellschaftliche Struktur und semantische Tradition," in *Gesellschaftsstruktur und Semantik: Studien zur Wissenssoziologie der modernen Gesellschaft*, vol. 1 (Frankfurt am Main: Suhrkamp, 1980): 1–72.

of adaptations to the environment. Since the environment is constituted by the system, this would not be possible. Rather, each social system evolves due to an internally generated process of change. The quantity of communications produces variations—Luhmann sees such variations as produced by a "deviant reproduction of elements of the system"[15]—which present numerous possibilities for redefinition of the system. Certain of these are selected, and the system is then restabilized. Each communication can be either affirmed or negated, and each of these two responses can itself lead to further communications that present a new set of semantic possibilities. In other words, each social system is in a constant state of expansion and contraction (evolution is not a linear process) that might be prompted by any one of its many communications. Variation, selection, and restabilization—important Darwinian terms—all contribute to Luhmann's conception of the social system as evolving in a state of "dynamic stability." It is "dynamic" in that it only exists as a consequence of the continually self-generating process of ephemeral communications, and "stable" in the sense that all systems have a coherence that enables them to be regarded as systems at all. Yet each social system is in a constant state of flux.

Up to this point I have treated Luhmann's account of systems as a *general* social theory. However, while his work covers a wide historical range, it is constructed as a theory of modernity; a central thesis of his work is that the emergence of communicative systems generated by semantic codes is a specific feature of modern society. Modernity is thus *functionally* differentiated—in contrast to pre-modern society, which is organized around principles of social stratification. Within social theory the term "function" is often associated with the structural functionalism of Talcott Parsons.[16] Luhmann studied with Parsons, but he understands function in semantic terms. Specifically, "a function is nothing other than a focus for comparison. It marks a problem...in such a way that multiple solutions can be compared and that the problem remains open for further selections and substitutions" (138). The idea of functional differentiation could thus be described as a theory of multiple rationalities, and bears comparison with the familiar equation of modernity with the splitting up of discourse into the separate spheres of science, ethics, and

---

15. Luhmann, *Die Gesellschaft der Gesellschaft*, p. 461.
16. See Talcott Parsons, *The Structure of Social Action* (New York: McGraw Hill 1937) and *The Social System* (New York: Free Press, 1951).

aesthetics.[17] Luhmann equates modernity with the rise of professional, specialized, and autonomous discourses of, for example, education, law, politics, art, or science, which operate according to their own distinctive codes. Communication is thus fractured in a second sense; not only is it open to suspicion and misunderstanding, thanks to its distance from the interiority of the psychic system, but it is also fragmented into a sequence of incommensurable semantic functions. To employ Luhmann's term, modernity is "polycontextural," and this has epistemological consequences, too. For an axiom of Luhmann's thinking is that knowledge is generated from within social systems; social systems "observe" on the basis of their own communicative semantic codes. This also applies to systems theory itself, which, far from presenting some master discourse, is itself another system, observing other systems from its system-bound perspective. Since modernity is functionally fractured, there cannot be a totalizing theory of modern society. As Luhmann notes, "contemporary society...cannot abide a final word....It knows no positions from which society could be adequately described for others within society."[18]

This characterization might also be construed as a theory of the postmodern, but for Luhmann such a lack of a "universally applicable rationality," far from constituting a distinctive historical phase, merely signifies modernity's coming to terms with its own differentiated status. For Luhmann, modernity is thereby defined in terms of the predominance of self- or second-order observation: "it examines the question of what an observer can and cannot see with their distinctions. We find ourselves in the land of motive and suspicion—the novel, the critique of ideology, psychotherapy."[19] This point has been developed further by Dirk Baecker in relation to that quintessentially modern term "culture."[20] As Baecker argues, the concept arose out of modernity's self-observation in terms of its difference from others: "'Culture' is accordingly the formal means of working through the problem that there are other cultures. It is a means of drawing a distinction.... Whatever might have existed worldwide in terms

17. See, for example, Jürgen Habermas, *The Philosophical Discourse of Modernity: Twelve Lectures*, trans. Frederick Lawrence (Cambridge: Polity, 1989).

18. Niklas Luhmann, *Observations on Modernity*, trans. William Whobrey (Stanford, CA: Stanford UP, 1998), p. 18.

19. Ibid., p. 19.

20. Dirk Baecker, "Globalisierung und kulturelle Kompetenz," in *Wozu Kultur?* (Berlin: Kadmos Verlag, 2001), pp. 11–32.

of forms of life and patterns of sociability, a 'culture' only emerged when another 'culture' was encountered....A 'cultural contact' is thus less the meeting of two forms of life than the production of modes of behavior that enabled such an encounter."[21] Only through difference—and Baecker has in mind European colonial expansion from the sixteenth century onward—could the concept of culture come into play.

This theory runs counter to certain other influential theories of post-modernity. I am referring here to theories of *contemporary* society that emphasize the postmodern shift toward a massive process of de-differen-tiation. Figures such as David Harvey have highlighted the postmodern merging of the cultural and economic spheres, while Lyotard's famous analysis points to the conflation of scientific research and economic and political interests.[22] Luhmann acknowledges that systems intrude on one another, but for such intrusions—which he terms systemic "irritations"—to have any impact, they have to be re-coded in the terms of the system in question. While contemporary society is functionally differentiated, there are multiple interactions *between* systems, a process described as "inter-penetration" or "structural coupling." At a certain point, different social systems may converge, but this does not mean a total congruence or loss of operational autonomy: "interpenetrating systems converge in individual elements—that is, they use the same ones—but they give each of them a different selectivity and connectivity, different pasts and futures."[23] An obvious example is the case of art. The dependence of art upon the art market does not, contrary to expectations, put into doubt the autonomy of the art system. Rather, this should be regarded as an instance of the structural coupling of the art and economic systems. I shall return to this later, but it is necessary first to examine Luhmann's general account of the art system.

Art as a Social System
In keeping with his larger project, art, like the law, the economy, politics, or science, constitutes a specific social system of modernity. In other words, it is a self-defining system of communicative operations. Luhmann traces

21. Ibid., p. 17.
22. David Harvey, *The Condition of Postmodernity* (Cambridge: Polity, 1990); Jean-François Lyotard, *The Postmodern Condition: A Report on Knowledge*, trans. Geoff Bennington and Brian Massumi (Manchester: Manchester UP, 1984).
23. Luhmann, *Social Systems*, p. 215.

its early origins to the Renaissance, although it only fully emerged in the late eighteenth century. In other words, he approaches art in terms of his *broader* outline of the shift from a pre-modern stratified society structure, based on class distinctions and hierarchies, to a functionally differentiated modernity. The key question is therefore how art differentiates itself from other systems. Luhmann's response is that "the function of art can be traced to problems of meaningful communication" (139). The specific semantic theme of art is the relationship between the non-social domain of conscious perception and the social domain of communication—in other words, perhaps the most basic question of all concerning society. These two belong to semantically differentiated systems, a condition that both prompts the need for communication (and hence social systems) and also ensures that there is always the possibility of miscommunication. In this regard, "art uses perceptions and, by doing so, seizes consciousness at the level of its own externalizing activity. The function of art would thus consist in integrating what is in principle incommunicable—namely, perception—into the communication network" (141). Luhmann reiterates this position in unambiguous terms on numerous occasions. The work of art is employed *exclusively* for communication—although he also recognizes that it can fail in this task, inasmuch as it participates in the risks involved in all communication. Thus, "art communicates by using perceptions contrary to their primary purpose" (22).

One cannot speak in terms of a hierarchy of social systems. No one social system has any priority over any other. Nevertheless, art in Luhmann appears to be concerned with the basic constitutive paradox of society *per se*—the communication of the incommunicable—in a manner that other social systems are not. This becomes manifest in a variety of ways. Most immediately it involves a disturbance of perception, for under normal conditions perception operates on the basis of an economy of vision: "omitting things from view. Seeing is overlooking" (22). Art thus directs perception toward the overlooked: "once we are warned, we start paying attention" (23). While it might appear that Luhmann is thinking primarily in terms of the visual arts, his account also claims to apply to literature, in which the medium is words. Thus, in poetry, connotation dominates over denotation, and the poem "communicates not through the propositional content of its utterances but . . . by virtue of the ornamental structure of mutually limiting references that appear in the form of words" (25). In literature—or "text art," as he terms it—this occurs through combining meaning, sound, and rhythm in which the "sensuous perceptibility of words" plays a central role. By such means, "text art," drawing on familiar meanings, "aims at disrupting automization and delaying understanding" (25).

With this, Luhmann forestalls an important potential criticism. In particular, his reference to perception might initially lay him open to the charge of reliance on a formalist notion of aesthetic experience, long disputed by social theorists of art. Yet, for Luhmann, perception is both less and more important than formalist accounts acknowledge. On the one hand, it is clear that in his reference to "text art" Luhmann is concerned with a cognitive process. At the same time, he stresses that perception exceeds the specific case of aesthetic experience; at a most basic level, reading is based on perception. This also answers a possible criticism that his emphasis on perception is inadequate given the history of twentieth-century art, with the production of ready-mades or conceptual art. Thus, even the anti-aesthetic work of the conceptual artists of the 1960s relies on visual perception. This echoes Terry Atkinson's critique of Lucy Lippard and John Chandler's well-known equation of conceptual art with the "dematerialization" of art.[24] Conversely, although the ready-mades of Duchamp, Warhol, and Koons appeared to erase the perceptual distinction between art and non-art, this non-perceptibility is less important than is often claimed. Luhmann takes issue with authors such as Arthur Danto, who, in the light of the *Brillo Boxes* of Warhol, saw art as subsumed within philosophy.[25] For while Warhol—or Duchamp—eliminated the possibility of distinguishing between artworks and non-art on the basis of sensuously perceptible properties, they did so using the *form* of the work of art. As Luhmann argues, ordinary objects do not insist on being taken for ordinary things, while the fact that *Fountain* or *Brillo Boxes* did, betrayed their function as works of art: "The function of art in such a case is to reproduce the difference of art. But the mere fact that art seeks to cancel this difference and fails...says more about art than could any excuse or critique" (145).

In keeping with the emphasis on art as a functional system of modernity, Luhmann draws his examples predominantly from modern art, literature,

24. See Terry Atkinson, "Letter to Lucy Lippard and John Chandler concerning the Article 'The Dematerialization of Art' (1968)." An extract from this letter is published in Alexander Alberro and Blake Stimson, eds., *Conceptual Art: A Critical Anthology* (Cambridge, MA: MIT Press, 1999), p. 9.

25. See Arthur Danto, "The Artworld," *Journal of Philosophy* 61 (1964): 571–84.

and music. Thus, the most prominent instances of art's concern with the theme of communication and its paradoxes are to be found in the Romantic philosophy of the symbol or in the aestheticization of the self, from the Georgian dandy to the modernist aesthete.[26] He also highlights the thematization of authenticity in the seventeenth century or of non-communication in Romanticism—important examples being Jean Paul's novels *Siebenkäs* and *Flegeljahre*. A similar significance is given to the Romantic fascination with the *Doppelgänger*, from which "the informed reader could infer that the author had split himself into two different personae that communicate with one another. As Schlegel puts it: 'Nobody can know himself unless he is both himself and another.'... Under such conditions one could exploit the dissolution of identity in order to represent both the difficulties and the failure of the ego's self-reflection as a problem of communication" (287). The *refusal* of meaning in modernist art and literature can be read in a similar manner, and this thereby reveals a crucial difference between modern and pre-modern art. In contrast to the Renaissance invention of perspective, for example, in which "the viewer is to view the image as they normally see the world, and perspective is the (invisible) means to seduce them into doing so," modern art thematizes observation and is consequently characterized as a second-order observation, i.e., the observation of observations.[27] Means, techniques of representation, become an end in themselves, in a process intended to achieve a disruption of automized patterns of meaning. This suggests parallels with Russian formalism, such as with Shklovsky's view that poetic speech "makes the construction of language perceptible" or "deautomizes perception."[28] Luhmann's writing can also be seen as privileging what Christoph Menke has referred to as the "aesthetics of negation," more familiar from the work of Adorno, Derrida, and others.[29] Luhmann dissociates himself explicitly from such positions, but this stems primarily from his skepticism toward theories

26. See Niklas Luhmann, "Weltkunst," in Luhmann, Frederick D. Bunsen, and Dirk Baecker, *Unbeobachtbare Welt: über Kunst und Architektur* (Bielefeld: Haux, 1990), pp. 7–45; here, p. 7.

27. Ibid., p. 9.

28. Viktor Shklovsky, "Art as Device," cited in Mikhail Bakhtin and Pavel Medvedev, *The Formal Method in Literary Scholarship*, trans. Albert J. Wehrle (Baltimore: Johns Hopkins UP, 1978), p. 89.

29. Christoph Menke, *Sovereignty of Art: Aesthetic Negativity in Adorno and Derrida* (Cambridge, MA: MIT Press, 1999).

based on ethical or normative imperatives, rather than from any incompatibility in the logic of his account.

The precise relation of Luhmann's work to such theories remains an issue for further discussion, but rather than pursue it at this stage I shall explore another important dimension to Luhmann's account, and this concerns his comments on art's *fictionality*. Basic to the function of art is its positing of an imaginary reality. This is in itself hardly a novel claim, except that Luhmann's interest focuses not on the nature of such fictional worlds, but on the consequences of such fictionality for the "real" world. It is important to note here that fictional has a special meaning in Luhmann. As he states, fiction is not simply a matter of "adding something to a monocontextual world" in an act of "self-assertion" on the part of the artist.[30] Fiction has a very particular relation to the real, for "every decision to fix something diverts one's gaze to the other side of the form, and draws attention to what might still be done or attended to."[31] In other words, the fictional draws with it attention to what is excluded—the real—and how. In particular, Luhmann claims, "the imaginary world of art offers a position from which something else can be determined as reality.... Without such markings of difference the world would simply be the way it is. Only when a reality 'out there' is distinguished from fictional reality can one observe one side from the perspective of the other" (142). The real is not a given, but rather constructed in virtue of its difference from the fictional. This is in accordance with Luhmann's general constructivist epistemology—a reality is the correlate of the observer. But where this position has been taken by many as involving a collapse of the distinction between fictional and real worlds—between philosophy and poetry, for example, or literature and history—there are no such implications here. Rather, art's fictional reality creates a "double of reality from which reality can be observed...whether in an idealizing, critical or affirmative manner" (143). It is the fictionality of art that underlies its ability to act as a critical practice and that permits reality to come into focus as a site of, for example, oppression, suffering, or disharmony. Moreover, while Luhmann is critical of the use of normative judgements, he identifies an ethical imperative, namely, that if it is not to be "empty self-assertion," art "has to be able to demonstrate its difference from reality and the benefits that can

30. Luhmann, "Weltkunst," pp. 13–14.
31. Ibid., p. 14.

be achieved from it."[32] In other words, if it is not to be an arbitrary fiat, the fictional world constructed by art has to be able to articulate critically its relation to the real.

Of course, it can be objected that this emphasis on the fictional offers a restricted view of art, in that much of the trajectory of avant-garde art, from Dada through to the minimalism of the 1960s, was dedicated to overcoming the difference between art and the real. Luhmann is, however, critical of this. The attempt to collapse the distinction between the imaginary/fictional and the real ultimately fails; it is by *insisting* on their identity with ordinary things that artworks, such as the minimalist objects of Carl Andre, for example, or the journalistic novels of John Dos Passos, foreground their status as works of art.

I have already noted that art occupies an elevated status in terms of its ability to communicate perception and to thematize the fracturing of communication. Its fictionality guarantees it a further crucial position, inasmuch as it instantiates the contingencies of modernity. It has become a commonplace of Critical Theory that aesthetic debates played a crucial role in articulating the sense of the distinctiveness of modernity. This emerged first in the *Querelle des Anciens et des Modernes* of the seventeenth century. As Klaus Lichtblau states, "The historical relativization of the aesthetic ideal of beauty highlighted not only the arbitrariness or polemical reversibility of the relationship of Old and New.... It also indicated the possible birth of a new classical style which no longer required the normative recourse to pre-given traditions."[33] Crucial, therefore, to the emergence of modernity was the concept of the new as a distinctive marker of the present; in terms of Luhmann's thinking, the guiding difference classic/modern or old/new served as the basis for a crucial self-description of modernity.

As I stated earlier, a central aspect of Luhmann's reading of modernity is also the emphasis on its decentered, polycontextural character. Not only does the fracturing of the social into a series of functionally differentiated systems undermine attempts to capture society as a totality; also, no particular system enjoys a privileged epistemological position. There is simply a collection of contingent perspectives onto the social that are generated from within different social systems. While he distinguishes between Old European and modern semantics, this temporal distinction is not so central to his concept of the modern; the passage to postmodernity is not to be located in a "waning of the new" or in the "aging of modernity," to borrow Peter Bürger's phrase, but rather in the recognition of that contingency.[34] In this context, while no system occupies a superior position in modern society, art's doubling of reality, in which such self-recognition is thematized and acted out, implies that it again fulfills a critical function of which no other system is capable.

Luhmann's point of departure is thus the contingency of all social systems; "everything can be done differently," and this starts with the first arbitrary operation that establishes a system (90). This fundamental contingency applies to art as well. "Whatever exists or is made in the world could be otherwise, too," and this includes art, which Luhmann terms an "ostentatiously improbable occurrence" (153). What he means is that the specific relationship between form and medium evident in a particular artwork is neither necessary nor explicable in purely causal terms. Hence his conclusion that "an artwork distinguishes itself by virtue of the low probability of its emergence" (153). Indeed, that there should be not only artworks but also a functionally differentiated art system is an equally improbable occurrence. Although Luhmann stresses the functional autonomy of the art system, its foregrounding of its own contingency leads to a wider recognition of the contingency of all social systems. This possibility of being otherwise is not an entirely arbitrary or free choice. A central operation of social systems is their reduction of contingency through generating a calculable set of expectations; although the initial establishment of a social system is highly improbable, its continued operation becomes progressively less so. This is what makes a social system a *system* rather than a random sequence of events. For Luhmann this is in part the function of the art industry. "[T]he art system supplies institutions in which it is not unlikely to find works of art," and this general process of structuring expectations—what Luhmann terms its "internal redundancies"—occurs through framing institutions and also through artworks themselves. Artworks thereby occupy a space between astonishment and recognition—or between the confounding and fulfillment of expectations.

This discussion also has to address a central difference between systems theory and the aesthetics of Critical Theory: namely, the absence of a normative dimension to Luhmann's work. This has been seen as its most

---

34. See Peter Bürger, "Das Altern der Moderne," in *Das Altern der Moderne: Schriften zu bildenden Kunst* (Frankfurt am Main: Suhrkamp, 2001), pp. 10–30.

problematic aspect, yet the absence of a normative dimension remains one of the cornerstones of his thinking. This is spelled out both in theoretical terms in *Society as a Social System* and in more informal terms elsewhere. In an interview from 1985, Luhmann states unequivocally: "Critical Theory lacks the complexity to be anything other than the provocation of an attitude of protest or resignation....It lends it admittedly a certain attraction, but also shows up its limitations. For example, one is in a position either not to see the monetary economy, the law, or the machinery of politics, or to see them only in terms of negative critique."[35] This deliberate standing apart from the political norms and aims of Critical Theory has undoubtedly laid Luhmann open to the charge of being an apologist for the social status quo, yet his position is more complex than that of conservatives such as Gehlen or Daniel Bell, inasmuch as he refuses any suggestion of the possibility—or even desirability—of a return to pre-modern social semantics.

Luhmann's emphasis on the functional autonomy of art consequently has no suggestion of the oppositional practice historically seen as the social obligation of the avant-garde and associated with the aesthetics of Critical Theory. Indeed, it has been argued that his emphasis on the autonomy of the art system gives his work a markedly formalist character.[36] This impression is also reinforced by his stress on the role of perception within the functional operation of art, yet the notion of autonomy here displays notable parallels with Adorno, despite the political and ethical differences between the two authors. In the latter's *Aesthetic Theory*, aesthetic alienation and artistic autonomy are the function of social and cultural division.[37] Indeed for Adorno, this is the constitutive contradiction of modern art: "Art's asociality is the determinate negation of a determinate society."[38] The more art sets itself in opposition to society, the more it reveals its social character as grounded in bourgeois ideals of freedom. As such, art, for Adorno, can never achieve total autonomy, and his writing is haunted by the fear that art will become absorbed within the circuit

35. Niklas Luhmann, "Biographie, Attitüden, Zettelkasten," in *Archimedes und Wir: Interviews* (Berlin: Merve Verlag, 1987), p. 126. On some of the wider issues concerning Critical Theory and its relation to Luhmann, see Wolfgang Malte Fues, "Critical Theory and Systems Theory," in Peter-Uwe Hohendahl and Jaimey Fisher, eds., *Critical Theory: Current State and Future Prospects* (New York: Berghahn Books, 2001), pp. 229–47.

36. See Erkki Sevänen, "Art as an Autopoietic Sub-System," p. 90.

37. Theodor W. Adorno, *Aesthetic Theory*, trans. Robert Hullot-Kentor (Minneapolis: Minnesota UP, 1997).

38. Ibid., p. 226.

of capital. One can translate such notions—though not their political imperative—into the conceptual framework of Luhmann. The constitutive paradox of modern art identified by Adorno reflects what Luhmann sees as the constitutive paradox of *any* social system, in which auto-reference and hetero-reference are mutually dependent. Moreover, while Adorno came to be preoccupied increasingly with the specific situation of modernism and the avant-garde, he saw the basic paradox of the asociality of art as central to its emergence as a separate social institution. Likewise, for Luhmann, as soon as art was established as a functionally self-defining social system, the tension between auto- and hetero-reference was a determinant of its basic logic. Hence his unequivocal assertion that "A retreat into pure self-reference in the face of the lamentable condition of the world would be a futile endeavor. Even the exquisite forms of *l'art pour l'art*, and precisely these, still remain forms."[39] In other words, they are still produced by means of the distinction between auto- and hetero-reference.

The Emergence of the Art System

In *Art as a Social System*, Luhmann traces the historical emergence of the art system, which arose at the same time as a wider shift toward functional differentiation in society. He argues that the rise of the idea of the artist in the sixteenth century was an important early sign of this shift; the figure of the artist could not be accommodated within the traditional class structure of European society and thereby anticipated the reorganization of society in *functional* terms. Luhmann also stresses the importance of the "pre-adaptive advances" that served as the necessary precondition for the emergence of a functionally autonomous system. Among such advances, ornament is perhaps the first and most fundamental. In general terms Luhmann sees the evolution of a distinct artistic domain, and hence social system, as prompted by "the fact that the artwork demands decisions concerning what fits (is beautiful) or does not fit (is ugly) for which there is no external orientation" (227). The logic of ornamentation anticipates that of the art system, although it does not necessitate the complex systemic differentiation of art, with the specialized roles attributed to artists, critics, theorists, patrons, dealers, and so forth. As Luhmann states: "A habitual pattern cries out, so to speak, for variation. A small alteration

---

39. Niklas Luhmann, "The Modernity of Science," in *Theories of Distinction: Redescribing the Descriptions of Modernity*, trans. Joseph O'Neil (Stanford, CA: Stanford UP, 2002), p. 65.

yields consequences; it requires further elaboration and supplementation, or else it must be eliminated as inappropriate—and this happens repeatedly in numerous attempts that might succeed or fail, establish a tradition or perish" (227). In other words, ornamentation is already driven by the recursive logic characterizing all systems; a necessary precondition for the art system was in place even in cultures where art as an autonomous system never emerged.

These are very general speculations, and they are supplemented by Luhmann's analysis of the specific historical factors that facilitated the emergence of the art system in Europe. Most important among these were developments in the pattern of courtly patronage in the fourteenth and fifteenth centuries, when artworks came to be valued *as artworks* and when concepts of evaluation—*acutezza, concetto, disegno*—permitted comparison *between* artworks (and also the production of a hierarchy between the fine and the mechanical arts). Hence art was no longer valued simply as part of some other social system, such as religion. Other developments were also crucial, such as "placing the art of the present within an account of its own historical development quite apart from the discussions about the value of ancient in contrast to modern art" or attaching value to the *process* of production as an instance of the operation of the system, which became manifest in the "artistic evaluation of the unfinished, of sketches, or of drafts as artworks in their own right."[40]

Luhmann also sees the rise of the art market in late seventeenth-century England and of the salon in eighteenth-century France as other key events, where "the patron no longer defined himself by social rank and aristocratic generosity but based himself instead on his expertise, that is, on function-specific capabilities" (164). As with the emergence of the artist, this prompted a shift from a stratified to a functionally differentiated society. It also presents an important instance of the structural coupling of two emerging systems, the economic and the artistic. But the crucial point here is that rather than leading to the subsumption of the one by the other, such structural coupling was an instrument in the *sharpening* of the distinctions between the systems of art and economics. This clearly runs counter to the dominant tendency of critical accounts of art, in which reliance on the art market is taken to indicate the undermining of the autonomy of art.

40. Niklas Luhmann, *Die Ausdifferenzierung des Kunstsystems* (Bern: Benteli, 1994), p. 15.

Such contrasts notwithstanding, much of the above parallels, albeit in a different idiom, well-established social histories of art, beginning with Arnold Hauser's tracing in the 1950s of the emerging institutions of art.[41] But for Luhmann, such shifts only count as further "pre-adaptive advances." Art had still not given up its claim to universality. Only with Romanticism and Hegel did art acknowledge its own differentiation from other social systems and cease looking for counterparts elsewhere in society. Thus, Hegel's conclusion, in the *Lectures on Fine Art*, as to the pastness of art, or the Romantic integration of art criticism into the art system, or the Romantic thematization of non-communication and non-self-transparency all point toward the formation of an art system in which, for the first time, art no longer draws on exterior resources for its authority.[42] Instead, the meaning of meaning, the meaning of the difference between perception and communication, and the meaning of the difference between art and its environment, become a focus of observation and self-observation. This places the emergence of the art system rather late in comparison with the more usual habit of connecting it to the emergence in the Enlightenment of crucial social and cultural institutions.[43] In contrast, for Luhmann, while such institutions—from galleries and the salon through to the idea of the artist as genius—provided important enabling contexts, only when art differentiated itself semantically can one speak of the functional art system of modernity.

I have suggested that the art system within Luhmann's work consists of more than just the production of artworks. Nevertheless, communication *through* artworks remains the necessary basis of the system. Luhmann writes:

> As an object that can be perceived, imagined (or described in literature), the artwork can be distinguished from other things. This distinction is constitutive of art, and it implies in advance an observer that uses this distinction (and no other). However, a differentiated, autonomously operating art system only comes into being when the individual artwork is distinguished from other artworks (and not just from other commodities

41. Arnold Hauser, *Social History of Art* (London: Routledge & Kegan Paul, 1951).

42. G. W. F. Hegel, *Aesthetics: Lectures on Fine Art*, trans. T. M. Knox (Oxford: Clarendon Press, 1998).

43. See, for example, Larry Shiner, *The Invention of Art* (Chicago: Univ. of Chicago Press, 2001).

that could be equally purchased). Art is transformed into the "imaginary museum" of Malraux.[44]

The communications embodied in artworks communicate with one another, and that "calls for criteria of comparison and standards of judgment."[45] Artworks remain central, and yet in Luhmann's theory the status and meaning of the work of art undergoes an important shift. Although an artwork is usually—though, of course, not *necessarily*—a physical object that endures through time, its ability to further the operation of the art system is linked to its appearance as a fleeting, evanescent event. As Luhmann states: "Operations...are nothing more than events. They cannot persist, nor can they be altered. They emerge and vanish in the same instant, taking no more time than is needed to fulfill the function of an element"; and later, "The art system has no reality except at the level of elemental events. It rests, one might say, on the ongoing dissolution of its elements, on the transitory nature of its communications, on an all-pervasive entropy" (49).

A number of important claims are being put forward here. First, the significance of artworks lies not in their physical, formal, or material properties but in their *communicative* role within the art system. This suggests similarities with hermeneutic and pragmatic histories of art of the nineteenth century, in which art was conceived of as a kind of event.[46] However, such histories remained caught by the tension between the temporal basis of art's appearance and its persistence as a physical object. For Luhmann, it is the former that is of far greater social importance. The social effect and meaning of the artwork is tied to its role as an ephemeral communication, and although it might continue to exist as a physical object, this is no guarantee that it will have any further communicative, and hence social, significance. And if it continues to function within the art system, this is because of its capacity to continue to prompt further communications. Thus, the artwork, when first produced and exhibited, constitutes a particular type of communicative event. If its production leads to further works, then it has functioned within the recursive network of the art system. It may of course lead to further communications beyond its immediate impact. The

44. Luhmann, "Weltkunst," p. 15.
45. Ibid.
46. See Hans Robert Jauss, "Geschichte der Kunst und Historie," in *Literaturgeschichte als Provokation* (Frankfurt am Main: Suhrkamp, 1970), pp. 208–51.

history of art is replete with such examples, from the frequent rebirths of classical Greek and Roman literature, architecture, and art to the constant revisiting of the work of artists such as Rembrandt, Goya, or Velasquez, for example. Each subsequent return or revisiting alters the meaning of the originals—placing them within an art system where once they did not belong or which might indeed not have existed when they were first created. As Luhmann states, "the artwork...only comes into being by virtue of a recursive networking with other works of art, with widely distributed verbal communications about art, with technically reproducible copies, exhibitions, museums, theatres, buildings, and so forth" (53). Indeed, there is no "pristine" state of the original artwork, only its meaning within the ongoing sequences of operations of the art system. Such a repositioning of the artwork as an immaterial element within a recursive network points to important ways of rethinking the historicity of art, and it also casts light on various shifts in art practice since the late 1960s. I deal with each in turn.

As a recursive network, any social system is constituted by virtue of its operation through time. More specifically, as a vehicle for the communication of meanings, a social system is bound to the inherent instability and futurity of meaning itself. Central to understanding the temporality of social systems is Luhmann's interpretation of meaning: "The phenomenon of meaning appears as a surplus of references to other possibilities of experience and action.... The totality of the references presented by a meaningfully intended object offers more to hand than can in fact be actualized at any moment. Thus the form of meaning, through its referential structure, *forces* the next step, to *selection*."[47] Hence, the experience of meaningfulness is founded on "an element of unrest. Meaning forces itself to change. Whether the result can be grasped as flux, process or motion is already a question of semantic processing."[48] Conversely, where there is no surplus of possibilities, one cannot speak of meaning, for meaning is the "difference between what is actual at any moment and a horizon of possibilities."[49]

There are obvious affinities here with deconstruction. The temporal deferment intrinsic to Derrida's concept of *différance* implies the same temporalization of significance. Luhmann himself has recognized such an affinity, yet the conclusions he draws are quite distinct. Where Derrida

47. Luhmann, *Social Systems*, p. 60.
48. Ibid., pp. 63–64.
49. Ibid., p. 65.

concludes that meaning is consequently never fully present, Luhmann stresses that meaning is actualized, but as an ephemeral moment that is always oriented to futurity. The implications for an understanding of art are numerous. Most significantly, perhaps, it is the futurity of meaning that accounts for the fact that art even has a history. More provocatively, this also leads Luhmann to see the dynamics of change as located *within* the autonomous operations of the art system. Hence, the bald assertion that "the evolution of art is its own accomplishment. It cannot be caused by external intervention" (235). This is a startling claim not only because it is within what purports to be a *social* theory of art, but also because it runs against the grain of most current accounts of art and its history. It appears as a throwback to the formalist histories of the nineteenth century. It is important therefore not to misread the nature of the assertion. Luhmann's emphasis on the possibility of interpenetration or the structural coupling of social systems leaves open the mutual interaction of art and other social systems. Nevertheless, once art no longer sought its justification in other social systems—or in external reality—it was involved in a process of "rapidly accelerating, self-generated structural change" (238).

Luhmann sees the artistic cultivation of concepts such as intuition, imagination, obscurity, ambivalence, cunning (*acutezza*), or wit (*Witz*) as attempts to generate internal criteria of selection—in contrast to, for example, the earlier concern with truth and falsehood, where art had not yet become functionally differentiated from science. The classic Marxist explanation of many of these concepts is to see them as ideological reflexes of larger social situations. A pertinent example of this would be Terry Eagleton's reading of the late eighteenth-century valorization of genius and imagination as linked to bourgeois ideologies of freedom and to their contestation of absolutist aristocratic power.[50] Luhmann has no specific theory of ideology in his work—although he has a theory of power and a constructivist epistemology—and as noted earlier he has no place for the normative criticism implicit in Marxist accounts of the rise of aesthetics.[51] At the same time, his account, for all its stress on endogenous evolution, is not as opposed to such theories as might first appear to be the case. For at stake is the question of the *extent* of the autonomy of social systems, and this echoes in certain respects the old Marxist debate concerning the

---

50. See, for example, Terry Eagleton, *The Ideology of the Aesthetic* (Oxford: Blackwell, 1990).

51. See Niklas Luhmann, *Macht* (Stuttgart: UTB, 2003).

relative autonomy of culture in its relation to society. Luhmann is thus not denying that a social system is a *social* system; the emergence of the art system was dependent on a set of social prerequisites, yet having emerged, the system of art evolved according to its own logic. The idea of an autonomous aesthetic experience, for example, could not have emerged at *any* time, but once having been established, its particular inflections and their subsequent modulations were internally generated. Like Adorno, Luhmann is at root claiming that art's autonomy—the autopoietic closure of the system—is a function of its sociality.

The Critical Significance of Systems Aesthetics

In considering Luhmann's systems aesthetics as a critical paradigm, a key issue has to be the question of its potential impact. Is it the case, as Robert Holub and others suggest, that it merely redescribes well-known insights in a new vocabulary, or does it compel a reassessment of the scope and limits of a social theory of art?

In order to begin to explore the critical difference that emerges out of an engagement with Luhmann's work, it is valuable to contrast it with the work of Michel Foucault and Pierre Bourdieu in relation to the question of historical change. Although not strictly speaking a sociological theory, Foucault's discursive and institutional theory is clearly heir to the sociological tradition stemming from Durkheim that conceives the social in terms of its institutions. So, too, for Foucault the history of discourse is the history of successive discursive or epistemic regimes. This conception is vulnerable to a number of criticisms, however, including its inability to account for the significance of *individual* actions, events, and utterances, or for the processes and causes of social change. Its emphasis on structures and rules lays out the domain of the possible but offers no explanation of how and why certain possibilities are actualized while others are not.[52] Hence, *The Order of Things* outlines the successive epistemic regimes of Renaissance and post-Renaissance Europe, but beyond a quasi-positivistic recording of the fact that one such regime was displaced by another in a sequence leading to the present, it neither explains in empirical terms *why* such epistemic shifts occurred, nor offers a theoretical model of the processes that would lead to them.[53]

52. A broad outline of these issues is provided in John Hall, *Cultures of Inquiry* (Cambridge: Cambridge UP, 1999).
53. Michel Foucault, *The Order of Things* (London: Routledge, 1976).

Bourdieu attempts to circumvent this by recourse to the concept of *habitus*, the dialectical relation between social structures and individual subjective agents.[54] He also replaces reference to objective social constraints with the much looser conception of "dispositions." Thus, the *habitus* is "a system of permanent and transposable dispositions, which, by integrating all past experiences, functions at any moment like a matrix of perceptions, judgments, and actions."[55] The mediating function of the *habitus* is also evident in its dual character: on the one hand, it is an internalized set of social structures and becomes "second nature," while on the other, it also takes on the character of a set of objective external constraints. Yet inasmuch as the *habitus* is nothing other than the regularized dispositions of the social collective, it is the social agent that actually *produces* the *habitus*. In other words, cognitive and social structures are engaged in a dialectic of mutual self-reproduction.

Bourdieu again runs into problems, however, in accounting for processes of *change*. For in his work change is the consequence of the *conjunction* of dispositions and external, objective events, yet this is seen primarily in terms of revolutionary events. Hence, the catalyst of change is the effect of an external cause rather than of some internal mechanism within the self-reproduction of the *habitus*. In *The Rules of Art*, he argues, for example, that "the initiative for change can be traced back, almost by definition, to new (meaning younger) entrants... by imposing new modes of thought and expression, which break with current modes of thought."[56] Using widely accepted spatial metaphors, Bourdieu speaks of the social space as "a field of forces that necessarily impose themselves on anyone finding themselves involved, like a field of struggle in the midst of which the participants face each other."[57] Quite apart from the privileging of social conflict and revolutionary change, Bourdieu seems to be relying on a hermeneutical theory in which the dynamics of the social field stem from the conscious interaction between subjective agents—and conscious position-takings of individual agents within what he terms "the space of possibles."[58] In addition, he appears to undercut his own attempt to

54. Pierre Bourdieu, *Esquisse d'une Théorie de la Pratique* (Paris: Seuil, 2000).

55. Ibid., p. 261.

56. Pierre Bourdieu, *The Rules of Art: Genesis and Structure of the Literary Field* (Stanford, CA: Stanford UP, 1995), pp. 239–40.

57. Pierre Bourdieu, *Raisons Pratiques: Sur la Théorie de l'Action* (Paris: Seuil, 1994), p. 55.

58. Bourdieu, *The Rules of Art*, p. 234.

mediate the structure—agent duality by seeing all ruptures and innova-tions as always already latent in the system. As he states: "For bold strokes of innovation or revolutionary research to have some chance of even being conceived, it is necessary for them to exist in a potential state at the heart of the system of already realized possibles."[59] The structural field thus comprises—in a quasi-Platonic and deterministic fashion—the totality of actual and possible practices.

Both Foucault and Bourdieu encourage an epochal conception of time. History consists in the succession of fields, regimes, or, to draw a parallel term from Thomas Kuhn, paradigms. Historical change thereby consists in the ruptures and shifts from one regime to another. In these cases either there is no convincing explanation as to how and why such shifts occur, or they are accounted for by resorting to a *deus ex machina* that casts into doubt the explanatory capacities of the theoretical model in question.

Transferred to the critical analysis of art, this encourages a lapse into one of the most basic yet problematic aspects of traditional art history: the reliance on an epochal understanding of art. The evident weaknesses of this are visible in numerous instances. An instructive recent example is T. J. Clark's outline of modernism, which, as Otto Werckmeister has pointed out, results in a monolithic image of modern art that equates it with revolution and consequently sees in the fall of the Berlin Wall a clos-ing of the modernist era.[60] Clark's weakness stems from a lack of attention to the complex and variegated politics of modern art, from anarchist traditions down to struggles for social democracy, which can hardly be regarded as rendered obsolete by the fall of Communism. However, the point is not the empirical lacunae in Clark's study—and one could also criticize Clark's complete lack of reference to the numerous right-wing avant-gardes—but rather the issue of his broader methodological frame-work and its consequences.

Luhmann inverts the traditional hierarchy within Critical Theory and the social history of art, by focusing on the role of the individual com-municative acts or operations that give rise to and then sustain a particular system. Instead of starting out with a priori determining structures, his approach emphasizes the social significance of the individual act. With

59. Ibid., p. 235.
60. T. J. Clark, *Farewell to an Idea: Episodes from a History of Modernism* (New Haven, CT: Yale UP, 1999). See Otto Karl Werckmeister, "A Critique of T. J. Clark's *Fare-well to an Idea*," *Critical Inquiry* 28 (2001): 855–67.

regard to the question of change, this turns out to be crucial. In contrast to the historiographic emphasis on large-scale ruptures and paradigmatic shifts, Luhmann's work locates change in the multiple small-scale and often hardly perceptible variations that occur from one communication to another. Social systems operate in a state of dynamic equilibrium; they persist through time yet are always evolving, and evolution occurs through the constant recursive operations of the system. Although operating on a high level of abstraction, Luhmann's work thereby foregrounds the significance of the micro-social in the interpretation of historical change, requiring a high degree of detailed empirical analysis. This would also include careful study of the varied factors leading to the *emergence* of individual social systems, something that Bourdieu and Foucault, for example, fail to do.

Luhmann's notion of systems also addresses other potential weaknesses in social theories of art and culture framed by Bourdieuian and Foucauldian notions of social structure. As George Kubler suggested in the 1960s, artistic and cultural development occurs by means of multiple simultaneous historical trajectories, each marked by their own temporalities.[61] This idea has been taken up in numerous ways since. Hal Foster's essay on the neo-avant-garde exploits the thematics of deferment to examine the relation between modernism and the postmodern.[62] Focusing in particular on the reprisal within the work of Dan Flavin, Carl Andre, Jasper Johns, and Marcel Broodthaers, of the political, ideological, and aesthetic impulses of the 1910s and the 1920s, Foster sees a deferment at work in which the practices of postmodernity comprise a working out of the postponed meaning of the original avant-garde. This also puts into question the myth of modernism as marking a new historical beginning.[63] More recently, David Hopkins has taken up the reprisal of Dada motifs in art from the 1980s to the present, examining the work of figures such as Matthew Barney, Paul McCarthy, and Keith Farquhar.[64]

61. George Kubler, *The Shape of Time: Remarks on the History of Things* (New Haven, CT: Yale UP, 1962).

62. Hal Foster, "Who's Afraid of the Neo-Avant Garde?" in *The Return of the Real: The Avant-Garde at the End of the Century* (Cambridge, MA: MIT Press, 1996): 1–33.

63. As Foster notes, "the notion of deferred action is useful for rather than break with the fundamental practices and discourses of modernity, the signal practices and discourses of postmodernity have advanced in a *nachträglich* relation to them" (ibid., p. 32).

64. David Hopkins, *Dada's Boys: Identity and Play in Contemporary Art* (Edinburgh: Fruitmarket Gallery, 2006).

The key question is how one accounts for such non-synchronicities. The theoretical weakness of a Foucauldian or Bourdieuian frame is that such phenomena can only be accounted for (and dismissed) as conservative survivals of the past. This is the instance of a well-known and more general critique of synchronic analyses, which focuses on their inability to account for the persistence through time of cultural practices. Moreover, while Freudian notions of *Nachträglichkeit* and Derridean notions of *différance* offer a powerful instrument for interpreting certain kinds of postmodern practice, they can do so only through the theme of repetition. Much of what Kubler and others were addressing, however, were not the numerous historical reprisals in art, but rather the fact that there coexist sets of practices that are aligned along different trajectories, operating according to distinct speeds, and with varying relations to the past. One of the most powerful demonstrations of this phenomenon was the restaging by the Guggenheim Museum and the Royal Academy of Arts in 2000 of the Exposition Décennale des Beaux-Arts at the Paris Exposition Universelle of 1900.[65] The exhibition highlighted the plurality of practices—artists exhibiting ranged from Franz von Stück and Gustav Klimt, to Sir Edward Burne-Jones, Sir Lawrence Alma-Tadema, and Pablo Picasso—which could not be easily divided into a straightforward opposition between avant-garde and conservative, but which rather threw into sharp relief the variety of relations to tradition and art-historical temporality operating at the same time.

I have dwelt on this notion because, arguably, Luhmann's thinking offers the means for a more sophisticated way of theorizing such a phenomenon. By conceiving the system of art as constituted by a multiplicity of operations through time, all of which are recursive responses to prior operations, Luhmann erases the distinction between synchronic and diachronic analysis, viewing both as aspects of the art system. As the complexity of the art system increases, so the possibility of varied temporalities *within* the system is heightened. The potential implications of this on thinking through the historiography of, for example, modernism are substantial. It suggests an alternative history of twentieth-century art, in which avant-garde practices play merely one role in a much larger history, a history that might also account for modernism's failures.

65. Robert Rosenblum, *1900: Art at the Crossroads* (London: Royal Academy of Arts, 2000).

Luhmann's emphasis on the temporal instability of meaning in social systems and on the importance of evolutionary change also offers an important way for reconceptualizing notable shifts in the cycle of the exhibition and distribution of art of the last twenty or so years. It has long been recognized that the production of artworks plays an increasingly incidental part of the art system; curating, social networking, and media marketing have come to occupy central place. As Angela Macrobbie has argued, the "speeding up or rapid acceleration of culture industry working practices" has led to the displacement of the independent "artist" by the deskilled cultural entrepreneur or the "incubator, the visual merchandiser, the cultural strategist."[66] This can be seen in, for example, the transformed role of the curator, formerly concerned with staging exhibitions of artworks, but now responsible for their production. Where once the exhibition was a *post hoc* response to artworks already in existence, this relation is now inverted. Curating has itself become a type of art production, and much contemporary art practice—the work of Rirkrit Tirvanija being a prominent example—is modeled on the idea of art-as-curation.

This tendency was already being commented on in 1972, when Lawrence Alloway used the metaphor of the network to describe the characteristics of contemporary art production, in which the making of artworks was no longer central to an art world dominated by dealers, publishers, and galleries.[67] As Alloway puts it, the output of the art world is no longer artworks but the distribution of artworks, in other words, the "knowledge industry, producing signifiers whose signifieds are works of art."[68] However, while Alloway put forward a number of suggestive *empirical* insights, he lacked an overall theoretical perspective that might have thematized and made sense of such phenomena. In contrast, Luhmann's systems-theoretical account allows us to view such developments as the outcome of the *intrinsic* logic of the differentiation of the art system.

Alloway noted the increased speed in the turnover within art production. The time separating the production of art from its appearance in galleries and other sites of exhibition and distribution was becoming

66. Angela Macrobbie, "'Everyone is Creative': Artists as Pioneers of the New Economy?" in Elizabeth B. Silva, ed., *Contemporary Culture and Everyday Life* (London: Sociology Press, 2003), pp. 161–94.

67. Lawrence Alloway, "Network: the Artwork described as a System" [1972] in *Network: Art and the Complex Present* (Ann Arbor, MI: UMI Press, 1984), pp. 3–16.

68. Ibid., p. 6.

increasingly diminished. Where museums used to exhibit only established (i.e., historical) art, or contemporary art emerging out of an established tradition (i.e., with a historical pedigree), they had abolished such a time lag, exhibiting not only new work but also entirely new artists.

Such a cyclical acceleration can also be determined from the position of the consumption of art. In particular, it can be explored by reference to what Zygmunt Bauman has described as "the using up" of art. In an article first published in 1998, Bauman describes the exaggerated transience of contemporary art, which he sees as the function of a process of over-consumption.[69] As Bauman states:

> [B]y the "using up" of the object of art in the process of its consumption I do not mean its destruction in the corporeal, physical sense—like in the case of the paperback bestseller bought in a railway newsstand at the beginning of the journey and thrown into the railway rubbish bin after its completion. What is at stake here is something else: the unavoidable fading of interest, loss of the "entertaining value," of the capacity to arouse desire and pleasurable emotions. A work of art approached as the source of entertainment tends to become tediously familiar.... it promises the wearisome sentiment instead of adventure.[70]

The impact of the work of art is increasingly transient, and Bauman points out the important role of "highly publicized, carnival-like" exhibitions in saving such works from fading away in a system increasingly oriented toward a "sensation by definition short-lived and until-further-notice."[71] This is a function of the wider condition of late modernity, described by Bauman as "the time of eternity decomposed into a string of episodes that admit of no other yardsticks or purpose than those of the instant satisfaction."[72]

Bauman's analysis of the temporality of contemporary art displays obvious parallels with Lyotard's identification of the future perfect as definitive of postmodern culture, now a well-established and accepted

69. Zygmunt Bauman, "On Art, Death and Postmodernity and What They Do To each Other," in *Stopping the Process: Contemporary Views on Art Exhibitions* (Helsinki: Kiasma, 1998), reprinted in Iwona Blazwick et al., *Fresh Cream: Contemporary Art in Culture* (London: Phaidon Press, 2000), pp. 20–23. All references will be to the latter edition.

70. Ibid., p. 21.

71. Ibid., p. 22.

72. Ibid.

trope.[73] I would like to suggest, however, that this phenomenon can also be illuminated further by recourse to a systems-theoretical account. Of key importance is Luhmann's treatment of the theme of evolution. In particular, he employs the twin concepts of "entropy" and "negentropy" to describe the evolutionary process. *Entropy*, the decay of a steady state or system into a disorganised array of elements, is countered by *negentropy*, the increasingly complex organization of the same elements within a system. For Luhmann all social systems stand poised between these two processes. On the one hand, due to the fleeting nature of communications there is always the risk that the system will disintegrate into entropic incoherence; people might simply stop going to exhibitions, writing about art, making artworks, and so forth. On the other hand, the recursive nature of the operation of social systems—the fact that each communication feeds back into the system as a response to a prior communication—means that there is always the possibility for the generation of still more communications, adding to the complexity of the system. It is this recursive, negentropic feature that underlies the evolutionary processes of variation, selection, and re-stabilization, and evolution involves a constant acceleration of the rate of change. As a functionally differentiated social system evolves, as the number of recursive operations grows, the possibility of variation increases in number and the rate at which they feed back into the system expands. Within the history of art since the fifteenth century, for example, this is evident both in the *quantity* of operations and in the *speed of operation* of the system. The number of artists and theories of art and so forth has grown exponentially, while significant historical changes have occurred with ever increasing rapidity. I would like to suggest that the situation described by Bauman, in which artworks are superseded and obsolete even before they have been produced, should be seen as a potent instance of the negentropic acceleration of the art system.

A standard explanation of this phenomenon is that it is a sign of the appropriation of art by the demands of popular culture. In other words, the temporality of the present is accommodated within the broader logic of postmodern theory. As Lash and Urry argue, "in the shift from organized to disorganized capitalism the various subjects and objects of the capitalist economy circulate...at ever greater velocity....With an ever quickening

73. Lyotard, *The Postmodern Condition*, pp. 71–84.

turnover time, objects as well as cultural artefacts become disposable and depleted of meaning."[74]

The constant quest for the new, the novel, and the bizarre, crucial to the promotion of consumerist consumption, is argued as having become central to the logic of art and cultural production. Going against the grain of contemporary critical theory, however, it is possible to read this process not as the result of the incursion of an alien logic, but as a consequence of the evolution of the art system as an autonomous social system with its own recursive operations. Art is "used up" not because it is consumed in some philistine manner, signaling its absorption into the culture industry, but because of the prodigious expansion of the art system; the complexity of the art system has resulted in a state of hyper-production and self-reproduction. What this suggests for the future of the art system remains an open question, but it raises some awkward questions that cannot be resolved by a nostalgic attempt to recapture art from the grasp of capital. It is art's own autonomous logic that is the root of the problem.

Conclusion

In reviewing Luhmann a basic question has to be posed: namely, what is gained by approaching art through the medium of systems theory? In general terms it can be seen as a provocation to some basic assumptions underpinning many current social theories of art. Such accounts have tended to foreground the macro-social frameworks anterior to and governing individual acts. Luhmann inverts this logic by starting with the micro-social events and practices that make up the larger social systems, but without absolutizing the individual producer. In so doing, Luhmann opens up the possibility of rethinking the nature of historical change, of what it even means to talk about the *history* of art. This might consist in the analysis not only of how the art system defined itself in reference to its environment but also of how its environment—with its own exclusions and inclusions—was also defined. Critical attention to the exclusions of art history is hardly novel in itself, but Luhmann's work invites reconsideration of the ethical and normative imperatives behind such a turn to the art historical margins.

74. Scott Lash and John Urry, *Economies of Signs and Space* (London: SAGE, 1994), pp. 2–3.

In addition, however, I have suggested that a systems-oriented social theory offers a novel set of insights into the nature of contemporary art production. In particular, one can argue that the emphasis on the evanescent event at the heart of the operation of the social system produces a theoretical account that mirrors the character, and especially the temporality, of contemporary culture. In Luhmann, contemporary art has met its theoretical counterpart. In opposition to most current views, his work suggests that many of the most striking characteristics of contemporary art reflect its hyper-autonomization rather than its convergence with other social systems. Although open to contestation, such a claim at least opens up new analytical possibilities, rather than functioning as one more restatement of a century-old debate.

Derrida and the Limits of Sovereign Reason: Freedom, Equality, but not Fraternity

Peter Gratton

"What must be thought," Jacques Derrida writes in the closing pages of *Rogues*, "is this inconceivable and unknowable thing, a freedom that would no longer be the power of a subject, a freedom without autonomy, a heteronomy without servitude, in short, something like a passive decision."[1] To certain readers of Derrida, this passage, coming near the end of *Rogues*, written some two years before he passed away, would mark the fundamental failure of his thought. "What must be thought...": an exhortation, an ethical injunction, but seemingly also a final plea at the end of a long career that, many believe, aimed at destroying the very fundaments of human equality and freedom, namely subjectivity, autonomy, and self-sovereignty. "What must be thought" points also to the future, to the future of a thought beyond Derrida himself, one who would be said ultimately to disappoint when it comes to thinking a freedom unaligned to all that we have taken freedom to be: a power, an ability, or at least the mark of a possibility of what one can accomplish, no matter the odds, no matter the political regime, even in the face of the governmentalities of modernity. Nothing would seem more unreasonable than that which is "inconceivable and unknowable," especially if we are to counter the problems of sovereignty in our day, in the "light and enlightenment of our day."[2]

Freedom and equality have been doubly positioned in a thinking of sovereignty. On the one hand, sovereignty has been seen as the *sine qua non* of freedom, since it is the self's auto-position, its autonomy, its ability

1. Jacques Derrida, *Rogues: Two Essays on Reason* (Stanford, CA: Stanford UP, 2005), p. 152.
2. Ibid., p. 145.

to rule over itself through its own coercive force managing its passions, its own unreasoning, which has been taken to be the predicate for an ability for the self to carry out its will into the world. The dignity of the person in Kant, but also the ruling (*archein*) of the self going back to Aristotle and Plato, has been aligned to the force of reason, to the reason of force over the turns of the self. It is this coercive ability of the self—whether enacted or not—that is the basis for thinking of an equality of one to another, of one sovereign self to another. On the other hand, this sovereignty of the self, its own self-rule and its equality with others, has been grounded in national sovereignty, one that will protect individual sovereignty as a right of citizenship. There is no need to revisit here all that has been reviewed elsewhere regarding the problems of nationalism and natalism, which have done anything but protect the dignity, the sanctity, and finally the sovereignty of each one. But—and this move is all important in the light and darkness of our day—this does not mean that we must, at every turn, attempt to resuscitate human dignity against sovereign cruelty via individual sovereignty, the supposed invulnerability and indivisibility of the self. We cannot simply fight one sovereignty we find abhorrent in its insidious biopolitical forms (political sovereignty) with one that finds for us, in a part of ourselves, so much to like, so much that we might want in the continuity and proclaimed sameness of the self (individual sovereignty). Certainly, we are often "in want of sovereignty [*en mal de souveraineté*]," wanting it even as its evil makes us ill.[3] National or popular sovereignty and self-sovereignty, at least since Rousseau, has called for the elemental prosthesis of one to the other, even where, in sovereignty's very movement, it should never be *in want*; sovereignty should never need anything else, if it is to be sovereign.[4] And yet the self and the nation-state is always already *in want of* sovereignty, always *in want of* the force and enforcement of its own law, its own autonomy, either with regard to the self or the nation-state. Sovereignty always needs its supplement, needs something

3. Ibid., p. 142.

4. Derrida carefully argued, both in *Rogues* and his 2001–2002 lecture course *La Bête et la souverain*, that one can never oppose "purely and simply" these fictions and presumptions of sovereignty, since "there is neither sovereignty nor the sovereign" ("Il n'y a pas LA souveraineté ni LE souverain"). Jacques Derrida, *La Bête et la souverain* (Paris: Galilée, 2008), p. 114 (caps in original text). Thus, he continues, "in politics, the choice is not between sovereignty and non-sovereignty, but rather between several forms of partitions [*partages*], divisions, and conditions that broaches [*entamer*] a sovereignty always presupposed indivisible and unconditional."

beyond itself, e.g., the government in the *Social Contract* of Rousseau, since a "democracy in the strict sense" could only exist, let us remind ourselves, "if there were a [sovereign] people of gods."[5] Sovereignty is also a power that is polyvalent, a force of law and law of force, as Derrida would call it, that has spread itself throughout the societies of modernity, sharing out its "right over life and death," as Rousseau put it succinctly in the *Social Contract*, a right that now means just as much to make live and let die as it does to make die and let live.

Conceptually, a sharing (*partage*) of sovereignty is impossible, since sovereignty in its most decisive moment is to be shared neither *de jure* nor in fact. It cannot, without being in utter want (*en mal*), share itself in language or give an account of itself, making itself accountable and measurable, which sovereignty in its utter want always already wants to avoid. This will be what Derrida calls sovereignty's constitutive and performative autoimmunity: the moment it sets out to immunize itself, to protect itself from the outside through its spreading out of force or by its use of language and narratives, it also brings about its demise as sovereignty. There is, in a sense, an impotence at the heart of power's height as sovereignty. But I want to be careful here—as does Derrida—to note that this should not bring a false hope for the final denouement of sovereignty. We have seen too much of that in recent years: the stories of the fall of sovereignty in the modern or "postmodern" age, in terms of the subject or the nation-state, had become in the 1990s part of the reveling of a new world order. Inversely, we have also seen concerns over the fall of sovereignty in light of the rise of other forms of power—economic (the rise and ubiquity of capitalism) or otherwise (disciplinary power, societies of the code, and so on). This means that we need to think sovereignty both in terms of its constitutive, performative autoimmunity but also in terms of the ways in which, as Derrida puts it, sovereignty changes "its shape and place."[6]

This change in "shape and place" is not, I would argue, simply due to the "state racism" by which the state sees as its work the saving and salvation of a nation of people. Nor is this change due only to the re-formation of monarchical sovereignty as national and popular sovereignty. With the "loss of authority" in the modern age, the performative backstop for

5. Jean-Jacques Rousseau, *On the Social Contract*, trans. Donald A. Cress (New York: Hackett Publishing, 1987), p. 87.

6. Jacques Derrida, *Paper Machine*, trans. Rachel Bowlby (Stanford, CA: Stanford UP, 2005), p. 119.

sovereignty has been laid aside. Each performative utterance—the words
that are *authorized* to declare an end to democratic debate, to declare war,
and so on—relies on previous performative utterances in a near endless
cycle of performative utterances of oaths and so on that still mark the cer-
emonies of power. These utterances then rely on previous performatives
going back, for example in the United States, to the foundational *ex post
facto* delineation of a right to declare a United States in a declaration of
independence. But the latter could still authorize itself, as does the Declaration of Rights of Man and Citizen, in terms of a beneficent Creator,
which earlier in the American declaration became an inverted divine right
used against King George III by the American colonies. With the loss of
authority in the modern age, about which Hannah Arendt writes perspicu-
ously, there is no ultimate legitimating authority. In any event, narratives
of power aside, the performances and performative utterances of sovereignty are no longer authorized *per se* by theological narratives: however
much they are still used, they have, as Arendt would claim, lost much of
their force, except as a shadowy set of complaints by religious reactionaries fully aware of this loss of force. Rather, sovereignty is self-authorized
by previous performative utterances and performances of power, all of
which is to say that, to put it simply, the "divine right of kings" and its
self-authorization has been replaced by the performances of the sword of
the Leviathan, the police and its apparatchiks that are the coercive force
of the law and the law of force in modernity. The Enlightenment, then, not
only gave force to reason, but with the concomitant loss of authority, came
to the fore the reason of force, the *raison d'état* in which "[a]buse of power
is constitutive of sovereignty itself."[7]

The changing shape and form of sovereignty is one often missed in its
conceptualization in light of the claims of Derrida, Agamben, and others
in recent years. To take one example, Jean-Luc Nancy, in a treatment of
sovereignty in *La création du monde ou la mondialisation*, follows up
on the logic of sovereignty's self-presumption as *Le Très Haut*, as that
which is higher than height, but also as the highest in a system in which it
can be categorized within a vertical hierarchy. Nancy argues rightly that
sovereignty has been figured as the summit, as the height of the political that is both higher than height, but also the summit by which it is
the sovereign in a given politics. He is clear that "sovereignty essentially

7. Derrida, *Rogues*, p. 102.

slips away [*échappe*] from the sovereign."[8] Nancy argues that the sovereign body belongs within a hierarchy of a political system, for example, feudalism, in which it is *primus inter pares*.[9] But sovereignty itself must escape this hierarchy; it cannot exist as the body at the height of a hierarchy since it "depends on nothing," is closed in upon itself, and founds itself through its own self-legitimation.[10] Sovereignty itself is *le très haut* as the detached summit, where it is "the Unequal itself. It is unequal to all kinds of equality or inequality."[11] It is, in sum, the "apprehension of the incommensurability between the horizontal [equality] and the vertical [hierarchy], between the base and the summit"; it does not even share with others finitude or mortality.[12] This at least is our worst apprehension about sovereignty, namely, its taking itself as the place beyond the spacing of the political, there where it has only a *"rapport à soi,"* through which it gives itself its own laws, constituting its "auto-positioning."[13] Sovereignty thus is always *ex nihilo*, founding itself on nothing other than its own *rapport* to itself. I won't go into all the semantic and powerful valences of sovereignty and its "twins" that Nancy treats well and at some length: *summus, superanus, supremus*, but also summation, the capital and capitalism that figures along and beyond the *summa linea*, which is to say, all the powers of measuring and the measuring up to itself of and as sovereignty.[14]

I bring up Nancy's analysis because it takes up a continuous line of thinking of sovereignty from Plato to Bodin, one that he rightly describes as a sovereignty that takes place in thought and as thinking.[15] But what worries me is that this conceptualization of sovereignty gives sovereignty too much and too little at the same time, that is to say, while it recognizes its ultimate failure, it also still sees sovereignty in terms of its medieval conceptualization; it repeats the *thèse royale* of the Bourbon period. Sovereignty, however, is not just *le très haut*, as Foucault argues quite well, but also the lowest, *le plus bas*, the most vulgar and "democratic" of forces in modernity. It is more or less than the lowest: it is a vulgarity to the political

---

8. Jean-Luc Nancy, *La création du monde ou la mondialisation* (Paris: Galilée, 2002), p. 160.

9. Ibid., p. 156.

10. Ibid., pp. 160–61.

11. Ibid., p. 148.

12. Ibid., p. 149.

13. Ibid., pp. 152–53.

14. Ibid., p. 145.

15. Ibid., p. 168.

in its most obscene and is, as Derrida rightly suggests, also its roguish power.[16] In thinking about democracy, as we will come to it, it is important to keep in mind democracy's vulgar elements: the *dēmos* that would make up a democracy. Another problem arises in Nancy's account. Let me quote from him on a thinking beyond or without sovereignty, of a "sovereignty without sovereignty," as he poses it, since though his intervention against sovereignty has much to offer, it also must give us pause, since it brings us back to some of the problems of natalism and nationalism that Derrida confronts in his deconstruction of sovereignty in his later work:

> The difficulty is to think the political without a subject: not without authority or the power of decision....This is an announcement of the problem of equality with which modern politics has been concerned, and sovereignty itself, which is defined as a summit that is not measured by any given height. Together, *liberty and fraternity* could represent this absence of the given height (of the origin [*fondement*], of the father).[17]

What Nancy brings us back to is the second part of the quotation from Derrida with which we began, namely, thinking a non-sovereign and therefore non-subjective freedom. The task of the remainder of this essay will be to tease out just what Derrida means by a "non-subjective" freedom, one that needs to be thought with and against conceptions of sovereignty either as *le très haut* or as the most roguish element, *le plus bas*. For Derrida and Nancy, freedom is an unconditional demand put upon the political itself, one that for politics and democracy (and there is no former without the latter, for Derrida) does not mean returning to a thinking of the subject in the classical sense. But neither does it mean thinking a "sovereignty without sovereignty," an unconditional freedom, along the lines of a thinking of fraternity and fraternalism, a Christian thinking of the sharing-out of the

---

16. What will become clear as I review the recent work of Derrida, especially *Rogues*, is that Derrida is not simply championing the rogue as a countersovereignty, or even a democracy that would be nothing other than what he calls a "voyoucracy," a rule by rogues, since this, too, as he makes clear, has its own law of force and force of law that is the mark of sovereignty. I underline this because I fear that Derrida's interest in *Rogues* may lead some to champion the rogue, when in fact Derrida valorizes the rogue as part of a deconstructive maneuver that will turn the figure of the rogue, of the *voyou*, back upon those who call all others a rogue, specifically the United States and its proclamation of certain regimes as "rogue states." For an excellent discussion of this part of *Rogues*, see Bill Martin's "Are there Rogue Philosophers? Derrida, at Last," *Radical Philosophy Review* 8, no. 2 (2005).

17. Nancy, *La création*, p. 167 (my emphasis).

political in terms of the dead father, one that brings us back to thinking community as communion.

In thinking toward a non-sovereign politics, if such a thing were possible, it would be necessary to rethink freedom and its aporias, as we've begun to approach them above. In the section that follows, we will pass through Derrida's elucidation of a non-sovereign freedom, one without autonomy, one without power and force, one that troubles and trembles the thinking of democracy but nevertheless ultimately confronts a long line of the fear and trembling of the politics of sovereignty.

Freedom, of course, has for an entire heritage of thinking the political been aligned with democracy and also a certain conception of sovereignty, the moment when a decision within a democracy is to be made. "This will be true throughout the entire history of this concept, from Plato's Greece onwards."[18] For Derrida, the autoimmunity of the democratic, the indeterminacy and self-criticism at the heart of any democracy worthy of the name, is nothing other than the "freedom of play, an opening of indetermination and indecidability *in the very concept* of democracy, in the interpretation of the democratic."[19] Derrida argues that there are two reasons for his turn in his later writing toward the concept of freedom: First, the vacancy or disengagement, the semantic indecision at the center of *demokratia*. "Democracy would not gather itself around the presence of an axial and univocal meaning that does not destroy itself and get carried away with itself."[20] Second, he also notes that the we should be oriented to all the places in thought where the interpretation and reinterpretation of freedom risks the disrupting of the sending off, the allegation or claim of democracy. "Wherever freedom is no longer determined as power, mastery, or force, or even as a faculty, as a possibility of the 'I can,' the evocation and evaluation of democracy as the power of the *dêmos* begins to tremble. If one values freedom in general, before any interpretation, then one should no longer be afraid to speak without or against democracy."[21]

This freedom in the concept of democracy is intrinsic to its "plasticity," that which gives rise to a democratic thinking of the democratic. "Democracy is what it is only by spacing itself beyond being and even beyond ontological difference; it is (without being) equal and proper to itself only insofar as it is inadequate and improper, at the same time behind

18. Derrida, *Rogues*, p. 22.
19. Ibid., p. 25.
20. Ibid., p. 40.
21. Ibid., p. 41.

and ahead of itself," he argues.[22] Derrida's thinking of freedom not only challenges a certain concept of the political, but also the politics of the concept. For Derrida, then, there is no democracy without deconstruction, as he argued in the *Politics of Friendship*; there is also no deconstruction without freedom.[23] As Derrida noted in his 2001–2002 seminar, *La Bête et le souverain*, "it's necessary to deconstruct, theoretically and practically, a certain onto-theology of political sovereignty" without dismissing "a certain thinking of freedom in the name of which deconstruction gets underway."[24] What is thus needed is "a wholly other thinking of freedom: on the one hand, a freedom that binds itself to and which belong (*qui se lie, qui soit liée*) heteronomically and precisely the the injunctions of the double bind and, on the other hand, therefore of a responsible endurance" of the double bind itself.[25] Derrida has long been attuned to indecidability, as we have seen, in political structures, concepts, and institutions, articulating the view that "ethics, politics, and responsibility, *if there are any*, will only ever have begun with the experience and experiment of the *aporia*."[26]

> I am exposed, destined to be free and to decide.... Between knowledge and decision, a leap is required, even if it is necessary to know as much and as well as possible before deciding.... "My" decision is and ought to be the *decision of the other* in me, a "passive" decision, a decision of the other that does not exonerate me from any of my responsibility.[27]

Derrida thus argues that any politics worthy of the name must be marked through and through by structural indecidability, double binds, and *aporias*, without clear passages and passes for what tomorrow. To dismiss the "ordeal of the indecidable" is, for Derrida, to replace politics in general and democracy in particular with a machine-like program that would make decisions and responsibility impossible.[28] The aporias of freedom and democracy do not paralyze politics, as many have feared and argued, but

22. Ibid., p. 38.

23. Jacques Derrida, *Politics of Friendship*, trans. George Collins (New York: Verso, 1997), p. 105.

24. Derrida, *La Bête et le souverain*, p. 402.

25. Ibid.

26. Jacques Derrida, *The Other Heading: Reflections on Today's Europe*, trans. Pascale-Anne Brault and Michael Naas (Stanford, CA: Stanford UP, 1993), p. 41.

27. Derrida, *Paper Machine*, p. 53.

28. Jacques Derrida, *Without Alibi*, trans. Peggy Kamuf (Stanford, CA: Stanford UP, 2002), p. 241.

actually make responsibility—and freedom—possible in the first place. This is what allows Derrida in *Rogues* to claim that "the *aporia* in its general form has to do with freedom itself."[29]

What are we to make of this claim, though, that the *aporia*—that is, the indecidability that gives rise to decisions worthy of the name—has to do with freedom itself? Freedom, whether positive or negative, *de facto* or *de jure*, natural or immanent to state apparatuses, has always been considered exemplary of the subject who is, first and foremost, a master and sovereign over itself. "In political philosophy," Derrida writes, "the dominant discourse about democracy presupposes this freedom as power, faculty, or the ability to act, the force or strength, in short, to do as one pleases, the energy of an intentional and deciding will."[30] To be free is to be sovereign, to be free to do what one wants, even if this freedom threatens to become license, to interfere in the self-mastery of others. Derrida thus argues that freedom can be understood as a turn of phrase for power, for the ability to choose, to decide, to determine *one-self*, to be master, and first of all master of one-self. "There is no freedom without ipseity and vice-versa, no ipseity without freedom—and thus, without a certain sovereignty."[31] But this freedom, Derrida argues, is always at war with itself, always threatening to do away with itself in its very freedom: freedom is always free to be otherwise than freedom, to free itself of itself. This is (its) autoimmunity. Nancy, for his part, articulates in *The Experience of Freedom* what Derrida calls the autoimmunity of freedom in the following way:

> The philosophical thought of freedom has been thoroughly subordinated to the determination of an ontology of subjectivity.... [But] freedom cannot be presented as the autonomy of a subjectivity in charge of itself and of its decisions, evolving freely and in perfect independence from every obstacle. What would such an independence mean, if not the impossibility in principle of entering into the slightest relation—and therefore of exercising the slightest freedom?[32]

Derrida treats this autoimmunity of freedom in *Rogues* through two interconnected strands of analysis: first, a philosophical investigation of the free play of concepts, including the concepts of freedom and democracy;

29. Derrida, *Rogues*, p. 54.
30. Ibid., p. 44.
31. Ibid., p. 23.
32. Jean-Luc Nancy, *The Experience of Freedom*, trans. Bridget McDonald (Stanford, CA: Stanford UP, 1993), pp. 4, 66.

second, a more obviously political—that is to say, at once strategic and performative—rendering of the concepts of freedom and democracy in response to political exigencies. In order to bring out the import of Derrida's conceptual and strategic interventions, I will treat these strands by turning to Derrida's reading of Nancy's *The Experience of Freedom* in *The Politics of Friendship* and *Rogues*.

Derrida begins his reading by reminding us that the relation between self-mastery and freedom is not just a modern conception, as Nancy suggests, but in fact extends back to the depiction of democracy in Aristotle and Plato, where it is said to be intimately related to both liberty (*eleutheria*) and free will or license as an "I can" (*exousia*). Because of this relation between freedom (*eleutheria* or *exousia*) and democracy, Derrida maintains that democracy is the only system in which one always already has the right, the license, to openly criticize everything, including the concept and history of the idea of democracy; this is both its threat and its chance. This self-deconstruction or auto-immunity gives rise to the aporia of democracy: the *dēmos* of democracy is always free to rid itself of democracy, or, to fend off this possibility, to limit democracy and curtail freedoms in order to save democracy from its supposed enemies. We have seen both alternatives play themselves out in recent years, for example, in Algeria in 1994, in Thailand in 2006, or anywhere in which the police apparatuses and security agencies expand and master the political in the name of protecting the democratic order.

For Derrida, Nancy is an ally for criticizing traditional notions of freedom anchored in the self-mastery of the subject. Nancy's text is exemplary for its attempt to think a non-subjective freedom, one based not in the mastery of the self, in ipseity, but in the throwness, the spacing, of existence, what might be called the *ex-ousia* of *exousia* or free will. Nancy argues that the metaphysical conception of freedom as mastery, as sovereignty, has been but another way of mastering freedom, a mastering of freedom in the name of mastery. Nancy writes:

> Keeping a space free for freedom might amount to keeping oneself from wanting to *understand* freedom, in order to keep oneself from destroying it in the *unavoidable determination of an understanding*. Thus the thought of freedom's incomprehensibility, or its unpresentability, might seem to heed not only the constraint of a limitation of power of thought, but also, positively, a respect for and a preservation of the free domain of freedom....[T]he metaphysics of freedom...often finds itself exposed

to the danger of having surreptitiously "comprehended" freedom…by having assigned freedom a residence in knowledge and, above all, in the self-knowledge of a subjectively determined freedom.[33]

The difficulty, Derrida argues, citing Nancy, "arrives when one must determine politically, indeed democratically…the spacing of a pre-subjective or pre-cratic freedom, one that is all the more unconditional, immense, immeasurable, incalculable, unappropriable insofar as it 'can in no way take the form of a property'."[34] Undeniably, Derrida argues, this takes a form of the impossible, an impossible that is at once reasonable, that is counting and accountable: to share the incommensurable of freedom in a "just, equitable, and measured fashion."[35] This is the traditional and well-known aporia of freedom and equality, the free play between the unconditional and the conditional that must be negotiated in any politics, indeed, in any democratic thinking of political and philosophical concepts. Nancy's claim in *The Experience of Freedom* is that "fraternity" names this very relation between the conditioning (equality) and the unconditional (freedom). "Fraternity is equality in the sharing of the incommensurable," Nancy writes.[36] This has been a constant, though often unavowed, theme throughout Nancy's corpus, from *The Experience of Freedom* to *La création du monde ou mondialisation*, in which, as we have seen, Nancy writes, "freedom and fraternity, together, could represent the absence of the given height" of sovereignty.[37]

But if what is shared out is already incommensurable, unmeasured, what use is the word "fraternity," which seems to put a certain measure, and a non-fortuitous exclusion of the feminine, into the very sharing of the incommensurable? This is what motivates Derrida's reading of *The*

33. Ibid., p. 44 (my emphasis).
34. Derrida, *Rogues*, p. 47.
35. Ibid.
36. Ibid., cited on p. 90.
37. In *The Sense of the World*, for example, Nancy argues for a thinking of fraternity that would name the very relation, the spacing of the common, between liberty and equality. A deconstructive politics, he says, requires an additional element beyond justice, liberty, and equality: "One could perhaps call this additional element 'fraternity' if it were possible to conceive of fraternity without father or mother, anterior rather than posterior to all law and common substance. Or if it were possible to conceive of 'fraternity' as law and as substance: incommensurable, non-derivable…in the dissolution of the Figure of the Father-already-Dead and his Thanocracy." Jean-Luc Nancy, *Sense of the World*, trans. Jeffrey S. Librett (Minnesota: Univ. of Minnesota Press, 1997), p. 115.

Experience of Freedom in *Rogues*. For Derrida, the "evocation and evalu-ation of democracy as the power [*kratos*] of the *dēmos* begins to tremble" when "freedom is no longer determined as power" or mastery, as is the case in Nancy.[38] But Derrida is also interested—and this interest provoked much of Derrida's later work—in this "trembling" of the *dēmos* of democ-racy. Traditionally conceived, the *dēmos* is inaugurated at the moment it imagines itself to be made up of equals, that is, those who are born free and equal.[39] The *dēmos* is the measuring out, the equalizing, of that which is by definition unconditional, namely, freedom. Ultimately, Derrida is worried that Nancy's "fraternalism might follow at least the temptation of a genealogical descent back to autochthony," that is, to a thinking of the *dēmos* that repeats a tradition that limits rights and freedoms to men of native birth, to the exclusion of women and immigrants from the rights of a familial circle.[40]

Derrida's critique of Nancy is at once strategic and conceptual. Nancy has argued, as he does in an appendix of fragments to *The Experience of Freedom*, that his use of fraternity is deconstructive, since it evacuates the term of its traditional meaning in order to reinvest it with another think-ing of the political.[41] This has been an approach familiar to those who have followed Derrida's readings of hospitality, the gift, and, of course, democracy. But Derrida notes, pointedly, "any time the literality" of the familial and phallocentric "implications ha[ve] been denied, for example, by claiming that one was speaking not of the natural or biological family (as if the family were ever purely natural and biological) or that the figure of the brother was merely a symbolic and spiritual nature, it was never explained" why one should hold onto this figure over any other, including those various figures of the feminine: women, mother, sister, and so on.[42] "One thus has to ask oneself," Derrida writes, "one has to ask Nancy, why he is so keen on keeping the word fraternity in order to the say equality in the sharing of the incommensurable" or freedom.[43]

For his part, Derrida argues that it is not enough to say that one is taking on the tradition in the combative sense, since the very use of certain

38. Derrida, *Rogues*, p. 41.
39. Ibid., pp. 45–50.
40. Ibid., p. 114. Derrida had already expressed this concern in *Politics of Friendship*, pp. 46–48n15.
41. Nancy, *Experience of Freedom*, pp. 168–69.
42. Derrida, *Rogues*, p. 57.
43. Ibid., p. 58.

terms cannot help but take on the tradition affirmatively, whatever one's intentions. This is the place of Derrida's conceptual politics: to point out not just the free play of concepts but also the way that they have sedimented into particular hierarchies throughout the tradition. The continued use and affirmation of certain terms, for example, fraternity, Derrida argues, risks foreclosing this free play of freedom and the democratic, that is an "experience of the impossible," the trembling of *différance* between fraternity and its other. Derrida argues that Nancy's acceptance of fraternity as the free sharing of the dead father is but a repetition, in another register, of a Christian and/or Freudian notion of community, or communion, as the sharing-out of the body of the dead father.[44] This part of the tradition is unacceptable, especially, though Derrida doesn't mention it, since Nancy calls for a fighting *for* fraternity. Nancy writes:

> Fighting "for" freedom, equality, fraternity, and justice does not consist merely of making other conditions of existence occur, since it is not simply on the order of a project, but also consists of affirming *hic et nunc*, free, equal, fraternal, and just existence.[45]

But what is left of the concept of democracy once the traditional foundations of the *dēmos* (birth) and *kratos* (the sovereign individual) have been called into question? Can we think of a democracy that would register an "experience of the alterity of the other, of heterogeneity, of the singular, of the not-same, the different, the dissymmetric, the heteronomous"?[46] In the end, these questions lead us to Derrida's articulation of the "democracy to come" and its relation to the question of freedom.

With the non-concept of the democracy-to-come, Derrida takes up and affirms a term that has resonances with ancillary tropes, including fraternity, that Derrida would want to critique. Derrida himself has worried about his use of the word "democracy," which in *Paper Machine* he says, "can only be use[d] anxiously."[47] But Derrida writes, for strategic reasons, that one must take on democracy in the name of democracy, especially since "any democracy is always influenced by the recognition of not being adequate to its model," a formulation that could not be said of fraternity. In

44. Ibid., p. 60.
45. Nancy, *Experience of Freedom*, p. 170.
46. Derrida, *Rogues*, p. 73.
47. Derrida, *Paper Machine*, p. 139.

fact, the former is taken up in a bid to question, critique, and displace the latter. Derrida asks in *The Politics of Friendship*:

> Is it still in the name of democracy, of a democracy to come, that one will attempt to deconstruct a concept, all the predicates associated with the massively dominant concept of democracy, that in whose heritage one inevitably meets again the law of birth, the natural or "national" law, the law of homophilia, civic equality (isonomy) founded on equality of birth (isogony) as the condition of calculation of approbation and, therefore, the aristocracy of virtue and wisdom, and so forth?[48]

And so the possibility is always raised of abandoning the name, of betraying the heritage of the name of a concept, in this case democracy, in order to live up to its name, Derrida argues. "[T]o keep this Greek name, *democracy*, is an affair of context, of rhetoric or strategy, even of polemics, reaffirming that this name will last as long as it has to but not much longer, saying that things are speeding up remarkably in these fast times, is not necessarily giving in to the opportunism or cynicism of the antidemocrat who is not showing his cards."[49] It is here that Derrida makes explicit his isonomy between deconstruction and democracy: "no deconstruction without democracy, no democracy without democracy."[50] It is also here that Derrida's generalized politics of the concept meets up with a specifically political intervention or invention.

In *Rogues*, Derrida thinks this through the problem of the vulgarity of the roguish *dēmos*, those appositional to the sovereignty of the *kratos* of democracy.[51] Though Derrida identifies himself as a rogue of sorts, it is this roguish trope that helps Derrida to take up the problem of the mob, those whose nationalisms Arendt reviewed at length in *The Origins of Totalitarianism*:

> The voyou [rogue] is always a part of mankind, always human, of our kind, and almost always a man....From a political point of view, the representatives of order, the forces of bourgeois or moral order, try to present as voyous all rebels, agitators, and insurgents, indeed all revolutionaries, whether they come from bad neighborhoods or from the

48. Derrida, *Politics of Friendship*, p. 103.
49. Ibid., p. 105.
50. Ibid.
51. Derrida, *Rogues*, p. 68.

suburbs, whether they erect barricades, as in 1848, 1870, or 1968, or commit acts of vandalism, crime, organized crime, or terrorism. This is as true for the revolutions of the left as for those of the right. Fascism, Nazism, populism, today's movements of the far right also often recruit from among a population that might easily be described as a voyoucracy, Criteria are often lacking in this area, which is also a *zone*, that is a belt, for distinguishing between voyoucracy and the people as plebeians, between democratic election, referendum, and plebiscite.[52]

Derrida, of course, is thinking of the role of the *banlieue*, the zones in and around French cities that, like the "ghettos" of the United States, have played as set pieces in demagogic rightist speeches in France, since it is in the *banlieue* where the other lives (even where the state has all but made life unlivable), a place nevertheless where a threatening underworld of gangs threatens the weak. In the United States, it is these places in which votes are least likely to count, or to be counted well. But it is also in these poorest of the poor regions of any state that populisms of a pernicious kind give rise to racism, there where the superfluous, *les hommes faibles*, find mechanisms for a backlash against the forces containing them in these zones, often in ways not amenable to a thinking of justice, though we must never forget that these crimes are nothing on the scale of the "white-collar" and other forms of criminality in the capital and in capitalism that go unpunished as the jails fill with the so-called criminal element of the *banlieue*. In sites *la-bas* and *en bas*, *le plus bas*, from the capital, the promise and the dangers of a democracy-to-come, of a democracy that counts all the votes and voices (*voix*), there is, as in the capital, an "indecidable limit between the demagogic and the democratic," between those *in want of sovereignty*, whatever "its shape and form" (as democracy or the voyoucracy of the criminal underworld), and those responding in the face of the other.[53] This requires another thinking of rights and also another thinking of citizenship beyond or within the nation-state, in short, "engag[ing] in another experience of belonging and in another political logic."[54]

When I speak of the democracy to come—this thing that can appear a little mad or impossible—I am thinking of a democracy that would no

52. Ibid., p. 67.
53. Ibid.
54. Jacques Derrida, *For What Tomorrow . . . : A Dialogue*, trans. Jeff Fort (Stanford, CA: Stanford UP, 2004), p. 94.

longer be bound in any essential way to citizenship. Here again, I come back to the same apparent contradiction: I am not against citizenship; it is necessary, and one must even fight for certain human beings who have been deprived of it, so that they might finally gain it. But the rights of man must also be extended beyond citizenship.[55]

In *Specters of Marx*, Derrida ties this thinking to what he calls the "new international," a haunting *from the future* of an international movement that Derrida argues is the only hope, the only "hope now," to borrow the felicitous and enigmatic phrase of Sartre's last interviews. As Bill Martin puts it, Derrida's writing is related to a double trauma: "a trauma not only from the future [as the *other* that interrupts the presence and present of the self], but indeed of *no future*."[56] As Derrida wrote in *Of Grammatology*, "the future can only be anticipated in the form of an absolute danger. It is that which breaks absolutely with constituted normality and can only be proclaimed, presented, as a form of monstrosity."[57] It is in the face of this possibility of "no future," of no future worthy of the name, that Derrida speaks of a responsible and non-naïve "hope now," of a hope from the future that impels us, *now*, to anticipate, to work, to think, that is, to be *engaged* in another spacing of the political that is represented in a "weak force [of] movements that are still heterogeneous, still somewhat unformed, full of contradictions, but that gather together the weak of the earth, all those who feel themselves crushed by the economic hegemonies, by the liberal market, by sovereigntism, and so on."[58] Let me quote at length from Derrida's *Specters of Marx*, because it is here that he ties together his thinking of the democracy to come with the thinking of the promise of an event of another thinking of the political beyond its capitalist mechanization:

> Even beyond the regulative idea in its classic form, the idea, if that is still what it is, of democracy to come, its "idea" as event of a *pledged injunction* that orders one to summon the very thing that will never present itself in the form of a full presence, is the opening of this gap between an

---

55. Ibid., p. 97.

56. Martin, "Are there Rogue Philosophers?" p. 154.

57. Jacques Derrida, *Of Grammatology*, trans. Gayatri Chakravorty Spivak (Baltimore, MD: Johns Hopkins UP, 1998), p. 5.

58. Jacques Derrida, "For a Justice to Come: An Interview with Jacques Derrida," in *The Derrida-Habermas Reader*, ed. Lasse Thomassen (Chicago: Univ. of Chicago Press, 2006), p. 268.

infinite promise (always untenable at least for the reason that it calls for the infinite respect of singularity *and* infinite alterity of the other as much as for the respect of the countable, calculated, subjectal equality between anonymous singularities) and the determined, necessary, but also necessarily inadequate forms of what has to be measured against this promise. To this extent, the effectivity or actuality of the democratic promise, like that of the communist promise, will always keep within it, and it must do so, this absolutely undetermined messianic hope at its heart, this eschatological relation to the to-come [*l'à-venir*] of an event and of a singularity, of an alterity that cannot be anticipated. Awaiting without horizon of the wait, awaiting what one does not expect yet or any longer, hospitality without reserve, welcoming salutation accorded in advance to the absolute surprise of the *arrivant* from whom or from which one will not ask anything in return and who or which will not be asked to commit to the domestic contracts of any welcoming power (family, State, nation, territory, native soil or blood, language...), *just* opening which renounces any right to property, any right in general... opening to what is coming... to the event that cannot be awaited as such, or recognized in advance therefore, to the event as the foreigner itself, to her or to him for whom one must leave an empty place, always in memory of the hope.[59]

Derrida has long noted, on the one hand, that the interminable analysis of the aporia of democracy as ultimately indefinable, deferred, and displaced, that is, democracy as *différance*, gives rise to indecision. But, for Derrida, "this indecidability is, like freedom itself, granted by democracy, and it constitutes... the only radical possibility of deciding"; it is the only *hope now* of the future.[60] In other words, the decision is the event of the "to-come" of democracy, its future, which is never satisfied with democracy as it stands, here and now. At this indecidable limit, we can see the true force, the force without force, of what Derrida calls the "passive decision":

If an event worthy of this name is to arrive or happen, it must, beyond all mastery, affect a passivity. It must touch an exposed vulnerability, one without absolute immunity... there where it is not yet or is already no longer possible to face or face up to the unforseeability of the other. In this regard autoimmunity is not an absolute ill or evil.... What *must* be thought is this inconceivable and unknowable thing, a freedom that

59. Jacques Derrida, *Specters of Marx: The State of Debt, The Work of Mourning, and the New International*, trans. Peggy Kamuf (New York: Routledge, 1994), pp. 111–12 (my emphasis).

60. Derrida, *Rogues*, p. 161.

would no longer be the power of a subject, a freedom without autonomy, a heteronomy without servitude, in short, something like a *passive decision*.[61]

Are we free to think, to experience, such a freedom? If it is no longer a matter of mastery, no longer a power of the "I can," then it is also no longer a matter of deciding *for* this freedom, of freeing the self for such a decision, of simply fighting *for* freedom or even a fraternity, of a decisionism or voluntarism that has no other relation than to the *solus* of the *ipse*. Deconstruction as an attunement to the autoimmunity of freedom and democracy is not a philosophy of the emanicipatory promise, of a teleological messianism with its theological fear and trembling, but a thinking of the free space of the promise itself, the radical perhaps within any system, institution, or living being open to the radical future, the democracy to come, the coming of the other:

> It is a question here, as with the coming of any event worthy of this name, of an unforeseeable coming of the other, of a heteronomy, of a law coming from the other, of a responsibility and decision of the other—of the other in me, an other greater and older than I am.[62]

Absolutely heterogeneous to any program—in fact, autoimmunity is that which calls for the "event of the irruptive decision"—the decision is indeed a weak force, always at risk and risking itself in the face of what or who knows what. What could be more undemocratic, less open and intelligible to the *dēmos* of democracy, than this and what Derrida called in *The Other Heading* a "'freedom' to be invented. *Every day*. At least. And democracy along with it."[63] To the democrat, to those who believe in freedom and think this freedom should be comprehended and experienced by all, this all may sound, as Derrida admits, like a dangerous obscurantism. But Derrida's deconstruction of democracy and freedom—rethought as the sending of a heritage still to come, of a democracy to come as this very sending—leads not to a political quietism paralyzed in the face of what Derrida suggestively calls the "*khōra* of the political."

Rather, taking on democracy and freedom—questioning power (*kratos*) and the measuring out of the people (*dēmos*)—is the unconditional claim

61. Ibid., p. 170.
62. Derrida, *Paper Machine*, p. 83.
63. Derrida, *The Other Heading*, p. 80.

made upon all those who take themselves to be the friends of freedom and democracy. And this claim would form nothing other than what Derrida called in "Faith and Knowledge" a "co-auto-immunity." This is the "death drive at work in every community," he writes, the "principle of self-protection" that also leads to the demise of a community rethinking itself in its "self-contesting attestation." "Keep[ing] the auto-immune community alive" means being "open to ... the other, the future, death, [and] freedom," that is, a being without sovereignty and a hope now apposing the reason of the strongest.[64] This co-auto-immunity, then, would be nothing other than the "community of the question" announced by Derrida long ago in "Violence and Metaphysics," that is, the questioning of the community, a non-sovereign freedom of questioning and the questioning of freedom.

64. Jacques Derrida, "Faith and Knowledge: The Two Sources of 'Religion' at the Limits of Reason of Alone," in *Acts of Religion*, ed. Gil Anidjar (New York: Routledge, 2002), p. 87.

THE TELOS INSTITUTE

The Telos Institute promotes the scholarly examination of topics in areas such as social theory, political philosophy, intellectual history, and contemporary culture in order to enhance the quality of intellectual discussion. Through regular conferences, the Telos Institute gathers scholars from around the world in order to offer new perspectives on current questions and to promote discussion of pressing but under-researched topics. The resulting research is made available through the affiliated journal, *Telos*, which also publishes documents and essays, frequently translated from other languages in order to make them accessible to the American and the international higher education community. Through support for scholarship, conferences, and publication, the Telos Institute makes a significant contribution to the scholarly world and adds to the quality of contemporary intellectual and political debate.

Support our mission by making a tax-deductible contribution to the Telos Institute. There are two ways to donate:

1. Donate *online* via PayPal on our website at www.telosinstitute.net

2. Donate *by check,* payable to "The Telos Institute" and sent to:
   The Telos Institute, 20 Main Street, Candor, New York 13743

Liberalism and Class Consciousness

Gábor T. Rittersporn

David Ost, *The Defeat of Solidarity: Anger and Politics in Postcommunist Europe*. Ithaca, NY: Cornell University Press, 2005. Pp. ix + 238.

Poland still celebrates the euphoric weeks of 1980 when a huge strike threatened to bring down the Communist government. While the euphoria is long gone, the strike's importance is unmistakable, marking as it did the beginning of the only political movement in the Eastern Bloc that was not defeated in a few days. Defying the Polish regime for a decade, even while outlawed under martial law, the movement was spearheaded by an organization without historical analogue. Solidarity styled itself as a trade union, challenging the Party-State's prerogative to shape industrial relations and wriggling out concessions for labor. Yet the putative union accomplished incomparably more, propelling the masses to political action, providing a sense of dignity and a cause for which to live. But what became of Solidarity under the New Regime? Why did the eminent champions of its ideals turn against it? Why did the trade union lose most of its constituency? Why did political movements under the Solidarity pedigree embrace illiberal options?

David Ost's *The Defeat of Solidarity: Anger and Politics in Postcommunist Europe* offers far more convincing answers to these questions than the entire library of books written to date on post-Communist Poland. The author avoids pondering whether privatization advances, whether the market economy is working, which elections are a success, and if countries of the former Eastern Bloc are progressing toward the best of all possible worlds. Ost shares some of his colleagues' illusions, only he sees much further, most notably when debunking the icons of Solidarity's erstwhile glory. For example, Ost provides some important insights as to the impact of dissenting intellectuals on Solidarity's denouement. From its earliest days, the movement profited from their advice, drafting programmatic documents, negotiating with the government, and helping Solidarity when it was forced underground. Dissidents, fascinated by the workers whose radicalism contrasted with the tactically cautious liberal opposition, brought the movement's message to the masses and, more widely, the world. Quite soon, however, the workers' radicalism became suspect. Prominent intellectuals started to claim that it stemmed from a lack of realism, from the masses' irrational urges, from a disdain for pluralism, or from submissiveness to charismatic leaders. While these intellectuals continued to support Solidarity, they feared that political liberalism and its program of neoliberal economy would likely conflict with the expectations of labor.

According to Ost, this led the liberal opposition to exclude Solidarity from the most important negotiations with the bankrupt Communist government. He also shows that both the movement's leaders and its rank and file sincerely subscribed to the liberal project, even when the masses started to suffer under the burden of new economic policies. (Introduced at a breakneck pace, these policies pauperized most of the population.) These burdens seemed regrettable yet inevitable to former partisans of Solidarity, whose social, educational, and cultural capital yielded newly elevated status. Growing contemptuous of protesting workers, they discarded the allies who brought them to power as irrational, ignorant, and dangerous. In so doing, they felt vindicated by their expertise, by received wisdom about the merits of market economy, and by foreign governments' approval. Ost describes this difficult situation. Solidarity (the movement) and its constituency continued to believe in the redeeming virtues of the neoliberal strategy, while the trade union of the same name lost credibility. One did little to defend impoverished workers, the other remained a political player. The former enlisted support precisely because it endorsed painful economic reform, even advocating speedier implementation and accusing former Communists of sabotaging the project by a subversion of the partially purged state apparatus. At the same time, political liberalism was suspected of having gone too far. Parties under Solidarity's flag managed to change governments, all the while retaining economic policies. After a while, the anti-Communist electorate even came to vote massively for former Communist reformers who promised to alleviate hardships.

Ost can not help but mock the liberal intellectuals who maneuvered themselves into the situation of the East German government, which, having lost the confidence of the people, might have found it easier to "dissolve the people and elect another," as Brecht suggested. The clear problem was that liberals were both unwilling to understand the masses and unable to tackle their discontent. The policies of former dissidents had everything to discredit rationalism, tolerance, openness to the world and other liberal principles. The more liberals vilified their opponents as reactionaries, the more the latter could legitimate illiberal programs such as nationalism, authoritarianism, xenophobia, religious fundamentalism, and antisemitism, all of which surfaced in the discourse of parties close to Solidarity. Ost condemns the elitism of Polish liberals, their dogmatism, and their narcissistic intransigence (constitutive of a cult of their own impotence). He denounces their readiness to perish politically rather than to face society as it happens to be. Solidarity also receives its share of blame, however. Ost attributes the trade union's failure to its leaders' eagerness to engage in politics and to the blindness of the rank and file who followed them. He recognizes that ultimately Solidarity fought for the same goal as its adversaries, the establishment of a market economy, by implementing a neoliberal strategy.

This political rivalry implies that the movement restrained the trade union, which was feared for having backed its members' protests. Strangely enough, this required little effort since union members generally accepted the reform. Their protests were directed at what political leaders designated and workers saw as Communist maneuvers subverting the market economy. Soaring unemployment and deepening misery were not enough to trigger large-scale combat protecting labor, and many workers surrendered because they were likely to find places in privatized enterprises, the efficiency of which many expected would guarantee better conditions. Many of Solidarity's former activists found jobs in the new state apparatus, while those who did not desert the union were helpless.

Ost concludes with one solution: Solidarity should have left the political arena to concentrate on its role as a trade union, rallying class-conscious workers and negotiating their economic rights. Ost argues (like quite a few reformers of the last century) that a self-conscious working class is a social group with a belief in its own subordinate position both in the market and in bargaining with business. It does not pretend to represent more than labor's particular interests and keeps away from politics. Polish workers do not necessarily understand this, resenting subordination and demanding more rewards. Ost thinks they would benefit from expert advisors channeling their resentment toward reaching arrangements with management. This said, Ost does not seem quite sure whether the market turn in Poland has political implications. Still, he faults liberal intellectuals for not orienting the masses toward brokering with employers, thereby betraying Solidarity.

Does Ost ask too much of liberal intellectuals? Did they not manage worker discontent in the 1980s? Did they not outline market reform well before the fall of the old regime? Did they not sell neoliberal economy to the masses as a panacea for all the wrongs they endured under Stalinist, neo-Stalinist, and post-Stalinist rule? Were they not, as Ost himself writes, convincing the masses that anti-Communism amounts to neoliberalism, and catering to the popular belief that business and labor can strike fair deals on the market? There was no reason for them to channel mass resentment toward economic targets under the new regime, as this was done before Communism's demise. The reform represented far more than economic change and the promise of better living standards, generally out of reach for workers struggling for reform. Workers targeted what was sold to them as economic transformation and subordinated everything to this end (as Ost would have them do), especially when they went to the ballot box to elect politicians pledging to conduct reform better than the liberal government. Their obsession with the economy, however, was irrational and not the espousal of illiberal politics. Liberalism's economic program was criticized as being too slowly implemented and not worth its hardships. The liberals' contempt for the masses left the people with no choice but to hope that anti-liberal parties would treat them better. Ost understands precisely this, that the latter were well-advised, rallying voters by proposing ideals diametrically opposed to liberal convictions, with the notable exception of the idea of a neoliberal economy.

Ost's proposition channeling worker discontent toward economic objectives is reminiscent of the Bolshevik scheme of self-criticism. The Bolsheviks encouraged labor, Party cells, and trade unions to question the ways in which their plant or branch was (mis)managed, complain about unfair or incompetent cadres, expose misconduct, and suggest improvements. Workers and militants could exercise self-criticism as vehemently as they wished, so far as they did not attack the management, the planned economy, or the regime as a whole. Many of their proposals were accepted, especially concerning industrial relations. However, this practice was predicated on the fiction of the unity of interest of, on the one hand, the Bolsheviks profiting from the system and, on the other, the rest of society suffering under said system. Ost insists on the need to focus on the particular interests of labor whose subordination to business must be as consciously accepted as the subjection the Bolsheviks imposed on their putatively class-conscious citizenry.

Is this conception not similar to the understanding of citizenship held by class-conscious intellectuals in Poland? Did they not accept the rest of society only insofar as it did not question their reform and leadership? Did their liberalism imply more than the magnanimous tolerance of sheep? Does the public interest count only as long as it corresponds to liberal interests? Ost harbors no illusions about Polish liberals, wondering if they were right to equate political liberalism with a radical strategy to enforce economic liberalism. He thinks true political liberalism could have sweetened the bitter pill Polish workers had to swallow simply by not humiliating the poor or denigrating their resentment. Liberals should have oriented discontent toward economic concerns and should have done their best to keep the masses out of politics by inculcating them with Ost's class consciousness, in somewhat the same manner as Lenin's followers who believed that the dark masses were to be educated by their enlightened troops. The Party-State treated people doubting the Bolsheviks' readiness in representing their interests quite harshly; the ignorant folk had to acquire class consciousness in order to understand its common cause with the Bolsheviks. To be sure, Polish liberals (or liberals *tout court*) would never go to such extremes, prepared as they are to step down if outvoted at elections. They also had no reason to worry when they were defeated, able as they were to quietly retreat to their ivory tower because the masses swallowed the pill. Even though the therapy was painful and the irritation continued, the patient consented. Illiberal governments faithfully implemented the program of neoliberal economy: it remained as unquestioned as ever.

Why should we believe the liberal intellectuals were losers? The Communist regime muzzled them, it persecuted them if they broke step, and it tolerated them only if they did not meddle in Party policy. Most of them had no choice but to put their skills to the service of an administration in which they were consultants at best. Suddenly, they became full members of the elite of political entrepreneurs, state servants, managers, technical experts, and academics, of the *beau monde* of producers of cultural goods and services. And neither was Solidarity defeated. It did not disappear from the scene. The trade union has declined and has to compete with other organizations, but remnants of the movement are strong enough to mobilize the electorate, to make and unmake governments.

The Polish experience shows that liberalism does not only mean the cult of the individual, of democracy, tolerance, morality, reason, civil society, and the belief in freedom, human rights, progress, and culture. It stands also for a world where educational, cultural, and especially social capital weighs more than the ballot, although it is scarcely accessible to the great majority of electors. In principle, liberalism became inseparable from a neoliberal economy that does not tolerate the weak, and which prospers best when the weak must struggle uphill in order to become a little stronger. Its rationality is the production of purchasing power (especially of those who are a little more equal than the others), no matter if it is through manufacturing war, peace, elite rule, or completely useless goods. This economy creates a universe where any good can be sold, including subjection, if buyers can be convinced they need it, if it distracts them and if they believe that it symbolizes status and distinction. Our world is now one where coexistence involves less personal decisions than the expert management of institutions, firms, and the flow of capital, human and inhuman alike. It is more and more the population's freedom to choose between procedures to which it will be subjected, among the entertainment it can enjoy between two votes. It is the liberty of the strong, while it is the right of the weak to toil in the hope of getting a little more flesh on his bones.

The Polish masses eagerly embraced this world as promising the purchasing power of their dreams. They worked hard and expected that one day their promise would be fulfilled, even though for the moment it brought more deprivation than riches. Polish workers may forget about the rights they had been fighting for at the time Solidarity was born. Ost suggests that they are self-conscious citizens if they are content with what they receive. He does not have to do much agitprop. Working people are remarkably acquiescent wherever one looks. There is no need to threaten them with Gulag camps. The strength of liberalism is its capacity to persuade people that they must pay for everything, and that the people would grow idle and irresponsible if they did not relieve entrepreneurs and the state from contributing to their housing, education, pension, and health care. So much so that the masses wonder less and less if business and government are responsible and diligent enough to provide them with workplaces instead of profiting from cheap labor in the poorest countries of the world. This project is all the more popular since it is predicated on easily digestible principles. Neoliberalism legitimizes the rules that everybody deserves the treatment he can buy and that the redemption of the poor is work, if he has the luck to have a job, whatever it pays.

The sense of liberal language cannot be deduced from the liberal self-image. It needs decoding. Hair-splitting linguists risk to understand liberal talk about reform as grandiose plans to change everything in order to leave everything as it happens to be. Nitpicking translators may think that the belief of liberals in their sympathy for simple folks boils down to promising dry bread for bargain prices and extra cheap tickets for pageants. Nagging interpreters may translate liberal discourse about tolerance and dialogue as tolerating the benighted masses as long as they speak the liberal dialect. Pedantic exegetes may be inclined to interpret liberal assertions about equal rights as the right to compete with conservatives to put the rest of society in its God-given place. Liberals sincerely believe their claims. Their claims are the only language to make sense of themselves and their universe, pretty much like the myths of the ancient Greeks that furnished a vocabulary to account for their world.

In prosperous societies radically anti-liberal movements are no match for liberals. As a rule they represent the lunatic fringe. Their appeal to base instincts and extremism are a strong contrast to liberalism's appeal to common sense and moderation. People favor calm and peaceful attempts to resolve problems, which seem intractable anyway. In parliamentary regimes illiberal parties survive because they are completely harmless. They must play the game if they want to remain on the scene and can gain some credit in troubled times. Their electors vote mostly to protest against unpopular policies of the other camps and only a minority of them truly long for the masochistic pleasures of hardened anti-liberalism. This is understood by illiberal statesmen who cannot help but continue the policies of their adversaries, withdrawing from the political stage when they are subsequently voted out. Some illiberal ideas are advertised by fully presentable conservative parties and governments, as witnessed in France. French intellectuals with liberal credentials, and also from the left (whatever they mean by that), class-consciously adhere to parties hijacking illiberal strategies, because they see few differences between progressivist and conservative discourses. They are right. The principles of freedom, human rights, and tolerance are powerful and honestly endorsed by conservatives. Conservatives may say fewer kind words about the masses than liberals, and they may speak more about the Motherland and Heaven and Hell. But the adherence of French intellectuals indicates that fairly extremist talk by conservatives about the care that business deserves, the dangers of immigration, the necessity of strengthening authority, and the need to make people work more amounts to proclaiming *urbi et orbi* what certain liberals confess *in petto*. Liberals are glad to let conservatives tighten the screws because they hope that most of the dirty job will be finished by the next elections. They are clever to achieve it at the price of a few concessions and at the sacrifice of turning a bit more assiduously the humanist prayer mill.

Genuine resistance to liberalism stands the best chances to be inhuman, brutal, and destructive. Savagery cannot be excused by the frustration of people who feel forever excluded from the consumer paradise. It cannot be justified by the devastation, in the name of liberal progress, of the traditional universe of people who want both of the best worlds: their old way of life and the consumer heaven. It cannot be defended as a revolt by people who turn against what they take for symbols of their humiliation by colonial and post-colonial rule and who seek redress for the denial of their faith and for the abuse of their human dignity. It cannot be vindicated as the fight of desperate people to recover their conquered lands. But frustration, lost horizons, and debasement explain something of the rancor of many people. More often than not, Hungarians, Czechs, and Romanians who scapegoat gypsies, as well as East Germans who assault Africans, are losers in the race for a place under the rising sun of neoliberalism. They boost their self-esteem through demonstrating superiority over allegedly second-rate people who are sometimes quite successful, like Caucasian traders in Russia. Russians beating up Asians and burning fancy cars after a soccer match lost to the Japanese national team want to take revenge on people they see as inferior yet nonetheless victorious over their country. The deluxe cars symbolize the wealth and lifestyle of the *nouveaux riches*, denounced as unpatriotic. Repugnant as they are, these incidents are nothing compared to the devastation and massacres perpetrated by self-appointed avengers and holy warriors.

No liberal intellectual can persuade these latter to relax and look class-consciously for a job at a local McDonald's. Talk of humanism and rights only provokes them. Liberalism has no narrative to rally them. In fact, liberalism has no grand narrative and it does not have to market one. Few voters can enumerate the human rights. People know better what they can earn or lose, where, how, when, and why. The need to make ends meet under heavy structural constraints motivates them more than high ideals. If there are mottoes that mobilize them, they are bound to advertise merchandise. This can be so attractive that they coexist with illiberal narratives and actually support them, as in Poland, Romania, or Russia. More often than not, trendy gadgets are more difficult to get hold of in places where narratives of the nation, religion, and race mobilize large masses. If such gadgets are available, they are likely to epitomize the foe. This does not mean that they are not coveted, however. The fascination engendered by reform in Poland suggests that one day the lures of the neoliberal paradise may ensnare the fighters' flocks, who risk feeling deceived if the holy war does not deliver the prosperity of their reveries.

Who can wait for that day? It will come too late for the innocents who may perish in senseless carnage. Can one afford the luxury to be liberal with the irreconcilable enemies of liberalism? One has to track them down all over the planet, with every possible means. One must be prepared for their strikes at the heart of the free world. They are difficult to trace. They may hide in our midst. A neighbor may shelter them. Heaven forbid that an acquaintance turns out to be one of them. Everybody must accept being screened and searched in their own interest. A new kind of class consciousness must unite true friends of freedom, recognizable by their endorsement of strict measures of security. Or not. The situation must be grave if liberal governments consent to international surveillance of phone conversations and electronic messages, even the websites people visit, including their most reliable subjects.

The East German secret police collected data on eight million individuals in forty years. Consider that twelve million people use the web-based Skype phone system at any given moment. East German Communists wanted to protect citizens in the name of socialist humanism, and, indeed, liberalism cannot be accused of more disrespect. It is in the name of human rights that liberalism protects humanity against itself. Liberals see strong reasons to doubt that people will follow their best interests if they are not disciplined, at least in market terms. One may ask if terrorists trust communication systems they know to be monitored. And one can fear that only enemies of liberal humanism are likely to wonder if pessimists, on account of man's diligence, will not be tempted to put surveillance data to uses other than the war on terror. The massive accumulation of records did not save East German Communism. They were of dubious utility when it came to fighting their adversaries. The belief in a better world proved more subversive than dissident agitation. The Promised Land was close, just behind the Berlin Wall and the barbed wire that protected the camp of socialist humanism against the failing class consciousness of their fellows.

Ost scores a point when he writes that the Manichaeism of the Cold War reduced one's options to the choice between a system depriving the masses of rights, including the right to enjoy the well-being of their choice, and the only system whose abundance was seen as the guarantee of boundless freedom. The dilemma has scarcely changed. The foes of liberalism have hardly more to offer than the worship of the Fatherland and the Elected People, the righteousness of the faithful, the purity of the race, the expedience of authoritarian rule, the cult of brute force, and the eternal glory of the warrior. The choice is meager and those who offer it disreputable. People trying to look for options beyond the liberal paradise can be easily confounded with rabid extremists. It would be a mistake to forget that Poland's liberal intellectuals prefer debate with people who hold their views, and accept the other primarily if they resemble their image of themselves.

Ost ends his book with a call to recast liberal ideology, an appeal perhaps heard by class-conscious readers who look for solutions in recipes of the *nouvelle cuisine* from faded issues of liberal newspapers. The masses may feel uncomfortable but they seem barely worthy of more than asking for higher pay. Ost may be close to the mark in this respect. If so, then there is no need to refurbish liberalism: it manifestly works without reform. In this respect, the cover of Ost's book features a fine photograph, taken by Ost himself, showing a street in a town of the Silesian Rust Belt, which Communism left in ruins. A lad is walking by in shoddy clothes, looking unhappy. Hopefully liberalism will recast the landscape, lining the street with postmodern condominiums. The residents will have some experience of unemployment, toiling diligently to pay mortgage, health insurance, the pension fund, the children's school, and drugs for their parents' heart condition. They will struggle to pay back loans and to keep up with the local Joneses. A young man will stroll around the place sporting a stylish outfit and a pair of chic sneakers. He will earn them through part-time jobs, just as he will earn his iPod, whose sweet melodies and diabolic rhythms will protect him from the noise of daily existence. He will class-consciously put up with his lot like the worm whom Brecht's angler invites to catch fishes together.

Think, Again: A Reply to Ulrich Plass

Gerhard Richter

In *Mixed Opinions and Maxims* Nietzsche offers sage advice on the topic of being misunderstood. He writes: "When one is misunderstood as a whole, it is impossible to remove completely a single misunderstanding. One has to realize this lest one waste superfluous energy on one's defense." I shall bear this wisdom in mind as I respond to Ulrich Plass's review of recent scholarship on the work of Theodor W. Adorno (*Telos* 146, Spring 2009), which includes my book *Thought-Images: Frankfurt School Writers' Reflections from Damaged Life* (Stanford University Press, 2007). Plass begins, without offering the reader any sense of my book's overall argumentation, by accusing me of excessive conceptual complexity. As the American philosopher John McCumber and others have convincingly shown, this clichéd tactic, typically proffered in a tone of moral superiority, amounts to the unacknowledged fetishization of a "metaphysics of clarity" that never can progress beyond its own status as a self-violating norm. But the real irony is that this very charge, which usually serves as a short cut to the labor of actual thinking, frequently has been leveled against Adorno himself. In *Minima Moralia* Adorno provides the following assessment of those who would marshal such an accusation: "[O]nly that which they do not first need to understand do they consider understandable; only that word which in truth is alienated and coined by commerce touches them as familiar."

Without providing any evidence to support his view, Plass proceeds by making the outlandish claim that my book "unwittingly diminished Adorno's *Minima Moralia* to a deconstructive inside joke." While I would be delighted to have my work inscribed in the venerable tradition of thoughtful meditations on jokes and wit that includes Freud's magnificent *Jokes and Their Relation to the Unconscious*, it would be difficult to construe my work as a joke book about the Frankfurt School, unless one were to find some perverse humor in Adorno's moral and philosophical engagement with National Socialism and with the cultural condition he terms "after Auschwitz." Plass goes on to assert that my book is "proof" that one must not "assimilate Adorno's dialectical thought with poststructuralist themes and tropes," lest one overlook the fact that between Adorno and Derrida stands Heidegger. In this context, Plass is quick to point out that I make what he calls a "superfluous reference" to a Heideggerean concept in my book. But subtle readers of the relation between Adorno and Heidegger have long appreciated that

Adorno's own polemic against Heidegger, *The Jargon of Authenticity*, may not be the most reliable guide to the connection between these two philosophers. In fact, there are important subterranean affinities between key elements in the theories of these thinkers, which serious scholars as different as Wilhelm Wurzer, Alexander García Düttmann, Fred Dallmeyer, and Hermann Mörchen have articulated in their various books on the complex relays between Heidegger's fundamental ontology and Adorno's negative dialectics. Even Jürgen Habermas acknowledges the importance of this connection when he concedes in his *Theory of Communicative Action* that "Adorno is in the end very similar to Heidegger as regards his position on the theoretical claims of objectivating thought and of reflection," such that in certain respects their works come "shockingly close" to one another. At any rate, one would be well-advised to conceptualize the relation between Heidegger and Adorno as an open question that deserves to be contemplated from ever new perspectives. Plass, however, has little patience with such subtle types of reflection, preferring instead to assure his readers that my book "gets the significance of Heidegger's thought for Adorno wrong." Ultimately, Plass muses, it is unfortunate that I fail "to provide evidence for [my] claim that philosophy is most socially and politically relevant when read as literature." One wonders which book Plass has been reading, as mine certainly does not make that claim. From the standpoint of an ethics of discussion, one must argue for one's claims, rather than simply assert them.

While every sentence that Plass writes about my book is embarrassingly wrong or grotesquely misleading, I will limit myself to just a few examples. To begin with, Plass misconstrues my argument as meaning that "it is not the content" that counts but *only* the form" (Plass's emphasis). This claim, had I actually made it, would not even have made sense in the context of my argument, as Plass easily could have verified. An equally absurd line of argumentation that he advances is the idea that I seek to "appropriate the notion of performance for [my] own style of writing" so that "[Richter], like Adorno or Bloch, is also an author of thought-images." Either Plass did not read a single sentence of my discussion on the genre of the thought-image, which makes clear that the form of my book is a different one, or he incomprehensibly misconstrued Martin Jay's endorsement on the back cover of my book, which suggests a link between my own mode of writing and that of the authors I treat. However, neither of these interpretations of Plass's statement can explain away the contradiction that obtains between Plass's claim that the style I employ in my book could have benefited from "a more disciplined adherence to the values of stylistic and conceptual clarity" (Plass leaves these terms undefined), on the one hand, and his suggestion that my writing mimics that of the thought-images that it treats, on the other hand. By that logic, the writing found in Benjamin, Bloch, Kracauer, and Adorno—the four authors of the thought-images that I read in my study—all do not meet Plass's lofty standards of conceptual clarity. Also, Plass surely must know that the "not-yet" is not simply an iteration of the Derridean category of the "to-come," as he seems to imply, but rather is a notion that plays a central role in Bloch's philosophy as the "Noch-Nicht" (the "Not-Yet"), and, as is well known, is a concept with which Adorno is in constant dialogue. Although Plass's hostility toward Heidegger, Derrida, and the post-phenomenological tradition is evident throughout the document (for example, in his later discussion of a recent book on Heidegger and Adorno), he makes a feeble gesture in a footnote—by citing two books that bring Adorno and Derrida together in a way that appears acceptable to him—to convince us that the derisive things he says about my attempt to think Adorno and Derrida together "does not mean that a deconstructive or Derridean reading of Adorno cannot be productive." He insists that the two texts he cites "demonstrate that the application of deconstructive tropes and a discerning eye for aporias and paradoxes can yield significant insights into Adorno's thought." Of course, recent scholarship on the connection between Adorno and Derrida, which stretches all the way from Christoph Menke's influential work to the recent volume *Derrida und Adorno: Zur Aktualität von Dekonstruktion und Frankfurter Schule*, edited by Eva L.-Waniek and Erik Vogt, has proceeded far beyond this rudimentary claim. But, more significantly, Plass seems not to notice that his remarks betray a fundamental misunderstanding of both Derrida and Adorno. After all, even a cursory reading of Derrida's work yields the insight—and Derrida is very explicit about this—that deconstruction is not a matter of simply "applying" something to something else, much less a so-called method to be applied to this or that external phenomenon at will. In fact, Derrida on many occasions explicitly called into question the notions of "application," "applying," "applicability," and so forth. Rather, deconstruction, instead of performing an external intervention in, say, the mode of a traditional ideology critique, examines that which within an object or a thought *already* is at odds with itself, already contradictory and self-questioning. Nor does Plass's language make sense from the perspective of Adorno's project. In Adorno's version of a negative dialectics, what is to be thought, among other things, is the difference or non-identity between *Anwendung* and *Vermittlung*, concepts that, in turn, are mediated by, rather than "applied" to, each other, as if transformative critique were a matter of a simple *Anwendung*. Plass is deaf to the dialectical nature of the mediatedness of those objects and ideological formations—among them, the very concepts "application" and "mediation"—upon which Adorno's thought so rigorously fastens and which he so often exposes as (always differently modulated) iterations of the Non-Identical. Even those among Adorno's readers who could not quite make it through *Negative Dialectics* and *Aesthetic Theory*—to say nothing of *Hegel: Three Studies*—will tend to appreciate the significance of this constellation to Adorno's project.

The Conservative Movement in America: Redeeming the Time or Serving the System?

Mark Wegierski

Paul Edward Gottfried, *Conservatism in America: Making Sense of the American Right.* New York: Palgrave Macmillan, 2007. Pp. xviii + 189.

What reflective conservatives see as the attenuation and destruction of tradition and traditionalism in Western societies has proceeded apace along a variety of paths. In this cogent study, Paul Gottfried looks at the shape this process has taken in the United States, where ruling elites have directed a so-called "conservative movement" that would capture the efforts and resources of many of those at least putatively opposed to the present-day regime. Gottfried describes how the initial founding of the "conservative movement" in the 1950s (mainly by William F. Buckley, Jr., and Russell Kirk) was based on some authentic traditionalist impulses. Nevertheless, Gottfried argues, elements of contrivance—and the frequent "purges" carried out by Buckley against those considered "unacceptable extremists"—made it easier in subsequent decades to reconfigure the "conservative movement" in directions of ever greater conformity to the prevalent regime.

He also clarifies that the basis of Buckley's "purges" before the 1980s was usually for being "soft on Communism" and *not* for antisemitism. For example, the John Birch Society was "excommunicated" when it came out against the Vietnam War. It is a testimony to the almost infinite flexibility of the "conservative movement" in rewriting its own history, that the current received wisdom is that Buckley had always based his "purges" on removing so-called "haters" from the movement. Was anarcho-capitalist Murray Rothbard an antisemite?

The influx of neoconservatives in the 1980s resulted in a massive reconfiguration of the ideological and intellectual lineaments of the "conservative movement," which only sporadically opposed these changes. Some of the reasons for the absence of resistance may have been the lack of confidence or belief in their own ideas, the search for respectability by many of the so-called mainstream of the movement, and the precarious reliance on foundation funding and the (Ronald Reagan and George H. W. Bush) government bureaucracy for their jobs. When Buckley handed over *National Review*, the dominant "movement" organ, to neoconservative control, the transvaluation of the "conservative movement" was all but finalized, and the neoconservatives swept all before them.

Gottfried brings commendable attention to the considerable shallowness of the official conservative rhetoric today. His description of the vacuous nature of conservative polemics against liberals who allegedly hold "no values" is insightful. It does not take too much philosophical effort to demonstrate that it is a conflict of one belief against another, and *not* of those who hold values against those who have none. This conservative tactic, argues Gottfried, has vitiated a more pertinent critique that certain values of "the social Left" are being massively imposed on society.

He also deploys a helpful analogy that the conservative movement in America today organizationally somewhat resembles the Communist Party structures in America and some Western European societies in the 1950s and earlier. While self-described conservatives feel a great sense of isolation from the general culture, those who take their bearings from the movement are conditioned to follow whatever "party line" is announced from the people at the top. They also frequently rely on the movement for their jobs and social connections. So a handful of neoconservative potentates can drive their hapless minions in any direction they want.

Gottfried interestingly ends the book with a quote from historian John Lukacs: "But now we're all social democrats!" (149). The quotation is highly symptomatic of a questionable assumption underlying the book's argument—that is, the assumption that the neoconservatives do not truly represent capitalism. It might have been more effective for Gottfried to argue that there are at least two main variants of capitalism—the bourgeois capitalism, mostly of the nineteenth century, and the managerial capitalism that is part of the managerial-therapeutic regime (sometimes called "late capitalism" by its critics). Presumably, Gottfried's hope is for the restoration of certain bourgeois mores, but that would seem to be a more difficult endeavor than an argument for a quasi-aristocratic aesthetic revulsion of more reflective, cultured persons (whatever their class origins or socio-economic status) against the current system, or for a populist rallying of what has been called "working-class authoritarianism." The putatively anti-capitalist "politics of cultural despair"—however much it may be disparaged by the present-day regime as constituting a typology of classical fascism—may be the only *possible* decent response to a society so thoroughly flooded by various debased forms of art and entertainment. And the path of populism—of protectionism and of immigration-restriction against cheap foreign labor—is almost inherently anti-capitalist. There does not appear to be an intrinsic link between the upholding of the interests of the lower-middle- and working-classes and the upholding of capitalism in late modernity. While it cannot be denied that the right to private property and the distinction between the public and private spheres are of enormous significance, not only to most forms of traditionalism but indeed to almost any vision of a more decent society, to necessarily link them to the upholding of present-day capitalism is rather questionable.

It is difficult to imagine how a society like the United States could necessarily become more capitalist than it is today. If every taxpayer in society were allowed to keep a somewhat greater share of the money they made, would this necessarily result in an improvement to society and culture? To think that rallying in the direction of a more intensive "capitalism" could lead the United States in a neo-traditionalist direction is highly questionable.

In his otherwise frequently insightful book, Gottfried has elided the matter that a critique of capitalism may be the beginning of greater insights about society. Indeed, it could be argued that many elements of what is transpiring today have arisen precisely out of the triumph of the capitalism of the consumerist/consumptionist society, which absolutely loathes the lifestyles of the abstemiously living, the smallholders, and the decent toilers, whom it denounces as greedy "petty-bourgeois" or authoritarian-minded "hard hats." It is implied if not stated outright by most current economic theorizing that if most people were to try to live according to the classical capitalist principle of "gratification-deferment," then the economy today would promptly collapse. The consumptionist type of capitalism has wreaked havoc on tradition and traditionalism, especially through mass-mediated pop culture. Indeed, it could be argued that it is only in the aftermath of the 1960s that capitalism truly reached the condition suggested in Marx and Engels's *Communist Manifesto*: "All that is solid melts into air, all that is holy is profaned."

Gottfried complains in his book that the "conservatism" of the "conservative movement" does not appeal to any concrete groups or classes in society. Nevertheless, it could easily be argued that the annihilation of various traditional classes, including the working class, is one of the salient characteristics of late modernity. The fragmented scene of late modernity has created an amorphous, diffuse situation where the most socially and culturally influential people are media pundits and various entertainment celebrities. Organizationally, society is dominated by public administrators (above all the mass-education system, from ECE to postgraduate studies) and corporate managers. Contemporary mass education and the mostly pseudo-psychological theorizing that typically underpins it have ensured that there is little possibility that a "counter-ethic" based on a more civilized, cultured, and humane ethos could ever emanate from public schooling.

The social, political, and cultural ramifications of our mediatized and consumerist society are often not fully explored, as most self-described social and cultural critics tend to be of "the social Left." Thus, what is probably the key feature of contemporary capitalism, the attenuation and annihilation of tradition and traditionalism in Western societies, is understated or mostly ignored—or is in fact itself celebrated as part of an ineluctable "progress." Many cultural critics on the Left (most prominently, Noam Chomsky), while having a certain insight into such aspects of the current-day system as its quasi-totalitarian nature, frequently trade in massive demonologies of an allegedly "corporate-ruled" society that is a monstrous blend of militarist "fascism" and big business. This leads them to downplay what reflective conservatives perceive as the real threats and challenges of late modernity to a more decent human social existence. To characterize the aptly named "society of the spectacle" as a form of a supposedly "eternal fascism" is absurd!

The relentless mediatized drive of consumer society in antinomian directions may be seen as the base for the frenetic changes in the ideological superstructure, including the metamorphosis of the "conservative movement." Hence, for example, the constant promotion of various forms of antinomianism and multiculturalism in popular, highly profitable musical subgenres, such as rap and hip-hop, or in the more euphonious music of Madonna, Shakira, and Beyoncé. Examining this culture industry and its political consequences may provide a more effective explanation of social and culture change than the conspiracy theories that circulate on the left.

Trying to focus the opposition around the concept of the "Right" may not necessarily be the only direction to be taken. Clearly, almost every Western society today needs a genuine Right. Yet there are also various possible streams of thought, such as "social conservatives of the Left." The term "Right" may be too narrowly political. There is a wider range of "non-conformist" criticisms of late modernity, such as those voiced most prominently by the ecological/environmentalist movement, as well as by certain neo-mystical thinkers, such as C. G. Jung, Joseph Campbell, and Ken Wilber. Notwithstanding the fact that much of its thought has been instrumentalized by the current system, the Frankfurt School's criticism of consumer society, and especially the critique of desiccated rationalism expressed in Horkheimer and Adorno's *Dialectic of Enlightenment*, can also lead to an unexpected neo-traditionalist turn.

Contemporary culture involves an ever more frenzied pursuit of lower pleasures and consumerist status symbols in the wake of the atrophy of a sense of a more anchored, rooted, and meaningful existence. Questioning this culture is the first step toward the possibilities of neo-traditionalism. This is all the more urgent as the current system moves increasingly unchallenged toward a "*sub rosa* social totalitarianism," imposed through the interlocking structures of mass media, mass education, and the consumption society.

At the same time, the system has so drastically weakened some Western societies that we may witness apocalyptic-dystopic outcomes as a result of challenges from outside the West, notably Islamic extremism. The continuing, unrelenting assault on the social and cultural base from which most of the military in the

United States originates will further contribute to a strategic decline. The weakness of genuine patriotism necessitates the constant drumbeat of a rather unreflective, ersatz patriotism—as typified by Rush Limbaugh—from which movement conservatives take their bearings. Most self-described American conservatives are likely to be as deeply immersed in pop culture and its various manifestations as the avowed left-liberals. The only thing that they can reasonably hold onto is their ideology. They typically have a considerable amount of spiritedness but usually comparatively little sense of reflection. For example, given the configurations of society today, any media pundits who support military endeavors are immediately seen by conservatives, left-liberals, and most of the public at large, as putatively "right-wing." Not surprisingly a desiccated definition of conservatism is part of a generally desiccated society. Gottfried helps us understand part of these vicissitudes of "conservatism" in the United States.

Islam and the Secular World Order

Shafiq Shamel

Bassam Tibi, *Political Islam, World Politics and Europe: Democratic Peace and Euro-Islam versus Global Jihad* (New York: Routledge, 2008). Pp. xiv + 311.

"The concern is to accommodate the 'return of the sacred' for a better future without a 'clash of civilizations'" (22). This vision stands at the center of Bassam Tibi's analysis of a post-bipolar world order. In light of the events of September 11, 2001, in the United States, March 11, 2004, in Madrid, November 2, 2004, in Amsterdam, and July 7, 2005, in London, as well as the uprising in Paris in October and November 2005 and the Danish cartoons controversy in 2006, Tibi claims that a shift has taken place in world politics: from a nuclear East-West polarity to an asymmetrical confrontation between Islam and the West. "The return of the sacred," Tibi argues, is emerging "as a politicization of religion" (15). "Politicization of religion," however, is not merely understood as the enforcement of both faith and religious values via modern political institutions but, more importantly, as "the return of history" (18). In this context, "the return of history" means a revival of foundational principles that were the driving force of Islam in its early years and that gave Muslims a civilizational primacy, which was gradually replaced by supremacy of the West (militarily, culturally, economically, and technologically). Tibi believes this history to be the source of the present resentment of the West and regards the Islamist mobilization as an attempt "to resume the *da'wa* [proselytization] parallel to the pursuit of a de-Westernization" (171).

The most prominent and important Islamic concept that Tibi discusses is "jihad." In fact, the entire book is a scholarly analysis (from the perspective of the discipline of International Relations) that offers an explanation of Islamism and political Islam in terms of the transformation of the early Islamic concept of "jihad" into "jihadism" since the 1930s. At the same time, Tibi also proposes alternative possibilities—most significantly, the concept of Euro-Islam—for an Islamic identity compatible (and non-confrontational) with Western modernity. As such, the conceptual framework of his analysis reveals the inner dynamics of Islamic thought and foregrounds the significant role of Islamism in world politics. Tibi disputes the linking of post-2001 Islamist acts of terror in the United States and Europe to the "occupation of Palestine, Iraq, Afghanistan, and Lebanon" or to U.S. militarism: "It is a fact that jihadism was born in 1928 when none of these issues existed" (107). He distinguishes Islamism from early twentieth-century anti-colonial movements in the Middle East and regards as inaccurate the notion that the rise of religious extremism in the Islamic world constitutes a crisis in cultural identity arising in response to the cultural, political, and military dominance of the West. According to Tibi, both Islamism and (especially) jihadism have their roots in an ideology inherent in Islam rather than in colonial, post-colonial, or imperial politics:

> After having lived as a Muslim immigrant for four and a half decades in Europe, I claim to see a very weak European *asabiyya* replacing the earlier ugly Eurocentrism. This is a shift from one extreme to the other. I translate *asabiyya* as civilizational self-awareness. As a Muslim who is committed to freedom and rationality, and who fled the despotism and authoritarianism that is currently not only prevailing but spreading in the world of Islam, I do not like to see the political culture of Islamism establishing itself in the Islamic diaspora in Europe (189).

Drawing on the ideas of the fourteenth-century Arab philosopher and historian Ibn Khaldun, Tibi describes his conceptual framework for the analysis of Islamism *and* the West, as well as Islamism *in* the West, as "a civilizational approach" that places "civilizations within the study of history" (119). In so doing, he dissociates himself from Samuel Huntington's idea of the "clash of civilizations," which he characterizes as "a superficial political way," and is able to show how "the study of religion and Islam in world civilizations and world politics can be linked" (119). Without ignoring the threat of such a "clash," Tibi instead focuses on finding a way out of it. This is the major contribution of the book as it tries to rethink Islam in the Islamic world and Europe—as well as Europe and Islam in the context of intellectual, political, and religious reality in the contemporary world, particularly in Europe. Moreover, this approach also challenges Francis Fukuyama's *The End of History and the Last Man* by illustrating how Islamism, both as a participant in the democratic process and as jihadism, has come to occupy center stage in world politics. As such, *Political Islam, World Politics and Europe* provides an insightful perspective on the emergence of Islamism and serves as an alternative vision to the ideology of jihadism, namely, Islam as Euro-Islam. Unlike populist tendencies in both the Islamic world and the West, this vision is based on the premise that "the religion of Islam (faith and ethic)" is distinct from "Islamism as a political totalitarian ideology represented by a movement based in transnational religion" (xii).

The distinction between Islamism and Islam is especially clear in the context of Tibi's discussion of "jihad." While traditional jihad (literally, "to exert oneself") designates a "regular war" that is "subjected to rules" (according to the Qur'an, it is "governed by strict rules of conduct and by limiting targets"), for "*futuhat-*wars, as an Islamic expansion," jihadism represents "a doctrine of irregular war" (50–59). Jihadism, unlike jihad, does not make a distinction between Muslim and non-Muslim. Indeed, the massacre and assassination of Muslims across the world by the jihadists indicates how traditional jihad has been re-functionalized as a tool to eliminate divergent ideas about Islam. This notion of jihad, however, is considered to be entirely different from the call of the nineteenth-century thinker al-Afghani for "an anti-colonial jihad" that was "a real defensive war against colonial rule, not terrorism" (53). Furthermore, in rejecting the legitimacy of the reinvention of the jihad tradition by the Muslim Brotherhood (*al-Ikhwan al-Mus-limun*), an organization founded in 1928 in Egypt, whose ideas were shaped by Hassan al-Banna and Sayyid Qutb, Tibi cites "the tolerant Qur'anic verse from the sura *al-kafirun*: 'You have your religion and I have mine'" (59). Tibi's analysis provides valuable insight into the relation between political thought and action in Islam. This tendency, however, also marks the conceptual boundary of the book: instead of political or social reality, the intellectual concepts of Islam constitute Tibi's point of departure. In other words, the social, cultural, historical, and political matrix of the very diverse Islamic countries is almost entirely excluded from the analysis in an attempt to focus on Islamism both as an antidote to cultural modernity in the West and as a threat to the development of political democracy in the Islamic world.

Basing his analysis not only on the geographic proximity and shared history of the Islamic world and Europe, but also, more significantly, on the tens of millions of Muslims living in Europe today, Tibi vehemently rejects the view that treats Islamism and jihadism as phenomena of the Islamic world alone. According to Tibi, Islamists and jihadists, although a minority, have become an influential political and cultural force around the world. On numerous occasions, he underlines his objection to "the admittance of such a culture [i.e., Islamism] to Europe in the name of 'tolerance' or multi-culturalism" (35). Although he draws on Karl Popper's notion of Europe as an "open society," he also asserts his commitment to another insight by Popper, namely, "that intolerance cannot be admitted in the name of tolerance" (158). In doing so, he declares his strong opposition to both totalitarian Islamists and cultural relativists. Tibi's confrontation with cultural relativism in particular is based on the premises of cultural modernity advanced by Max Weber and Jürgen Habermas. He objects to any critique of the concept of Euro-Islam (an alternative to Islamism) as "Orientalism" and emphasizes frequently the necessity for rethinking both Islam and Europe's response to Islam and Islamists. In Tibi's view, there are only two options for Europe: "Either Europe succeeds in the politics of integrating Muslim migrants as European 'citizens of the heart,' or the Islamist and Salafist [a Sunni strand of Islam] leaders of this diaspora will manage to incrementally Islamize Europe" (156). Euro-Islam, as Tibi envisions it, "is aimed at the incorporation of the European values of democracy, laïcité, civil society, pluralism, secular tolerance and individual human rights into Islamic thought" (157). But, as Tibi acknowledges, this process cannot be accomplished without European policies to "replace the exclusion which is inflicted by Europeans on Muslims and which contributes to their defensive response of self-ethnicization" (189). However Tibi also asserts that the European concept of civil society is neither negotiable nor compatible with the Islamic law of *sharia*. Beyond social and cultural integration for Muslims in Europe, Euro-Islam entails a commitment to accepting the secular order of European politics.

The situation in the Islamic countries resembles the choice that Muslims face in Europe: Islamism *or* a rethinking of Islam. A transformation of Islam different from the Islamism of Salafist-Wahabi Islam—"mobilized to confront the secular authority structure of the 'Westphalian synthesis'"—will certainly involve a paradigmatic shift in Islam, both as a religion and a civilization (69). Ibn Khaldun's concept of *asabiyya* (*esprit de corps*) constitutes for Tibi the point of departure as he engages Islam from the viewpoint of International Relations and the political world order: "the strength or weakness of civilization depends upon the commitment of its members to civilizational core values" (158). Similar to the situation in Europe, the Muslims in Islamic countries likewise find themselves at a crossroads: Islamism *or* transforming Islam on principles of "rationalism." Such a process can, Tibi suggests, proceed as a "return of history" different from Islamist or jihadist ideology. Given that Hellenization constitutes an essential part of the heritage of Islam, which in the past has led to "cross-cultural fertilization"—i.e., "the introduction of Hellenism to Europe... via the rationalist line of thought in Islamic civilization" by such philosophers and thinkers as al-Farabi, Ibn Sina (Avicenna), and Ibn Rushd (Averroës)—Tibi considers the revival of this tradition of thought in Islam as the only viable strategy for overcoming the current cultural and civilizational impasse in the Islamic world (28). A commitment to this intellectual tradition would provide Muslims with the opportunity to embrace the dominant secular world order without compromising their cultural and intellectual identity. Al-Farabi's *al-Madina al-fadila* (*The Perfect State*), as Tibi explains, is based on a "secular understanding of the state" that "is also acceptable to non-Muslim parts of humanity" (33). "The acceptance of reason-based knowledge for Muslims," Tibi argues, "would for them smooth the way to secular democracy, human rights, peace among democratic nations, and above all cultural-religious pluralism" (33).

In contrast to Islamists' re-functionalization of the tradition of jihad in the form of jihadism, Tibi emphasizes the notion of "change" as inherently Islamic. Drawing on the Qur'an as well as on Islam's "tradition of Enlightenment" and "of being open to learning from others," he objects to the essentialization of Islam as culture and civilization (19). For him, a cultural and intellectual transformation of this magnitude can be only accomplished through major changes in the institutions of education in the Islamic world. In Islamic societies, the success of democracy, which Tibi argues to be "intrinsically part of a universal cultural modernity," depends directly on the primacy of secular education (221). "The educational indoctrination in the values of Islamism along with the shari'atization of Islam" in the Islamists' madrassas, as "the political instruments employed for Islamist ends," threaten the advancement of democratic values, such as "cross-cultural morality" and religious pluralism (221, 220). Tibi instead advocates Habermas's notion of "post-secular society" and considers the secularization of education the primary condition for democratization in the Islamic world (115). He agrees with a contemporary Moroccan philosopher, Mohammed Abed al-Jabari, that "a better perspective for Arabs can only be based on the revival of their rationalist heritage based on the tradition of Hellenization. The conclusion is that secular rationalism is not alien to Islam, and nor is it imported, as Islamists contend" (223). Tibi acknowledges throughout his analysis that his primary subject is Islam in the Arab world. Nonetheless, he discusses the emergence and development of Shia Islamism in Iran in order to show the relevance of Islamism for the emerging world order. As an alternative to both Sunni-Arab and Shia-Iranian Islam, Tibi highlights the evolution of Islam "in the Islamic civilizational periphery of Indonesia" and argues that "the most advanced understanding of a 'civil Islam'" is to be found there (70). But due to the conceptual focus of the book, this observation does not develop into a detailed analysis of the situation in Indonesia. Nor does the book address the role that the religion of Islam, as an intellectual force, has occasionally played in confronting politically and socially repressive dynasties or regimes throughout history.

Tibi contends that the Islamists' conviction of "Islamic principles of order" are universal and argues for such aspirations to be replaced by "reason-based modernity" as the only universally valid paradigm of cultural plurality (17). It is in this context that he objects to Habermas's notion of a "post-secular society" and firmly believes in "the separation of the worldly and the divine as one of the foundations of cultural modernity" (17). It is also precisely from this perspective that he calls "the Islamist accusation of 'epistemological imperialism'... a denunciation of cultural modernity and subsequently of the secular concept of order" (17). Tibi's commitment to secularism, as he frequently asserts, has precedents among Islamic thinkers going back to the tenth century. The real question for him remains, however, the universal validity of the worldview of cultural modernity in the contemporary world; and his response is positive. He particularly points to "Arab liberal thought"—an intellectual tendency also present in other parts of the Islamic world—at the end of the nineteenth and at the beginning of the twentieth centuries (22). Given the conceptual focus of his analysis, however, Tibi does not reflect on the critical issue in this context: namely, the roots and the nature of the gradual shift from "liberal" and secular thought to "the return of the sacred" and Islamism as a compelling paradigm of cultural identity for Muslims at the end of the twentieth and the beginning of the twenty-first centuries. In other words, *Political Islam, World Politics and Europe* is primarily marked by a sense of urgency concerning the rise of Islamism as a threat to the secular political order of international politics and the ways it *should* be dealt with, both in the Islamic world as well as in the West, rather than engaging local, regional, and international political factors that influenced its emergence and shaped its development until the present moment.

Derrida and Other Animals

Matthew Congdon

Jacques Derrida, *The Animal That Therefore I Am*. Trans. David Wills. Ed. Marie-Louise Mallet. Fordham, NY: Fordham University Press, 2008. Pp. xiii + 176.

The scene of philosophical interest in nonhuman animal life seems to have always been lacking in robust theoretical resources. The philosophical canon from ancient Greece onward contains only a few rare exceptions, and even in the past century, when research on nonhuman animals seems to have gained new momentum, this interest has remained confined primarily to conversations having to do with the moral status of animal life, with these discussions roughly divided into two major camps: animal rights discourse and a utilitarian critique (*à la* Peter Singer) of that rights discourse. Against this historical backdrop, Jacques Derrida's *The Animal That Therefore I Am* attempts to interrogate, complicate, and think differently this picture of the philosophical problematic of nonhuman animal life, through a range of discussions of the status of "the animal" in philosophical discourse and in ways that move beyond the moral-status question, using as its touchstone five major figures from the Western philosophical tradition: Descartes, Kant, Levinas, Lacan, and Heidegger. By taking a characteristically deconstructive approach to the question of the limit between what is properly human and what defines animality—multiplying, rather than ignoring, the differences that separate human beings from other animals—Derrida's text belongs to the first strokes of a new wave of philosophical approaches to animal life.[1]

The material in this text, gathered and edited by Marie-Louise Mallet, represents approximately ten hours of lectures (including three prepared papers and one informal, improvised discussion of Heidegger) delivered by Derrida at the 1997 Cerisy conference on "The Autobiographical Animal," which was dedicated

---

1. Along with Derrida, we might include the work of Donna Haraway and Cora Diamond as well as some recent texts that have attempted to build upon and respond to *The Animal That Therefore I Am*, such as Leonard Lawlor's *This Is Not Sufficient: An Essay on Animality and Human Nature in Derrida* (New York: Columbia UP, 2007) and Cary Wolfe's introduction to Stanley Cavell et al., *Philosophy and Animal Life* (New York: Columbia UP, 2008), which attempts to draw out the affinities and differences between Derrida's and Diamond's lines of thinking.

to his own work. While David Wills's translations of chapters one and three—"The Animal That Therefore I Am (More to Follow)" and "And Say the Animal Responded?"—have been available for several years,[2] having the entire series of lectures collected in one volume makes an immeasurable difference, as the texts come together and constitute a sequence, building upon and referring to one another, gesturing toward remarks to come. Moreover, the previously unavailable material from chapters two and four—"But as for me, who am I (following)?" and "I don't know why we are doing this"—contains the bulk of the close readings of philosophical texts that provide the heart and hard work of the lectures as a whole, without which we would only be able to speak in generalities about Derrida's work on the philosophical problematic of animal life.

The text opens with Derrida's already well-known (and already infamous) reflections on the experience of being seen naked in the eyes of his cat as it follows him to the bathroom each morning. Derrida chooses to reflect upon the experience of this *particular* cat, upon its "unsubstitutable singularity," as opposed to reflections upon "the animal as such," as it provides Derrida with the motif of an irreducible aconceptuality of animal life[3] and serves as the deconstructive wedge in his readings of Descartes, Kant, Levinas, Lacan, and Heidegger, all of whom make "of the animal a *theorem*, something seen and not seeing" (14). Armed with this notion of irreducible aconceptuality, Derrida sets out to demonstrate the way in which thinkers throughout the history of philosophy have attempted and failed to account for animal life by means of varying conceptual schemata delineating the capacities separating human subjectivity from nonhuman animality. Such failed accounts have involved various versions of a disavowal of what is "animal" in the human subject, thereby marking the fundamental and central disavowal that constitutes what is "proper to man."

Derrida's text is motivated by a hypothesis that runs as follows: The past two hundred years have witnessed an unprecedented and accelerated transformation in the way human beings interact with and subjugate nonhuman animal life, instigated by new developments in zoological, ethnological, biological, and genetic forms of knowledge. This has been accompanied by a reciprocal disavowal and dissimulation of the transformation itself on the part of its human propagators; while contributing to this transformation, human beings have done everything they can to keep its grim consequences safely out of sight.

The unequivocal way that Derrida asserts this hypothesis responds to a frequently repeated criticism of his writings, namely, that his idiosyncratic philosophical style often makes it unnecessarily difficult to unearth and appreciate his

2. Chapter 1 had previously been made available in *Critical Inquiry* 28 (2002): 369–418, and chapter 3 was included in Cary Wolfe, ed., *Zoontologies: The Question of the Animal* (Minneapolis: Univ. of Minnesota Press, 2003), pp. 121–46.

3. As Derrida writes, "Nothing can ever rob me of the certainty that what we have here is an existence that refuses to be conceptualized [*rebelle à tout concept*]" (9).

concrete argumentative assertions, given their embeddedness within pages of hesitations, esoteric textual allusions, and seemingly extraneous rhetorical gestures. What we have here, however, is a case in which it is difficult to accuse Derrida of mincing his words, as the primary components of this "unprecedented transformation" are stated without ambiguity. He cites animal experimentation, industrialization of meat production, artificial insemination and genetic manipulation on a massive scale, the reduction of animal life to production and reproduction within a restricted economy of consumption, all of which takes place "in the service of...the putative human well-being of man" (25).

Here, Derrida invokes the much-abused comparison between today's treatment of animals and the Nazi Holocaust, a rhetorical maneuver that should make us wary, perhaps uncomfortably so, considering the pitfalls risked by such an invocation: (1) the fact that this comparison, drawn too quickly, always risks a shallow insensitivity to, and exploitation of, an event far too unique and incomprehensible to be meaningfully compared to any other event; and (2) such a comparison adds very little to our actual understanding of the problem of the treatment of animals and the ethical implications surrounding it, amounting to a feeble *reductio ad Hitlerum*. To be fair, Derrida is not unaware of these pitfalls, as he cautions, "One should neither abuse the figure of genocide nor too quickly consider it explained away" (26). While it is not clear that his ensuing justification of his invocation of the Holocaust gets him entirely off the hook, the picture remains provocative. Alongside the extinction of species, which is accelerating at an alarming rate, we also are witnessing a kind of negative genocide: farmed animals are not simply exterminated but kept alive and made to reproduce at an exorbitant rate, so that, "being continually more numerous and better fed, they could be destined in always increasing numbers for the same hell, that of the imposition of genetic experimentation, or extermination by gas or fire" (26).

Derrida sharpens the import of this hypothesis concerning the transformation that has occurred over the past two hundred years by arguing that it is currently passing through a "critical phase" (29). It was about two hundred years ago, Derrida points out, that Jeremy Bentham initiated a shift in the way that animal life is philosophically discussed. Contrary to the questions traditionally asked about animals and used to demarcate the status of the human animal—such as "Can they think?" "Can they reason?" or "Can they speak?"—Bentham's line of inquiry addresses animals' capacity *to suffer*, a kind of capacity for *in*capacity. Bentham's question "Can they suffer?" leaves Derrida with no room for doubt and involves an implicit invocation of pity and compassion toward the suffering of animals. As such, the past two centuries have been characterized by a struggle between, "on the one hand, those who violate not only animal life but even and also this sentiment of compassion, and, on the other hand, those who appeal for an irrefutable testimony to this pity" (28–29). The critical phase we are passing through acts as a kind of injunction, a call to think through a war waged over pity that is "not only a duty, a responsibility, an obligation, it is also a necessity, a constraint that, like it or not, directly or indirectly, no one can escape" (29).

Both sides of the "war waged over pity" seem to emerge and to derive their resources from the same hegemonic discourse, namely, one that begins with Genesis in asserting the mastery of humankind over nature. Those who want to respond with compassion to the suffering of animals still attempt to situate themselves within a discourse of universal rights that, "while founding law and right, will have led at the same time to the denial of all rights to the animal, or rendered radically *problematic* any declaration of animal rights" (88). Descartes, Kant, Levinas, Lacan, and Heidegger represent the "peaks in the mountain range" constituting this discourse and, as such, warrant an extended deconstructive examination that will shed light on the contemporary "critical phase" of human and nonhuman relations.

Derrida's critical strategy remains consistent throughout his readings of these five "peaks." His critique of the division between human and animal does not consist in smoothing over or effacing the limit that separates human and nonhuman animals. Instead, his strategy consists "in multiplying its figures, in complicating, thickening, delinearizing, folding, and dividing the line precisely by making it increase and multiply" (29). To be sure, part of his approach involves several reminders of the animality of human life that certain philosophical conceptual frameworks disavow, but this only occurs by way of a multiplication, rather than a denial, of the differences in the human-animal problematic, thereby showing that the differences separating the creature that calls itself "man" and the creature this man calls "animal" cannot be conceived in simple oppositional terms. Derrida's complication of these limits occurs primarily in two ways. First, he indicates the way in which animal diversity is obscured by the signifier "the animal," employed by thinkers from Aristotle to Heidegger, which places all nonhuman animals, from mollusks to higher primates, in the same homogenous category. In order to draw attention to this point, Derrida develops a neologism, "*l'animot*." The term is jarring in spoken French, as it seems to confuse the singular article "*l'*" with the plural noun "*animaux*," replacing the last syllable with "*mot*" or "word." The neologism serves as an alarm that sounds each time we would normally use "the animal" as our signifier, reminding us of the confusion between singularity and plurality that this signifier evokes, and pointing toward its own status as a *mot*, simply a word. Second, Derrida complicates and multiplies the differences further when he calls into question the rigor and purity of our attribution to the human subject of those various capacities that we deny to animals. That is, rather than "giving back" to the animal the capacities it has been denied, Derrida calls into question our own claim to those very same capacities.

Derrida targets Descartes as the initial propagator of a kind of purely human subjectivity, specifically, a *cogito* that is detachable from animality in the sense of sensuous experience and embodiment. His methodological doubt, which razes everything except clear and distinct ideas, leaves behind only a purely human "I think" in its wake. The image suggests to Derrida a disturbing "tableau of a world *after* animality, after a sort of holocaust, a world from which animality, at first present to man, would have one day disappeared: destroyed and annihilated by man" (80). His characterization of Kantian, Levinasian, and Lacanian conceptions of subjectivity proceeds along similar lines insofar as they "reprise" the Cartesian pure human ego that must disavow what is animal within the human. Kant's transcendental unity of apperception relies on notions of auto-referral and autonomy that imply clear black-and-white separations from animality, and the Levinasian ethical subject, the face, is both fraternal and human, placing the animal outside of the ethical circuit. And Lacan (to whom the entire third chapter is dedicated) remains within a discourse that is "quite literally Cartesian" (123) insofar as he maintains a strong distinction between the animal's capacity for *reaction* and the distinctly human capacity for *response*, which implies a continuation of the Cartesian conception of the animal as machine. The discussion of Heidegger takes on a very different and much more informal tone, as it presents an attempt at a faithful transcription of a recording of an improvised conversation that closed the Cerisy conference.[4] The strategy of reading, however, remains in line with the readings from the preceding lectures. Each figure represents for Derrida a different form of the same kind of gesture: a questionable attribution to the human subject of some capacity that is adamantly denied to "the animal." Correspondingly, his approach in each case consists in asking: Can we so purely and rigorously attribute to the human subject those capacities that we deny to "the animal"?

While the importance of Derrida's readings of these figures should not be underestimated, as they demonstrate just how much needs to be rethought in order to more sufficiently account for animal life in philosophical and political conversation, they also seem to leave us wanting some hint of a positive picture. Indeed, Derrida's focus upon the various exclusions of animality that constitute subjectivity and ethics leaves us wondering what philosophical ground *has* been laid that would lead to a more robust consideration of animality. The text seems to beg for a deeper exploration of positions that might be considered much closer to Derrida's, or at least positions that more actively seek to include animality within philosophical discourse. Derrida hints at exceptions to the Cartesian legacy of animal exclusion—most notably Nietzsche and Kafka (and very briefly and somewhat hesitantly, Hegel)—but full discussions of such figures never arise. The one exception to this tendency is Derrida's brief discussion of Adorno, in which he relies heavily upon Adorno's critique of the subjection of animality and nature in transcendental idealism. Paraphrasing Adorno, Derrida writes, "for an idealist system . . . animals virtually play the same role as Jews did for a fascist

4. In her foreword, Mallet briefly discusses the difficulties involved in attempting to faithfully capture the ad hoc and viva voce character of this informal discussion (xi–xii).

system. Animals would be the Jews of idealists, who would thus be nothing but virtual fascists" (103). Derrida and Adorno appear to have essentially the same evaluation of Kant on this point: the Kantian "I think" picks up and reaffirms an injunction as old as Genesis, namely, that properly human subjectivity shall have dominion and mastery over nature and all animal life. But his engagement with Adorno is brief, and one begins to wonder what it would look like for Derrida to engage more fully with any of these "less typically Cartesian" figures.

While the text remains a propaedeutic to a further thinking through of animal life—and, as such, does *not* indicate a positive philosophical or ethical program— it is also not the case that Derrida leaves us with *no* conceptual tools with which we might begin to think differently the philosophical question of animal life. It would thus seem worthwhile, and perhaps even demanded by the text itself, to point toward some of the repeated tropes in Derrida's text that at least *hint* at what a deconstructive ethics of animality might entail, and to suggest some ways in which they might be taken up in a positive light.

First, his criticism of the extension of rights to animals—which points out that the *Universal Declaration of Animal Rights* does "not possess the authentic status of a right, which in principle must always imply a means of constraint" (87)— makes it clear that something other than rights discourse is needed.[5] And indeed, Derrida is driven to ask, "Must we pose the question of our relations with the *animot* in terms of 'rights'?" (88). Of course, his criticism of the concept of animal rights does not take the form of Peter Singer's utilitarian appeal to the greatest happiness of the greatest number as a guiding principle, which does away with the need for rights. Thus, if there is a positive ethical outlook embedded in Derrida's text, it will not take either of the forms most evident in today's discussions of the moral worth of nonhuman animals.

Derrida seems closest to identifying a site of ethical contact with animal life when he speaks of suffering: "Being able to suffer is no longer a power; it is a possibility without power, a possibility of the impossible. Mortality resides there, as the most radical means of thinking the finitude that we share with animals" (28). Within suffering resides the most potent manifestation of our shared mortality and fundamental negativity. His attempt to multiply rather than efface the differences between human and nonhuman animals appears to result in a reversal, as he is led back to claim a kind of shared feature or sameness that links our human existence with that of nonhuman animals: we share finitude, mortality, a capacity to suffer. But what does it mean to share finitude, to have in common the very feature of our being that marks the contingency and fragility of life? Would this lead us to an ethics of structural interdependency, or would this remain too unreflectively metaphysical to emerge from a deconstructive text?

---

5. Conveniently, the full text of the 1989 *Universal Declaration of Animal Rights* is included in the "Notes" section of *The Animal That Therefore I Am*.

A positive ethical program never fully emerges from these lectures, and as a result *The Animal That Therefore I Am* remains a characteristically Derridean text: it can point out the danger of our conceptual exclusions, and even humble us before a fundamental aconceptuality presented by the unthought irreducibility of "the animal," and it can clear the ground by demonstrating the deep *lack* of resources available to us in our thinking through the philosophical question of nonhuman animal life. But the text does not, and indeed *cannot*, tell us unequivocally how to proceed, how animals *ought* to be conceptualized, treated, or thought in relation to humans. Alas, as Marie-Louise Mallet points out in her foreword (ix), while Derrida often spoke of producing a full-length text addressing the many questions of animality, it never came to fruition, and what we have in this book remains an introduction, or deconstructive propaedeutic, to further ethical, political, epistemological, and still other modes of thinking about the question of our relation to other animals.

social research

AN INTERNATIONAL QUARTERLY OF THE SOCIAL SCIENCES

FREE INQUIRY AT RISK
UNIVERSITIES IN DANGEROUS TIMES
Arien Mack, Editor
Volume 76, Nos. 2-3 (Summer-Fall 2009)

ISSN 0037-783X. $18 ind/$40 inst. Annual subscription print+online: $47 ind/ $155 inst./$36 students with valid ID. Print only: $42 ind/$145 inst. Foreign postage: $22/year or $8 for 1st back issue + $5 each add'l issue. Order online for electronic-only. Agent/bookseller discounts available. Payment by check (in US$, drawn on a US bank, payable to Social Research), AmEx, Visa or MasterCard, or ask for us in independent bookstores. Editorial and business office: 80 5th Avenue, 7th fl., New York, NY 10011. Phone (212) 229-5776; Fax (212) 229-5476. socres@newschool.edu

VISIT US AT WWW.SOCRES.ORG